Standard BASIC Programming with True BASIC™

AVERY CATLIN

University of Virginia

PRENTICE-HALL, INC., Englewood Cliffs, New Jersey 07632

Library of Congress Cataloging-in-Publication Data

CATLIN, AVERY.
Standard BASIC programming with True BASIC™.

Includes index.
1. BASIC (Computer program language). 1. Title.
QA76.73.B3C38 1987 005.13′3 86-16912
ISBN 0-13-841578-1

Editorial/production supervision and
interior design: **Mary Jo Stanley**
Cover design: **Ben Santora**
Manufacturing buyer: **Ed O'Dougherty**

Printed in the United States of America

10 9 8 7 6 5 4 3 2

ISBN 0-13-841578-1 025

True BASIC™ is a trademark of True BASIC, Inc., Hanover, N.H.

PRENTICE-HALL INTERNATIONAL (UK) LIMITED, *London*
PRENTICE-HALL OF AUSTRALIA PTY. LIMITED, *Sydney*
PRENTICE-HALL OF CANADA INC., *Toronto*
PRENTICE-HALL OF HISPANOAMERICANA, S.A., *Mexico*
PRENTICE-HALL OF INDIA PRIVATE LIMITED, *New Delhi*
PRENTICE-HALL OF JAPAN, INC., *Tokyo*
PRENTICE-HALL OF SOUTHEAST ASIA PTE. LTD., *Singapore*
EDITORA PRENTICE-HALL DO BRASIL, LTDA., *Rio de Janeiro*

Contents

Appendices

Preface

Standard BASIC Programming is designed to teach students how to write programs in True BASIC, one of the first commercial versions of American National Standard BASIC. Since its conception at Dartmouth College, BASIC has become one of the most widely used computer languages. Unfortunately, many different versions of BASIC have been developed, and they vary considerably in scope and syntax. If instructors who teach BASIC are unable to find a suitable book that covers their selected version of the language, they are faced with the serious problem of language differences between the textbook and the reference manual. Equivalent program statements in the textbook and the reference manual will not be the same, and students will be confused.

One solution to the problem is to use a standard version of BASIC. A proposed American National Standard (ANS) for BASIC was released for comment in 1984. This ANS BASIC is a comprehensive language that is well suited for writing practical programs, but at the same time retains much of the simplicity and ease of use of the original BASIC. If the proposed standard is adopted, as seems likely, vendors will be encouraged to modify their BASIC languages to conform to the standard, and the many different versions of BASIC should gradually disappear. Thus it seems particularly appropriate at this time to use ANS BASIC to teach introductory programming.

This is not a book on computer literacy, but rather a book on programming. While it covers many aspects of True BASIC syntax, it is not meant to take the place of the True BASIC language reference manual. It teaches students how to write practical programs in a modern version of standard BASIC.

Even though the subject matter is programming, most of the students who use this book will not become professional programmers. Almost all of them will use personal computers in their business or professional lives. They will run application programs much of the time, but will occasionally find a need to write small programs, probably in BASIC. Thus while designed primarily to teach programming, the book is also designed to give students a better understanding of the capabilities of modern computers.

The material is suitable for a one-semester or two-quarter course in a college or university curriculum. By omitting several chapters (for example, the chapters on graphics, matrices, and indexed databases), the book is a suitable text for a one-quarter course. Students are expected to have completed high school mathematics. While the book is written for the general college student, its advanced examples are drawn mostly from the business world and are based on the everyday use of computers in business.

Several areas have been given special emphasis:

Careful adherence to ANS BASIC standards.

An early introduction to modular program development through the use of independent subprogram units—functions and subroutines.

Extensive use of example programs to show how BASIC statements are used.

The importance of good program style, or how to write programs that are easy to read and understand, and thus easy to maintain.

An early explanation of program debugging techniques.

Examples of techniques for storing and retrieving information using data files and databases, probably the most important commercial use of computers.

A textbook is written to teach, to explain those small but difficult points that may not be understood by a student, even after attending lectures. Every effort has been made to write clear and complete explanations. After years of experience teaching college students, the author has found certain ideas that students have difficulty understanding, and these ideas are explained in detail.

Some points requiring special attention are

The difference between a variable name and a variable value.

Just how do variables store information.

The difference between a number and a string of digits.

The use of indexed variables, especially for students with limited mathematical ability.

The concept of program files and data files, how they are alike and how they differ.

What happens when a disk file is over-written or erased.

The concept and scope of local variables.

The different methods for passing information to functions and subroutines.

Programming cannot be learned just by reading. The book assumes that each student will have access to a computer and will write programs. Material is presented in such a way that students can start writing programs during their first week of class. A list of important points, a dozen or more self-test questions, and several programming problems are included at the end of most chapters. Test data for these problems, as well as all example programs in the book, are available on a floppy disk for IBM PC-compatible computers. You can obtain this disk from the publisher or from the store where you purchased this book. Information on how to use the disk is contained in a text file named README and in Appendix K.

Acknowledgments

Many people contributed to the development of this book. It was used for four classes in draft form before publication. The students in these classes made many contributions through their questions and comments. My graduate teaching assistants helped find and correct errors in both text and programs, and my thanks goes to them:

Phil Dickens	Bob Linthicum
Jim Thomas	Chris Zacjarewicz
Kyle McGlotten	Jim Wiltshire
Cheryl Rose	Tom Blair
Pat Heck	Faith Leifman
Jim McPherson	Bryan Catron
Rebecca Funderburg	

Critical reviewers are an important asset when writing a new textbook. I was fortunate to have the help of five dedicated and experienced teachers who helped me turn the first draft into a much better book. My thanks to:

Mark Pellegrino	Norwalk Community College
B. Douglas Aims	Sierra College
George Miller	University of Washington
Edward Harter	Pacific Lutheran University
J. Patrick Fenton	West Valley College

Writing a book in one's spare time means that not enough time is left for other things. My special thanks to my wife, Edie, for her support and understanding during all those weekends and vacations when I spent so many hours in front of a computer terminal.

1 Getting Started

1.1 INTRODUCTION

Before starting to write computer programs, you must decide which language to use. We explain why True BASIC (a version of American National Standard BASIC) is a good choice. You must learn how to operate your computer, which we assume is an IBM PC-compatible personal computer. We also discuss how you will use this book during the learning process.

1.2 WHY LEARN BASIC?

Most of the people who use personal computers are not professional programmers. They use a computer as a tool to help them accomplish some particular task. They need to learn to program in order to become more familiar with the computer and to write small programs for particular jobs. Their computer language requirements are different from those of the professional programmer. True BASIC is an ideal language for their use, being both easy to learn and powerful enough to handle difficult jobs.

Many professional programmers and computer scientists will tell you that BASIC is not a suitable language for writing large programs. They may be correct if they refer to one of the simple, early versions of the BASIC language. But True BASIC, the language we will be using, is an advanced version of BASIC that combines the ease of use of simple BASIC with the structure and power of more sophisticated languages.

Here are some of the advantages of almost every version of BASIC:

It is easy to learn.
It is easy to use.
It has a simple syntax.
Its programs are easy to modify.

For these and other reasons, BASIC has become the most popular programming language for personal computers. Today more people write programs in BASIC than in any other computer language.

There are some disadvantages to a simple version of BASIC:

It produces slow programs.
It lacks good control statements.
It lacks a named subprogram capability.

True BASIC completely eliminates these disadvantages, making it a suitable language for both casual users and writers of large programs.

1.3 FIRST STEPS

This book will show you how to write programs in the True BASIC language. Whenever we want to give an example that we know will work on a specific computer, we will use the IBM Personal Computer as our model. There are a number of personal computers on the market that are IBM PC-compatible to varying degrees. Most of our examples will run equally well on these machines. We used an IBM PC/XT, a Compaq portable computer, and an AT&T PC 6300 to write and run the sample programs in this book.

We will concentrate on teaching programming, not on covering every detail of the BASIC language. You can supplement this text book with the *True BASIC Reference Manual,* published by the Addison-Wesley Publishing Company, Inc. The language reference manual is the final authority on correct syntax of True BASIC statements and commands.

The language reference manual is not designed to teach you how to program in BASIC—that is the objective of this book. Your manual should be kept up to date because most computer languages are constantly changing and new versions are issued every year or so. You should refer to it for detailed information that is not covered in this book, especially information on advanced or specialized uses of True BASIC.

We assume that you have access to a personal microcomputer that supports the True BASIC language. Computer programming can be learned only by doing, not just by reading. As you read the text, type in the example programs on your computer or load them from disk. If you want an IBM PC-compatible floppy disk containing all the example programs and test data for the practice programs, contact the publisher or the store where you purchased this book.

You must learn first how to turn on your computer, insert a floppy disk (if necessary), and start the True BASIC system. If your computer is connected to a network, you may not need to use a floppy disk, but you will have to learn how to access the network and enter your account number and password. One of the most frustrating initial steps in learning to write computer programs is learning to use your computer.

Before starting to use your personal computer, read carefully the operating instructions prepared by the computer manufacturer or by your institution. These instructions should tell you all that you need to know to get started. If you have problems, ask your instructor or another student for help. In many institutions, there are other users of the same type of computer equipment, and they will probably be glad to help you get started. Only after you become familiar with your computer equipment will you be able to concentrate on learning to write BASIC programs.

1.4 HOW TO USE YOUR COMPUTER

In this section, we tell you how to turn on your computer, start using the True BASIC system, and turn the computer off when you are finished. If possible, ask someone to help you the first time. Read your computer manuals and instruction books for more information. Remember, the second time you use the computer is much easier than the first time.

Let's assume you have an IBM PC-compatible computer with at least one disk drive. It uses the MS-DOS (or PC-DOS—they are essentially the same) operating system, version 2.0 or later. If you have two drives, you should use the drive called drive A. On an IBM PC, this is the left drive. On an AT&T PC 6300, it is the bottom drive. On some other computers whose drives are mounted horizontally, it is the top drive. As you can see, there is no universal agreement in the computer industry as to which drive is drive A and which is drive B. Consult your computer manual if the drives are not labeled.

Insert a disk containing the operating system and True BASIC in drive A, close the drive door, and turn on the computer. After the computer does some checking, it may ask you for the date, which you must enter in the MM-DD-YY format. It will then ask you for the time, and you enter it in the HH:MM format. Note that a colon is required to separate hours and minutes. Some IBM PC-compatible computers have a built-in clock that automatically sets the date and time.

The computer next displays the prompt **A>** which indicates that drive A is the selected drive and that it is waiting for instructions. Type HELLO (in either uppercase or lowercase characters) and press the Enter key (often marked ↵ or Return). The True BASIC system will be loaded, and when it is ready, it will display the prompt **OK.** You may now write a BASIC computer program.

When you are finished writing programs, you can leave the True BASIC system by typing BYE in response to the **OK** prompt and pressing the Enter key. You will see the **A>** prompt again, and if you are through using the computer, remove your disk from the disk drive, and turn off the machine.

A set of general specifications for True BASIC on IBM PC-compatible computers is given in Appendix A. Some of these specifications will make little sense to you until you learn more about the language. You should know, however, that this appendix exists and is available for reference.

1.5 HOW TO USE THIS BOOK

The first six chapters of the book constitute Part I and should be read in sequence. They give you enough knowledge of BASIC to write many programs. The next three chapters are Part II and cover three important advanced topics in BASIC programming. We introduce the concept of subprogram units in Chapter 7 and then use these units in Chapters 8 and 9. We recommend that the chapters in Part II be read in the order in which they are presented. The last five chapters cover specialized features of the True BASIC language and make up Part III. This part uses concepts introduced in earlier chapters.

We have included examples of True BASIC statements and example programs throughout each chapter. As mentioned earlier, these example programs are available on a floppy disk for IBM PC-compatible computers. If this disk is in drive B, enter the command TYPE B:README from MS-DOS to receive instructions on how to read these programs. The same instructions are printed in Appendix K.

We urge you to run all the example programs, typing them in from the book if you do not have them on disk. Don't be afraid to modify them—even if you make mistakes, you will learn more about programming. Several programming assignments are listed at the end of most chapters. These assignments can and should be used for further practice and to help you evaluate your progress.

SELF-TEST QUESTIONS

1. Where can you find additional information on the True BASIC language, beyond what is covered in this book?
2. What operating system is used by IBM PC-compatible computers?
3. Should the operating system disk used to "boot" the system be inserted in drive A or drive B?
4. What is the correct format for entering the date when requested by the operating system?
5. What is the correct format for entering the time?
6. If a prompt B> is displayed on the screen, which disk drive is the active or selected drive?
7. What command is entered to start the True BASIC system?
8. What command is entered to terminate the True BASIC system and return to the operating system?
9. Should commands be entered in uppercase characters or lowercase characters?
10. What prompt is displayed by the True BASIC system?

2 Writing Simple Programs

2.1 INTRODUCTION

Computer users have developed their own special vocabulary, so we first define several computer terms. We then show you how to write a simple computer program in True BASIC and how to make the computer execute the program instructions (run the program). We introduce program statements that accept information typed on the keyboard and that display this information on the screen.

We next discuss the editing facilities available in True BASIC for writing computer programs. We introduce several commands that are used to create, run, and save new programs and to retrieve old programs.

2.2 DEFINITIONS

A *computer system* consists of a computer (the electronic unit that executes program statements) and associated equipment, as well as one or more programs required to make the computer operate. The computer and its associated equipment is called *hardware,* while the programs are called *software*.

Let's start by defining some of the hardware objects you will use, as shown in Figure 2-1.

Computer—this term refers properly to the central processing unit (CPU), which performs actions based on program instructions, and its associated electronics. The term is often used, however, to refer to the complete computer system.

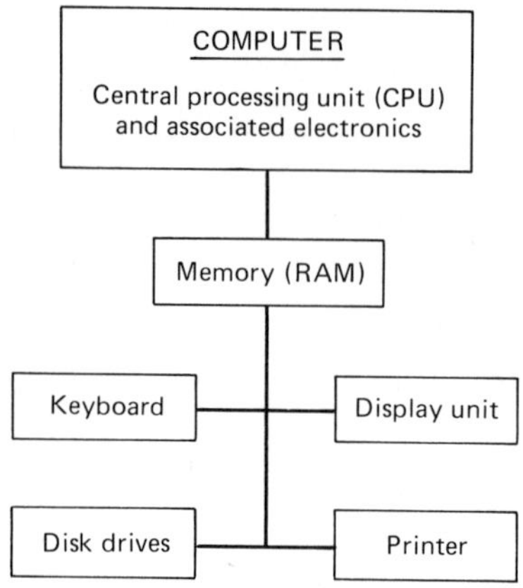

Figure 2-1 Diagram of a computer system.

Memory—a collection of electronic devices or chips inside the computer where information is stored. **When you turn off your computer, all information stored in memory is lost.** Memory is sometimes called RAM (for random access memory).

Keyboard—the typewriterlike device with keys that you press to enter characters into the computer. When you press most keys, a character also appears on the display unit screen.

Display Unit—the televisionlike screen on which characters are displayed. These characters may be sent to the screen from the keyboard or from the computer.

Disk Drive—a device like a record player, with magnetic disks on which information is stored in a relatively permanent form. The disk may be fixed in place and shared by several users through a computer network, or it may be your own personal and removable disk, called a *floppy disk*. Information stored on a disk is not lost when you turn off your computer. If a floppy disk is physically damaged, however, its information may be destroyed. A disk is slower than memory, which means that it takes longer to write information on a disk than it does in memory, and reading from a disk is also slower.

Printer—a mechanical device, connected to your computer or to a shared computer network, that prints characters on paper as they are received from the computer.

We also define several computer software terms.

Program—a series of instructions to the computer, telling it how to carry out a specific task. For example, the task might be to sort a list of names and print out the sorted list on the printer. The individual instructions are called *program statements*. In the example, a program statement might be used to print a single name. The program itself may be stored in memory or in a file (see next definition) on a computer disk.

File—a collection of characters or other information, usually stored on a computer disk. Each file is identified by a name, and a directory of all files is maintained automatically on the disk. We have already discussed storing a computer program in a file on disk. Any other collection of text characters, such as a term paper or even a letter to a friend, may be stored in a file. Information may also be stored on disk in a form that cannot be displayed directly on the screen, but that can be read and used by a BASIC program.

Statements—instructions in a computer program that cause the computer to carry out a certain action. For example, the statement

```
PRINT "ABC"
```

tells the computer to print or display the letters ABC on the display unit screen. The letters are not displayed until the program containing the statement is executed or run (see next definition).

Statements may be written in either lowercase or uppercase letters and True BASIC will ignore the difference.

Commands—direct instructions given by the user to the computer. Whereas a statement is an instruction that is part of a computer program, a command is an instruction that is given directly to the computer. For example, the command

```
RUN
```

tells the computer to execute the program statements in memory. Commands may be written in either lowercase or uppercase letters.

2.3 A SIMPLE PROGRAM

Here is our first True BASIC program, containing three statements. We present it now so you can see what a program looks like, and we discuss it in detail later in this section. As you might expect, this program displays the message **Hello!** on the screen.

```
! Example Program 2-1.
PRINT "Hello!"
END
```

The Command Window

When you enter the True BASIC system, you will notice that the screen is divided into two parts. The smaller part, at the bottom of the screen, is called the history or *command window*. It is here that you enter commands and see the results when a program is run. The prompt

```
OK.
```

in the command window means that the system is waiting for you to enter a command.

The Program Window

The top part of the screen is called the editing or *program window*. When you press the F1 function key on an IBM PC computer keyboard, the cursor (a flashing underline or box symbol) will move from the command window to the program window. The F2 function key moves the cursor back to the command window. All function keys are on the left side of the keyboard.

You can write or edit program statements only when the cursor is in the program window. A nonflashing box on the left margin is called a *line tag* and shows where the statement will be written.

A BASIC program consists of one or more statements. Statements may be written in either uppercase or lowercase letters. Each statement begins at a line tag. You may insert a blank line any place in a True BASIC program to make the program easier to read.

No Line Numbers

Many versions of BASIC require that you write a numeric label, called a line number, at the beginning of each statement. **Line numbers are not required in True BASIC** and we will not use them in this book.

The Enter Key

You type in each line of your program by pressing the appropriate keys on the keyboard. The cursor shows where the next character will be displayed. You must end each line by pressing the Enter or Return key on your keyboard. On the IBM PC keyboard, the Enter key is marked with a bent arrow:

↵

We will call this key the Enter key. It is similar in action to the old typewriter carriage-return key, although on a display unit it moves the cursor to the left margin of the screen. Its function when writing a program is to tell the computer that you have finished typing a statement. The computer then accepts the statement and the cursor moves to the beginning of the next line, indicating that the computer is ready for you to type in another statement.

When you press the Enter key, you generate a nonprinting character called a *carriage return* and the cursor moves to the left edge of the screen. When the computer receives a carriage return, it generates another nonprinting character called a *line feed* and the cursor moves to the next line. This pair of characters, the carriage return and line feed, marks the end of each program statement.

All this explanation can be condensed into one simple instruction—**always press the Enter key when you have finished typing a BASIC statement or command.**

The ! or REM Statement

Here is our first program again:

```
! Example Program 2-1.
PRINT "Hello!"
END
```

The first line contains a REMARK statement. This is a comment or explanation that is placed in a program for the convenience of the programmer and anyone else who reads the program. The exclamation point (!) and any words that follow it are ignored by the computer. The word REM (for remark) can be used instead of an exclamation point.

The PRINT and END Statements

The PRINT statement displays the characters within quotation marks on the display unit screen. In computer terminology, this set of characters is called a *string constant* and must be enclosed in quotation marks. The END statement is used to indicate the end of the program. It is required in all True BASIC programs.

To run this program after you have finished writing the statements, press the F2 function key. You will return to the command window and see the OK prompt. Type the True BASIC command

```
RUN
```

(in either lowercase or uppercase letters) and your program will execute, displaying the word "Hello!". You can enter commands only when the cursor is in the command window and the OK prompt is displayed.

Here is a similar program:

```
! Example Program 2-2.
PRINT 22.5   ! print a number
END
```

The value displayed (22.5) is called a *numeric constant* and is never enclosed in quotation marks. Spaces are required in True BASIC statements to separate words and numbers, just as they are required in ordinary sentences. Extra spaces between words and numbers usually cause no harm. Notice that we write the key words of our program statements in uppercase, a practice we will follow in the future.

We write a REMARK statement, beginning with the exclamation point, after the PRINT statement. Remarks may be included in programs as separate lines or as comments at the end of program statement lines. In the latter case, you must use an exclamation point rather than the word REM.

2.4 ANOTHER PROGRAM

Let's write another, slightly longer program. Before writing a new program, you should erase the old program from the screen and from memory. If you don't, you will get a mixture of old program statements and new program statements. Return to the command window (if you are not already there) by pressing the F2 key and enter the NEW command to erase screen and memory. You will see the old program erased from the program window, and at the same time it is erased from memory. After entering the NEW command, the cursor will move automatically to the program window, and you may begin writing a new program.

The INPUT PROMPT Statement

This new program asks the user to type in his or her name, and the computer displays that name on the screen. It looks like this:

```
! Example Program 2-3.
! Program to display a name.

INPUT prompt "Type in your name...": Name$
PRINT Name$
END
```

The third line of the program is a blank line that is created by just pressing the Enter key. It makes the program a little easier to read. The next line introduces a new statement, an INPUT statement with a PROMPT. This statement does two things: it displays on the screen the words within quotation marks (the prompt) and then waits for the user to type a reply of one or more characters, followed by pressing the Enter key. All characters typed in, before the Enter key is pressed, are associated with the word Name$, which is called a variable.

We will discuss variables at some length in the next chapter, but for the time being, you can think of Name$ as the name of a mailbox (actually a memory location) where a string or collection of characters can be stored. This string of characters is called the value of the variable Name$. We say that the characters typed in from the keyboard are stored in the variable Name$. The PRINT statement in the fifth line then displays this stored value on the screen.

The Plain INPUT Statement

An INPUT statement can be used without the word PROMPT and the prompt phrase in quotation marks. In this case, a single question mark is displayed on the screen to indicate that input is expected. Most programs are easier to use and understand if a prompt is specified in each input statement. If an input statement does not include a prompt, use a separate print statement to tell the user what to do.

Here is an example:

```
! Example Program 2-4.
! Input statement without prompt.

PRINT "Type in your name after the question mark."
INPUT Name$
PRINT Name$
END
```

2.5 EDITING PROGRAMS

To edit a program means to change it, most often by modifying or deleting existing statements or by inserting new statements. True BASIC allows you to edit the program, called the *current program,* displayed in the program window.

Cursor Movement Keys

A number of special keys on the IBM PC keyboard are used for editing. These are on the right side of the keyboard. We begin by listing several keys for moving the cursor. If these keys produce numbers instead of the actions listed here, press the Num Lock key to deactivate the numeric keypad and allow the cursor movement functions to work.

left arrow	moves cursor one character to the left
right arrow	moves cursor one character to the right
up arrow	moves cursor up one line
down arrow	moves cursor down one line
Home	moves cursor to start of the program
End	moves cursor to end of the program
Ctrl left arrow	moves cursor to start of the current line
Ctrl right arrow	moves cursor to end of the current line
PgDn	displays next page (17 lines) of program statements in the program window
PgUp	displays previous page of the program

The designation ''left arrow'' means to press the key marked with a left arrow. It is confusing because there are several such keys close together on the keyboard—we mean the keypad key, which is also marked with the digit 4. The designation ''Ctrl left arrow'' means to hold down the control key (usually marked Ctrl) and simultaneously press the left arrow key.

The Insert Key

Use of the Ins or Insert key requires a more detailed explanation. This key switches or changes the mode of typing from insert mode to overwrite mode. When you first start True BASIC, if you move the cursor to some point in your program and press a character key, that character is inserted in the text at the position of the cursor. The character beneath the cursor and all characters to the right are moved one position to the right. You are in the insert mode, and the cursor symbol is an underline character.

Pressing the Ins key switches to overwrite mode. Now when you press a character key, the character under the cursor is replaced by the new character. You will notice that the cursor has changed to a large rectangle or box. The Ins key acts like a toggle switch—each time you press it, you change from one mode to the other.

You may want to insert a new line rather than characters. If you place the cursor over a line tag when in either the insert or overwrite mode and press the Enter key, a new blank line will be inserted in your program just above the cursor. You can then type in a new statement.

How to Print a Blank Line

For example, you might insert the statement PRINT on a line by itself, just above the statement PRINT Name$ in Example Program 2-3. The program will then read

```
! Example Program 2-5.
! Program to display a name.

INPUT prompt "Type in your name...": Name$
PRINT
PRINT Name$
END
```

The PRINT statement, used by itself, produces a blank line in the output displayed by the program. If you want to produce two blank lines, include two PRINT statements in your program, each statement on a separate line.

The Delete Key

The Del or Delete key deletes the character under the cursor. If you want to delete several characters, hold the key down and it will repeat automatically. To delete a statement line, place the cursor over the line tag and press the Del key. The entire line will disappear.

Function Keys

We have already discussed two of the function keys, the *F1 key* and the *F2 key,* which move the cursor between the command window and the program window. Another important function key is the *F10 key,* the help key. You can press this key at any time to get help on a specific topic. When the prompt ''Help:'' is displayed, enter the name of the command on which you want help. If you don't know, enter the word TOPICS, and a list of topics for which help is available will be displayed.

The other function keys are discussed in detail in Chapter 6 and are listed in Appendix B. As you have time, start to learn about the function keys and use them as you write programs. You will find that they simplify many editing tasks.

2.6 COMMANDS

True BASIC commands are direct instructions to the computer telling it to do something immediately. They are always entered from the command window in response to the OK prompt. Even though we show commands in uppercase characters, lowercase characters may be used.

You will need to use many of the commands in this section as you write your first computer programs. As you type the commands, you will gradually find yourself memorizing them. A complete list of all True BASIC commands is given in Appendix C.

Simple Commands

The command

```
HELP
```

displays information on the screen. You will be given general information and told how to get more specific information.

The command

```
BYE
```

exits the True BASIC system. You return to the operating system, receiving the A> prompt. **Any program left in your program window is lost.**

The command

```
NEW
```

clears the program window. A program that has just been typed in or loaded from disk is in a section of memory called the *user workspace*. **The NEW command also erases the current program from the user workspace.** It should always be used before writing a new program.

The command

```
FILES
```

lists the names of all True BASIC program files on the disk in your current disk drive. These files always have the suffix .TRU. The *current disk drive* is the one from which you started True BASIC by entering the command HELLO. It is usually drive A.

If your computer has two disk drives, you may choose to keep your programs on a disk in drive B (see the SAVE command). When you refer to the program files on a disk in drive B, you must use a file name that begins with the prefix "B:". Thus a True BASIC program file named SORT, located on a disk in drive B, would have a full file name of B:SORT.TRU.

The command

```
FILES B:*.TRU
```

tells the computer to list all True BASIC program files (those with the suffix .TRU) on the disk in drive B. The asterisk (*) is called a *wildcard* character and represents any sequence of characters and thus any file name.

A program that you have just written may be saved on disk by using the command

```
SAVE prefix:filename
```

If no suffix is specified for the file name, the usual program suffix of .TRU will be added. If you intend to save the program on the disk in drive B, be sure to use the prefix "B:". This prefix is not part of the file name.

The program is stored on your disk in a file that is given a name identifying the particular program. For example, the program we wrote earlier might be stored in a file named MYFILE.TRU on the disk in drive B, using the command

```
SAVE B:MYFILE
```

The MS-DOS (or PC-DOS) operating system limits file names to an eight-character name, plus an optional suffix consisting of a period followed by three characters. An optional prefix, consisting of a single letter and a colon, is used to designate the disk drive.

You will be safe if you use only letter or digit characters in the file name. **Remember that a blank space is considered a character and it cannot be used in a file name.**

Examples of legal file names are

CHAP12.TRU
B:QUIZ5.DOC
A:GRAPHLIB.TRU

Examples of illegal file names are

B:QUIZ5.TEXT	(suffix cannot exceed three characters)
A:GRAPHLIBR.TRU	(name cannot exceed eight characters)
HW ONE.TRU	(blank characters not allowed)

Many times you will want to load a program from disk into the user workspace. The command

```
OLD filename
```

retrieves the named file from disk. The suffix .TRU is assumed if not specified. For example, the command

```
OLD B:HOMEWORK
```

loads the file HOMEWORK.TRU from the disk in drive B. The file name specified is called the *current file name*. If you mean to load a file named HOMEWORK that has no suffix, use the command

```
OLD B:HOMEWORK.
```

where the trailing period indicates no suffix.

The current program is erased automatically when you load a program into the user workspace from disk. **If you want to keep the current program, you must be sure to save it on disk before loading another program.**

If you try to save a program, using the file name of a file that already exists on disk, you will get an error message. You should instead use the command

```
REPLACE
```

to save a new version of an old program. This command works only if you previously saved the program during the current session or if you originally loaded the program from disk with the OLD command. No file name is needed because the program is saved under its original name (the current file name).

If you have just typed in or loaded a BASIC program, the command

```
RUN
```

instructs the computer to execute the program. A program must be in memory in the user workspace (displayed in the program window) before it can be executed.

Actually, the RUN command causes two actions to take place. First, the program is translated from True BASIC into a sequence of instructions understood by the computer, a process called *compilation*. Then the compiled program is executed by the computer. With large programs, there may be a noticeable pause while the program is being compiled.

The Break Key

You may want to stop the execution of a program before it reaches its normal end. An interrupt or *break key* is provided in True BASIC. Hold down the Ctrl key and simultaneously press the Break key in the upper righthand corner of the keyboard. Program execution stops and the normal OK prompt is displayed.

Saving Your Program During Development

We urge you to develop the habit of saving your program on disk as soon as you have spent 15 minutes or so entering a new program. Use the SAVE command. If anything happens to stop your computer, such as a power failure or some mistake on your part that locks up the operating system, everything you have written will not be lost. Programs on disk are relatively safe, whereas programs in memory can be easily lost. As you continue writing a new program, or as you modify an existing program, use the REPLACE command often to save the latest version on disk.

Backing up Your Disk

Another good habit is to keep backup copies of all important programs on a second floppy disk. You can use the MS-DOS COPY command to transfer programs to the backup disk. This command is described in the MS-DOS (or PC-DOS) reference manual that came with your computer. Remember that floppy disks are easily damaged and wear out. Sooner or later, you will be unable to access a program stored on your program disk. A backup disk then becomes invaluable.

Other Commands

The command

```
UNSAVE filename
```

deletes a file from disk. Use this command with caution because **once a file has been deleted, it cannot be recovered.**

Another command to use with caution is the command

```
LIST
```

which lists your current program on a printer that is connected directly to your computer. If no such printer exists, however, the LIST command may lock up your computer and require you to reset it, causing you to lose any program in memory. This is just one more example of what can happen if you do not frequently save your program on disk.

It is sometimes convenient to merge or insert a disk file into your current program. The command

```
INCLUDE filename
```

inserts the named file into your program, immediately after the program statement designated by the cursor.

For example, you might keep a standard program heading in a disk file called HEADING.TRU. It might consist of the following remark lines:

```
! PROGRAM:   Prog01
! AUTHOR:    John Williams
! DATE:      March 15, 1987
! DESCRIP:   Display name on the screen.
!
```

Assume that the disk containing this file is in drive B. To include the heading file in your current program, go to the program window and create an empty line at the beginning of the program (see Section 2.5). Place the cursor on the line tag of this new line, press the F2 key to go to the command window, and enter the command

```
INCLUDE B:HEADING
```

The file HEADING.TRU will be inserted into your program after the new empty line. If you wish, you can then delete the empty line.

A specific command for IBM PC-compatible computers allows the boundary between the program window and the command window to be moved. The command is

```
SPLIT N
```

where *N* is the number of lines in the program window. The value *N* cannot be less than 0 or greater than 24. Here are some examples:

```
SPLIT 0    command window fills entire screen
SPLIT 24   leaves a command window of one line
SPLIT 17   default value, 8 line command window
           and 17 line program window
```

Saving the Screen Image

If a printer is attached to your computer, the LIST command will produce a paper listing of your current program. It is not as easy, however, to produce a paper record of the execution of your program. If all the information you want to capture on paper is displayed on the screen, use the PrtSc key to transfer an image of the screen to your printer. Hold down the Shift key and press the PrtSc key. Before printing the screen image, you can increase the size of the command screen by using the SPLIT 0 command.

If the information you want to capture fills several screens, you wil! have to transfer the screen displays one by one, using the PrtSc key each time. If no printer is attached to your computer, but it is connected to a network that includes printers, see the local authorities for specific printing instructions.

Many of the file manipulation commands can be confusing, and several of them are potentially dangerous. We suggest that you practice with a couple of short, unimportant program files until you are certain you understand how the commands work. A complete list of commands is given in Appendix C.

IMPORTANT POINTS

Line numbers are not required with True BASIC statements.

Always press the Enter key when you finish typing a BASIC statement or command.

A blank space is considered a character and can never be used in a file name.

When you type the command BYE, the current program will be lost if it has not already been saved on your disk.

Be sure to save or replace your current program before using the command OLD to load another program or the command NEW to write a program.

Once a file has been "unsaved" or deleted from your disk, it cannot be recovered.

Develop the habit of frequently saving or replacing your current program.

Keep backup copies of all important programs on a separate disk.

SELF-TEST QUESTIONS

1. What is RAM?
2. Is information stored on a floppy disk lost when the computer is turned off?
3. Is information stored in memory lost when the computer is turned off?
4. What is a disk file?
5. Are line numbers at the beginning of program statements required in True BASIC?
6. Which part of the screen is the command window, the upper part or the lower part?
7. What is the name of the small nonflashing box at the left margin of each program statement?
8. After you type the letters of a command, which key do you press to tell the computer to execute the command?
9. Which character or characters are used to denote the beginning of a REMARK statement?
10. What statement is required in every True BASIC program?
11. Which key do you press to move the cursor to the program window?
12. What program statement is used to accept characters typed in from the keyboard?
13. How do you indicate to the computer that you are finished typing information in response to a prompt?

14. When in the program window, which key or keys do you press to move the cursor to the start of the current line?
15. When in the program window, what happens when you press the key marked Home?
16. When you first enter the True BASIC editor (move to the program window), are you in the insert mode or the overwrite mode?
17. Which key do you press to move the cursor to the command window?
18. Which mode are you in, insert mode or overwrite mode, when the cursor is a flashing underline character?
19. What happens when the cursor is on top of a program line tag and you press the Enter key?
20. What action results when a statement consisting of the single word PRINT is executed?
21. How do you delete an entire line of your program?
22. Which function key do you press to get help?
23. When you enter the NEW command, what happens to your current program?
24. What command is used to list the names of all True BASIC program files on the disk in drive B?
25. What command is used to load the program file HW3.TRU from the disk in drive B into the user workspace?
26. Which key or keys do you press to stop a program that is already executing?
27. What command do you use to save a new version of an old program file?
28. You are working in True BASIC and have just saved a new program file named PROJECT.TRU on the disk in drive B. Explain how you would save a backup copy of this program file on another disk.
29. What command do you use to cause the command window to fill the entire screen?
30. What happens when you hold down one of the shift keys and press the key marked PrtSc?

PRACTICE PROGRAMS AND EXERCISES

In each of the following problems, write a True BASIC program that will produce the specified results.

1. Display the following lines on the screen.

   True BASIC, Inc.
   39 South Main Street
   Hanover, NH 03755

2. Display your name, local address, and telephone number on separate lines on the screen.
3. Ask a user (the person who runs the program) to enter his or her name and then display that name again on the screen.

   Test your program using the name William P. Blank.
4. Ask a user to enter three numbers in response to three prompts. Display these numbers again on the screen, one above the other, in reverse order (the opposite order from entry).

   Test your program using the numbers -7, 2 and 13.

5. Display the names of four of your friends on the screen. Display these names in double-spaced format (names separated by blank lines).
   Test your program using the names:

   Mary F. Jones
   Hannah G. Forbes
   Bill Bradley
   Peter C. Johnson

The following exercises are designed to give you practice using some of the True BASIC and MS-DOS commands.

6. Use the True BASIC editor to write a series of REMARK statements, like those at the top of page 17 or in the file HEADING.TRU on the example program disk. Name this series of statements HEADING.TRU and save it on disk.
   Then load one of your other True BASIC programs into memory from disk. Use the INCLUDE command to insert HEADING.TRU at the beginning of your current program. Save the new program on disk, and if a printer is available, list the new program on paper.
7. Copy a True BASIC program from your program disk to a separate backup disk. Look up the MS-DOS COPY command with the verify option and use this command to make the copies.
   If your program disk is in drive B and your backup disk is in drive A, the proper command to backup file HW01.TRU is

```
COPY B:HW01.TRU A: /V
```

8. Use the COPY command of MS-DOS to make a copy of one of the program files on your program disk. Give the copy a different name from the original program. Look up the DIR command of MS-DOS and use it to display the directory of files saved on your program disk.
   Enter the True BASIC system and use the FILES command to look again at the program disk directory. Use the UNSAVE command to delete the copied file that you have just created.

3 Assigning Values to Variables

3.1 INTRODUCTION

True BASIC uses labeled mailboxes (memory locations) called variables to store information that can be accessed from a program. We identify two types of variables—those that store numbers (numeric variables) and those that store characters (string variables). We explain how to assign values to variables and how to manipulate variables.

Information may also be stored in a section of memory identified by DATA statements. We show how to read this information and use it in a program.

We enhance our ability to display information by introducing new syntax and statements that provide more control over the format of screen displays.

3.2 ASSIGNMENT STATEMENT

A variable name in a computer program is the name of a memory location where information is stored. You might think of a variable name as the label of a mailbox for information storage. This mailbox is, of course, really just a small area of memory. A typical variable for storing a number might be named Cost. The rules for forming variable names are discussed in the next section.

Numeric Variables

The information stored in a variable is called its *value*. Thus you can assign the value 29 to the variable Cost or store the value 29 in the mailbox whose label is Cost. True

BASIC allows you to use the variable name Cost for only one memory location or mailbox—it should not be used for any other purpose in your program.

The assignment statement or LET statement is used to assign a value to a variable. In our example, this statement would be

```
LET Cost = 29
```

Note that the equal sign (=) is used here as an assignment symbol, not as an equality symbol. The distinction will become clear later. Also note that the word LET is required in True BASIC, in contrast to some other versions of BASIC where its use is optional.

Our mailbox has certain unusual properties. When another value is placed in the mailbox (or a new value is assigned to the variable), the original value is overwritten and destroyed. It cannot be recovered. Thus the statement

```
LET Cost = 86
```

replaces the original value of 29 with the new value of 86.

We said that the equal sign is not an equality symbol when used in this manner. Look at the following example:

```
LET Cost = Cost + 10
```

This statement tells the computer to take the value now in the mailbox Cost (this value is presently 86), add 10 to it, and place the resulting value back in the mailbox. The variable Cost now has the value of 96. As you study this example, you see that it is obviously not a mathematical equality.

Please read over this section again if you have any questions about the difference between a variable and its value. Two points to remember are

A variable can have only one value at a time.

Assigning a new value to a variable destroys the old value.

Here is a simple program that uses the assignment statements just discussed

```
! Example Program 3-1.
! Use of assignment statements.

LET Cost = 29
PRINT Cost
LET Cost = 86
PRINT Cost
LET Cost = Cost + 10
PRINT Cost
LET Cost = Cost - 25
PRINT Cost
END
```

This program displays the following numbers:

```
29
86
96
71
```

Initial Values

What happens if you execute a program statement like

```
PRINT Cost
```

and you have not yet assigned a value to Cost? True BASIC assigns an initial value of zero to a numeric variable, and thus a zero will be printed. It is good programming practice, however, always to assign an initial value to a program variable before it is displayed or used in calculations, even though True BASIC does not require this step.

3.3 VARIABLE NAMES

A variable name must begin with a letter of the alphabet. It may contain up to 31 characters. We recommend that you use only letter characters and digit characters. **A space or blank character is not allowed in variable names.**

Lowercase and uppercase versions of letters are treated as the same character in variable names. Our usual practice is to use an uppercase letter for the first character and lowercase letters for the other characters. A reserved word in True BASIC (such as PRINT—see Appendix D for a list of reserved words) cannot be used as a variable name.

You should choose appropriate variable names that describe the physical entities that they reference. For example, a variable used to hold the sum of several numbers might be named Sum, while a number used to hold the balance in a bank account might be named Balance.

True BASIC has two types of variable names. The variable we have been using, Cost, is the name of a numeric variable. This type of variable can have only numeric values, such as 29 or 109.23 or −1300 or 0.000025.

String Variables

The other type of variable name is used for string variables. A string variable name differs from a numeric variable name by having a dollar sign ($) as the last character. Maximum length is still 31 characters, including the dollar sign. Remember that a string is any sequence of characters (even a sequence of digits) and that this sequence of characters is the value of the string variable. The value must be enclosed in quotation marks, as in the example

```
LET Phrase$ = "a test string"
```

The initial value of a string variable in True BASIC is the null string, meaning that it contains no characters. Thus a string variable may have a value of "abc" or "covered boxes" or "12345" or even a null value denoted by "".

Here are two program statements that illustrate the difference between numeric and string values:

```
LET Cost = 225.75
LET Cost$ = "225.75"
```

In the first statement, the variable is of numeric type and its value can be used in arithmetic calculations. This value is stored in the computer as a number. In the second statement, the variable is of string type and its value consists of six characters—five digits and a decimal point. This value can be displayed on the screen with a PRINT statement, but it cannot be used in calculations. It is stored in the computer as six characters.

Note especially that these two variables, Cost and Cost$, are not the same and are not equal to each other, even though their values look similar. **A numeric variable is never equal to a string variable.**

3.4 NUMBERS

True BASIC defines only one type of number. It makes no distinction between whole numbers, which mathematicians call *integers,* and numbers containing a decimal part, which are called *real numbers*.

Exponential Notation

Numbers may be written or displayed in decimal format, such as 13.375, or in exponential format. The latter format is especially useful for very large or very small numbers. Thus the number 1,475,000,000,000 can be written as 1.475e+12 or 1.475E+12. This format is shorthand notation for 1.475 multiplied by 10 raised to the twelfth power (or 1.475 multiplied by a number consisting of a one followed by 12 zeroes). The plus sign is optional—the number can also be written as 1.475E12. Small numbers can be represented in a similar fashion, the number .0000228 being written as 2.28e−5, which is 2.28 divided by 10 raised to the fifth power.

Sometimes when you write large numbers in other applications, you insert a comma between every three digits, as shown here:

```
2,125,000,000
```

This format cannot be used when you type in a number— **the commas are not allowed.** Other common formats for numbers, such as $19.95 or 75% are **not** allowed when entering numeric values (the dollar sign and percent sign are not valid characters in numbers).

Depending on the size of a number, True BASIC will make an automatic choice to display the number in either decimal or exponential format. When you use a number in a program, as a constant or as the value of a variable, you can write it in either format.

A user can enter a number, in response to the INPUT statement, in either format. Further information on how True BASIC displays numbers is in Appendix E.

3.5 ARITHMETIC OPERATIONS

Arithmetic expressions are used in BASIC to make numeric calculations. These expressions may contain arithmetic operators, numeric constants, and numeric variables. Here are the arithmetic operators and their symbols:

- \+ for addition
- − for subtraction
- * for multiplication
- / for division
- ^ for exponentiation

The symbols for addition and subtraction are familiar. Some examples follow:

```
LET Sum = Sum + 1
LET N1 = N2 - N3
LET Ans = A - (B - C)
```

The symbol for multiplication is an asterisk (*) and must always be used. While the expression 2*X* in mathematics means 2 times *X* , in BASIC it must be written 2**X* (or 2 * *X* —the spaces are optional). The symbol for division is the familiar slash (/).

For example, the program

```
! Example Program 3-2.
! Use of arithmetic operators.

LET X = 3
LET Result = ((X * 7) - 2) / 5
PRINT Result
END
```

displays the result 3.8.

As another example, let's calculate the total cost of an item that has both a sales tax and a handling charge.

```
! Example Program 3-3.
! Calculate total price for an item.

LET Price = 13.90
LET TaxRate = 0.1   ! 10 percent
LET Handling = 1.00
LET Total = Price + (TaxRate * Price) + Handling
PRINT Total
END
```

This program displays a value of 16.29.

Exponentiation means "raising to a power". The variable *X* multiplied by itself is called "*X* squared" and is written *X* ^2. On most computers the exponentiation symbol is displayed as a caret (^), although some computers may display an uparrow.

An example is the program

```
! Example Program 3-4.
! Use of exponentiation.

LET X = 5
PRINT X^3
END
```

which displays a value of 125.

A similar program can be used to calculate the area of a circle. The constant PI is a system constant with a value of approximately 3.14159.

```
! Example Program 3-5.
! Calculate the area of a circle.

LET Radius = 12.2
LET Area = PI * (Radius ^ 2)
PRINT Area
END
```

This program displays the result 467.595.

Order of Precedence

There is a rule called the order of precedence for arithmetic operators. It says that operators are evaluated from left to right, first exponentiation, then multiplication and division, then addition and subtraction. Expressions within parentheses are always evaluated first. By using this rule, we can determine just how True BASIC will evaluate an expression.

For example, in the statement

```
LET X = 2 * 5 + (9 / 3) ^ 2 - 7
```

the first scan evaluates the expression in parentheses (9/3) and produces a value of 3, resulting in the equivalent statement

```
LET X = 2 * 5 + 3 ^ 2 - 7
```

The second scan performs the exponentiation, raising 3 to the 2 power and producing a value of 9. The equivalent statement then becomes

```
LET X = 2 * 5 + 9 - 7
```

The third scan multiplies 2 by 5, giving a result of 10 and an equivalent statement of

```
LET X = 10 + 9 - 7
```

The last scan performs the addition and subtraction and assigns a value of 12 to X.

An alternative way to write arithmetic expressions is to use lots of parentheses. For example, we could have written our original statement as

```
LET X = (2 * 5) + ((9 / 3) ^ 2) - 7
```

We then follow the rule of evaluating the contents of inner parentheses first and quickly calculate the value of the expression. If you use lots of parentheses (as we will do in our example programs), you seldom need to worry about the order of precedence.

As an example of how parentheses can change the value of an expression, look at the following program:

```
! Example Program 3-6.
! Use of parentheses.

LET A = 5
LET B = 7
PRINT A - 2 / B + 3
PRINT (A - 2)/(B + 3)
PRINT A - (2/B) + 3
PRINT A - (2/(B + 3))
END
```

This program will display the following results:

```
7.71429
.3
7.71429
4.8
```

You can see that placing parentheses at different locations produces different results.

True BASIC arithmetic expressions can be used with numbers in a wide range of sizes. Expressions are calculated to at least ten digits. For the IBM PC computer, the largest number is about 3.6E+308, and the smallest number is about 1.1E−308 (see Appendix A for exact values).

If a number is too large in absolute size (greater than 3.6E+308 or less than −3.6E+308), you will get an overflow error. If a number is too small (closer to zero than 1.1E−308 or −1.1E−308), True BASIC will substitute zero for the number.

3.6 STRINGS

As explained earlier, string variable names must end with a dollar sign. These variables contain string values, which are character sequences of varying length. The maximum length of a string in True BASIC is about 32,000 characters. Usually you have no need to be concerned about exceeding this maximum length.

In addition to its maximum length, every string has a current or *dynamic length*, the actual number of characters currently stored in the string variable. Information on dynamic length is also stored in the string variable and can be accessed with a special string function (the LEN function, described in Chapter 5).

The assignment statement may be used to assign a value to a string variable. For example,

```
LET Phrase$ = "What is your name?"
```

Remember that the string value or constant must be enclosed in quotation marks.

Including Quotation Marks in String Constants

If you want to include quotation marks within the string, use a double set of quotation marks. For example, the program fragment

```
LET Phrase$ = "He said ""Hello""."
PRINT Phrase$
```

displays the sentence

```
He said "Hello".
```

The Null String

A string with a dynamic length of zero is called a *null string* —it has a null value. It can be created by the statement

```
LET Example$ = ""
```

where no character (not even a space) is enclosed by the two quotation marks. Note that the null string is different from a string containing a single blank or space character. The latter string can be created by the statement

```
LET Example$ = " "
```

Remember that every string variable is set initially to a null string.

Using Substrings

True BASIC allows you to access parts of string variables. These parts are called *substrings*. The expression [a:b], added to a string variable name, designates a substring that starts at the character in position "a" and ends at the character in position "b". The first character in a string is at position 1.

If the variable Phrase$ has a value of

```
What is your name?
```

then the substring Phrase$[6:7] has a value of

```
is
```

and the substring Phrase$[14:17] has a value of

```
name
```

The notation Phrase$[a:b] makes it easy to refer to a part or substring of the string variable Phrase$. The limits "a" and "b" must be integers or numeric expressions. If "a" has a value of less than 1, the value 1 is used instead. If "b" has a value greater than the length of the entire string, the string length is used instead. If the value of "a" is greater than the value of "b", a null string is produced.

The substring notation can also be used in an assignment statement. For example, the program

```
! Example Program 3-7.
! Assign a value to a substring and
! thus change the value of a string variable.

LET Trip$ = "travel in town"
LET Trip$[8:9] = "to"
PRINT Trip$
END
```

displays the phrase

```
travel to town
```

You can actually insert a new substring that is of different length from the original substring. For example, the statement

```
LET Trip$[8:9] = "into"
```

in the program displays the phrase

```
travel into town
```

You can also use substrings to separate a string into two or more parts. Consider the case where you have a string containing both an account number and a name, such as

```
163259,John Ivory
```

The number always contains six digits and is separated from the name by a comma. Assume this string value is assigned to the string variable Line$:

```
LET Line$ = "163259,John Ivory"
```

You can separate the account number from the name and display it by using the statement

```
PRINT Line$[1:6]
```

which displays the string value

```
163259
```

If we assume that the string Line$ is no longer than 100 characters, the name can be extracted by using the statement

```
PRINT Line$[8:100]
```

which displays the string value

```
John Ivory
```

This ability to separate strings into substrings has many important uses in business applications.

Concatenation of Strings

A useful operation with strings, similar to the addition operation with numbers, is *concatenation*. This means adding one string of characters to the end of another string of characters. The ampersand (&) is used to indicate string concatenation in True BASIC.

For example, the program

```
! Example Program 3-8.
! Concatenate three strings.

LET FirstName$ = "Mary"
LET LastName$ = "White"
LET Name$ = FirstName$ & " " & LastName$
PRINT Name$
END
```

will display the name

```
Mary White
```

A one-character string, consisting of a single blank, is placed between the strings FirstName$ and LastName$.

The LINE INPUT Statement

If you are using the INPUT statement to enter a string value from the keyboard, the characters typed in cannot include a comma because the INPUT statement interprets a comma as the end of input. The general form of the INPUT statement is

```
INPUT Var1, Var2, Var3,...
```

where the variables may be either numeric or string. A user must use commas to separate the several values that are assigned to variables. For example, the program

```
! Example Program 3-9.
! Entering multiple values with INPUT statements.

PRINT "Enter names of two employees:"
INPUT Name1$, Name2$
INPUT prompt "Salaries? ": Salary1, Salary2
END
```

produces the following sample dialog between user and program (text entered by user is underlined):

```
Enter names of two employees:
John H. Smith, Mary Johnson
Salaries? 13500, 14000
```

If you need to enter a string of characters containing one or more commas, you must either enclose the entire string in quotation marks or use the LINE INPUT statement.

This latter statement can only be used with string variables. In many applications, only a single string variable is used in the LINE INPUT statement to simplify the program structure.

A prompt can be included in the LINE INPUT statement, as it is in the INPUT statement.

```
! Example Program 3-10.
! Enter and display a name.

LINE INPUT prompt "Type in your name...": Name$
PRINT Name$
END
```

A name containing a comma, such as James Brown, Jr., will be accepted by the LINE INPUT statement and assigned to the variable Name$.

The LINE INPUT statement has another useful property. It accepts a null string value (the user just presses the Enter key) and assigns that value to a string variable. This type of entry is often used in programs to signal a particular user response. The regular INPUT statement will not accept a null string value.

3.7 READING VALUES FROM MEMORY

The programs we have discussed require string or numeric values to be entered from the keyboard. An alternative form of input is to read values from a section of computer memory where they have been stored.

The DATA Statement

DATA statements are used to store string or numeric values in memory. String values must be enclosed in quotation marks if you wish to include leading or trailing blanks, or any characters other than letters, digits, a period, plus or minus signs, or internal spaces. In particular, a string containing a comma must be placed in quotation marks. Individual values are separated from each other by commas in the DATA statement.

Some typical DATA statements are

```
DATA 10, Computer, 15, Disk Drive
DATA 8, Chair, 2, "Table, 3 ft. by 8 ft."
```

Note that DATA statements may be placed anywhere in a program before the END statement. When you run the program, one of the first actions that the computer takes is to examine the DATA statements and store their values in a special section of memory.

The READ Statement

One or more READ statements are used to read these stored values into variables. Variables in a READ statement are also separated from each other by commas. For example, the following READ statement can be used with either of the preceding DATA statements:

```
READ Quantity1, Name1$, Quantity2, Name2$
```

The computer keeps track automatically of which values have been read and which is the next value to read. Reading starts with the first value in the first DATA statement. In the foregoing examples, if the first DATA statement is read, the first value 10 is placed in the first variable Quantity1, the string value ''Computer'' (but not the quotation marks) in variable Name1$, and so forth.

The single READ statement can be replaced by several READ statements and the results will be identical. For example

```
READ Quantity1
READ Name1$, Quantity2
READ Name2$
```

If you try to put a nonnumeric string in a numeric variable, you will get an error message. You can, of course, put digit characters in a string variable, but you must remember that these digits represent a string value, not a numeric value.

If the number of variables in READ statements is greater than the number of values in DATA statements, you will get an error when you try to read a value that does not exist. No error occurs if the number of values is greater than the number of variables, although the extra values will not be read.

Here is an example program that reads three numbers from a DATA statement, calculates their sum, and prints it on the screen:

```
! Example Program 3-11.
! Use of the DATA statement.

READ First, Second, Third
LET Sum = First + Second + Third
PRINT Sum

DATA 15.3, -181.7, 225
END
```

This program displays a value of 58.6.

READ and DATA statements are often used with the READ statement in a loop, as discussed in the next chapter. We introduce the statements here and expand on their use in Chapter 4.

3.8 MORE ON PRINTING

We have used the PRINT statement in several examples to display a single variable value or an expression value. This statement can also be used to display several variable values.

The Comma Separator

Commas are used to separate the variables First, Second, and Third in the example program. These separators tell the PRINT statement to display the three values in separate print zones, where a *print zone* is a subdivision of the screen width. The default width of a print zone in True BASIC is 16 columns, but this width can be changed as shown later. Each variable value is displayed at the beginning of a print zone.

```
! Example Program 3-12.
! Use of print zones.

LET First = 5
LET Second = 10
LET Third = -20
PRINT First, Second, Third
END
```

The example program displays the numbers in a format like this:

```
 5          10         -20
```

ZONEWIDTH and MARGIN

The print zone width and effective screen width can be determined and changed by program statements. The statement

```
ASK zonewidth Width
```

assigns the value of the current print zone width to the variable Width.

The statement

```
SET zonewidth Columns
```

allows you to change the print zone width from the current value to the value of expression Columns. The expression must be numeric, usually a numeric variable or constant. Print zone width cannot be less than one column or greater than the screen width.

Two similar statements

```
ASK margin Width
SET margin Columns
```

determine and change the right margin of the display screen. The default margin value for most display units is 80, giving a screen width of 80 columns. The screen width cannot be less than one column and must be at least as wide as the current print zone width. We introduce these two statements at this point because they are related to the ZONEWIDTH statements, but we will not use them in programs until a later chapter.

Here is a modified version of the previous example:

```
! Example Program 3-13.
! Changing the print zone width.

LET First = 5
LET Second = 10
LET Third = -20
PRINT First, Second, Third
PRINT
SET zonewidth 8
PRINT "New print zone width is 8"
PRINT
PRINT First, Second, Third
END
```

The modified program produces this display:

```
 5          10         -20

New print zone width is 8

 5      10     -20
```

Our program has reduced the width of each print zone to 8 columns.

The Semicolon Separator

If semicolons are used to separate the variables, the statement

```
PRINT First; Second; Third
```

produces the display

```
 5  10 -20
```

A semicolon separator tells the PRINT statement to put the numbers as close together as possible. You will note that a space is left in front of the 5 and the 10. This space is for the numeric sign that is not displayed if the number is positive but is displayed if the number is negative. Another space is left after each number.

String values are displayed in much the same way as numeric values. Since strings have no numeric sign, the semicolon separator leaves no space between adjacent string values. If you want a space, you must add it.

```
! Example Program 3-14.
! Use of semicolons with strings.

LET First$ = "Mary"
LET Last$ = "White"
PRINT First$; " "; Last$
END
```

displays

```
Mary White
```

Compare the output of this program with that of Example Program 3-8. They both display the same phrase, but use different methods. Example Program 3-8 uses string concatenation, while Example Program 3-14 uses semicolon separators in a PRINT statement. These two programs illustrate the point that there is often more than one way to write a computer program to produce the same result. In this case, neither method is clearly superior to the other.

The Trailing Semicolon

A semicolon at the end of a PRINT statement, which is called a trailing semicolon, has a different meaning—it suppresses the carriage return and line feed that normally follow a PRINT statement. For example, the statements

```
PRINT "A"
PRINT "B"
```

display

```
A
B
```

while the statements

```
PRINT "A";
PRINT "B"
```

display

```
AB
```

You can use a PRINT statement with a trailing semicolon in place of the PROMPT clause in an INPUT statement. If you want to suppress the question mark normally displayed by an INPUT or LINE INPUT statement, use a prompt consisting of a null string. Here is another way to write Example Program 3-10.

```
! Example Program 3-15.
! Use of trailing semicolon and null prompt.

PRINT "Type in your name...";
LINE INPUT prompt "": Name$
PRINT Name$
END
```

This technique might be used if you have such a long prompt string that the LINE INPUT statement is longer than the normal screen width.

Simple PRINT USING Statement

Another way to control the format of information displayed on the screen is to use a special print statement called the PRINT USING statement. We introduce a simple form of that statement and discuss additional forms and capabilities in Chapter 10.

The PRINT USING statement uses a format string to control the appearance of items displayed on the screen or printed on paper. We will use this statement to display only a single numeric value.

The format string in our simple version is a string constant, consisting of a sequence of numeric format characters (the "#" character) and an optional decimal point. Enough format characters must be included in the string to accommodate the largest numeric value that will be displayed.

The number of format characters after the decimal point specifies the number of decimal digits that will be displayed. The numeric value is right-justified in the format string field and if necessary, padded with zeroes on the right. The value is rounded if it contains too many decimal digits. If the format string is too short, an error message consisting of a string of asterisks (*) is displayed.

Here is an example program showing how this simple version of the PRINT USING statement works:

```
! Example Program 3-16.
! Use of the PRINT USING statement.

PRINT using "####": 125
PRINT using "####": 1285.9
PRINT using "####": 34562
PRINT
PRINT using "###.##": 12.5
PRINT using "###.##": -12.521
PRINT using "###.##": -133.33
END
```

This program produces the following display:

```
 125
 1286
 ****

  12.50
 -12.52
 ******
```

The comma and semicolon characters provide a limited formatting capability with PRINT statements. The simple PRINT USING statement gives slightly more capability. We will discuss other ways to achieve greater format control in Chapter 10. In the meantime, experiment with these statements until you have a better understanding of how the display format can be controlled.

IMPORTANT POINTS

A variable can have only one value at a time.

Assigning a new value to a variable destroys the old value.

A numeric variable is never equal to a string variable.

Commas are not allowed in numbers.

The LINE INPUT statement can only be used with string variables.

SELF-TEST QUESTIONS

1. What is the assignment operator or symbol in True BASIC?
2. Is the keyword LET required in an assignment statement?
3. How do you differentiate between a numeric variable name and a string variable name?
4. Is the statement LET B = B/2 a valid True BASIC statement? If not, why not?
5. What happens to the old value stored in a variable when a new value is assigned to the variable?
6. What is the initial value of (a) a numeric variable, and (b) a string variable?
7. Can a space be included as part of a variable name?
8. How many characters are allowed in a variable name?
9. Which of the following expressions are valid variable names?
   a) Ending
   b) 2ndEnding
   c) Spare Tire
   d) NoSuchLuck
10. If the variable Value$ is assigned a value of "12", can you evaluate the expression (Value$ + 2)? If not, why not?

11. What, if anything, is wrong with each of the following statements?
  a) LET Value = 1,230,000
  b) LET Value = 1.23e6
  c) LET Value = 15%
  d) LET Value = $12.95

12. Evaluate the following expressions:
  a) LET X = 1 − 2 / 2
  b) LET X = 2 ^ 3 − 1 / 2
  c) LET X = 1 + 2 − 3 * 4 / 2
  d) LET X = 2 + 2 / 2 + 2

13. Can a string variable named Long$ be assigned a string value containing 500 characters?

14. If the string variable Name$ has been assigned the value "Bill Wilson", what is the value of the substring Name$[6:11]? What is the proper substring notation for the first name "Bill"?

15. If Prefix$ has the value "for" and Suffix$ has the value "ever", what is the value of the expression (Prefix$ & Suffix$)?

16. Is the statement

```
LINE INPUT Value
```

a valid True BASIC statement? If not, why not?

17. Can a DATA statement be (a) the first statement in a program, or (b) the last statement?

18. If the first READ statement in a program is

```
READ A
```

and the first DATA statement is

```
DATA 3, -2, 7
```

what value is assigned to the variable A?

19. If a program has one READ statement and one DATA statement, what happens if the number of variables in the READ statement is greater than the number of values in the DATA statement?

20. Given the program

```
LET Star$ = "*"
PRINT Star$, Star$
END
```

in which column will (a) the first asterisk be displayed, and (b) the second asterisk be displayed?

21. What statement is used to change the print zone width from the current value to 10 columns?

22. What is the effect of a trailing semicolon at the end of a PRINT statement?

23. What display is produced by the statement

```
PRINT using "##.##": Number
```

when Number has (a) a value of 17.2, or (b) a value of −17.2?

PRACTICE PROGRAMS

1. Assign the value 10259 to the variable A and the value 137321 to the variable B. Display the sum of these two variables on the screen.
2. A DATA statement contains three numeric values. Display the average of these three values on the screen.

   Test your program using the statement

   ```
   DATA 1001, 12.3, -2.59
   ```

3. Ask a user to enter his or her first name, middle initial, and last name, all on separate lines. Store these values in three separate variables. Then display the complete name on the screen, with a single space between names and initial, and a period and space after the initial.

   Test your program by entering the three values

   Constance
   W
   Green

4. Ask a user to enter a number and then display the cube of the number on the screen. Your screen should look like this (entered number is underlined).

   ```
   Number? 5
   Cube of 5 is 125
   ```

   Test your program using the numbers 5 and −7.
5. A DATA statement contains five string values, each consisting of a single character. Assign these characters to variables and display them on the screen in the following pattern:

   ```
   Q A F H T
   A
   F
   H
   T
   ```

   Note that the first data value is only displayed once.

   Test your program using the statement

   ```
   DATA Q, A, F, H, T
   ```

6. Ask a user to enter three numbers and store them in variables A, B, and C. Calculate and display the value of the expression ($B^2 - 4AC$).

   Test your program using the values A = 4, B = 7, and C = 3.
7. Ask a user to enter two numbers and then display their sum and difference on the screen. The screen display should look like this:

   ```
   Enter two numbers: 13.2, 7.5
   Sum is 20.7  Difference is 5.7
   ```

Test your program using the number pairs

13.2, 7.5
128.3, 301.7
56, 7

8. A temperature in degrees Fahrenheit (F) can be converted to a temperature in degrees Celsius (C) by using the formula

$$C = \frac{5(F - 32)}{9}$$

Ask a user to enter a temperature in degrees Fahrenheit and display the corresponding temperature in degrees Celsius. The screen should look like this:

```
Fahrenheit temperature? 59
Celsius temperature is 15 degrees
```

Test your program using Fahrenheit temperature values of 59, 32, and 212 degrees.

9. A farmer has a 14 foot diameter silo that is 60 feet high. Ask a user to enter the height of silage that has been stored in this silo. Display the number of tons of silage in storage. Assume corn silage that has an average weight of 45 pounds per cubic foot.
Test your program using a height of 46 feet.

In the following problems, use the PRINT USING statement to display dollar amounts rounded to the nearest cent.

10. Ask a user to enter the size of a room (width and length, in feet) and the price of carpet per square yard. Add a charge of $2.00 per square yard for delivery and installation. Display the total cost of carpeting the room. The screen display should look like this:

```
Length of room in feet? 18
Width of room in feet? 2
Price of carpet per square yard? 2.50
Cost of installed carpeting is 348.00
```

Test your program using the following data:

Length	Width	Price
18	12	$12.50
11	11	$14.35
10	8	$9.75

11. The present value (P) of an amount (A) produced by compounding interest annually for N years at a percentage interest rate of I, is given by

$$P = \frac{A}{(1 + I/100)^N}$$

Ask a user to enter the amount of money in dollars, the interest rate in percent, and the number of years. Display the present value of this amount. The screen should look like this:

```
Amount? 10000
Interest in percent? 11.5
Number of years? 12
Present value is 2708.33
```

Test your program using the following data:

Amount	Interest	Years
10,000	11.5%	12
5,000	8.3%	9

12. Ask a user to enter the amount of an initial deposit in a savings account. Assuming an interest rate of 8 percent, compounded annually, calculate and display the amount of money in the account at the end of ten years.

Test your program using initial deposits of $100, $1,200, and $5,000.

4 Program Control Statements

4.1 INTRODUCTION

Computer programs become more powerful and useful when they are capable of repeating actions (looping) and making decisions (branching). We introduce both concepts and explain how to use the different looping and branching statements.

We also introduce relational operators and logical expressions, fundamental concepts in any discussion of computer decision making. We show how to use logical expressions to control the reading of DATA statements. We then discuss two common types of computer programs—one type counts and sums a sequence of numbers, the other type identifies the largest and smallest numbers in a sequence.

4.2 FLOW OF PROGRAM CONTROL

Statements are executed sequentially, one after another, in a simple BASIC program. In the sample program that follows, first a PRINT statement is executed, then three INPUT statements, then another PRINT statement, and finally an END statement. The result of the program is to print the sum of three numbers entered from the keyboard.

```
! Example Program 4-1.
! Print sum of three numbers.

PRINT "Enter number when prompted by '?'"
INPUT A
INPUT B
INPUT C
PRINT "The sum is"; A + B + C
END
```

Writing the program in this manner becomes unsatisfactory if you want to find the sum of many numbers. Computer programs often need to repeat the same statement or sequence of statements over and over again. The technique used to accomplish this repetition is called *looping*.

The DO and LOOP Statements

Looping requires two kinds of statements: one to tell the program to repeat a block or group of statements and the other to tell it when to stop repeating.

Look at the following example:

```
! Example Program 4-2.
! Print sum of positive numbers.

LET Sum = 0
PRINT "Enter one or more positive numbers."
PRINT "Enter a negative number to stop."
INPUT Number
DO while Number >= 0
   LET Sum = Sum + Number
   INPUT Number
LOOP
PRINT "The sum is"; Sum
END
```

We have introduced two new statements, DO and LOOP. These statements enclose a *block of statements,* one or more adjoining statements, that are executed over and over again. Whenever the LOOP statement is reached, control is transferred back to the DO statement. At this point, a check is made to see whether the value of Number is zero or positive. If the value is negative, control is transferred out of the loop and the statement following the LOOP statement (the ''PRINT Sum'' statement) is executed.

For example, if a value of -1 is entered for Number, the DO statement transfers control to the statement after the LOOP statement. This statement is ''PRINT Sum'' and the value of Sum is displayed.

The first INPUT statement, outside the loop, accepts the first number entered by the user. If this number is negative, no sum is calculated. The INPUT statement inside the loop is used for subsequent entries. Note the use of indentation to set off the block of statements in the loop.

Another type of statement is used by a computer program to decide which of two blocks of statements to execute. This process is called *branching*.

The IF and ELSE Statements

Here is a sample program that illustrates branching:

```
! Example Program 4-3.
! Branching example.

INPUT prompt "Answer Y or N...": Reply$
```

```
IF Reply$ = "Y" then
   PRINT "The answer is yes."
ELSE
   PRINT "The answer is no."
END IF
END
```

Again we have introduced several new statements. The combination of IF and ELSE statements allows the choice of one of two blocks of statements. If the value of Reply$ is "Y", then the condition in the IF statement is true and the first block of statements (in this case, just a single PRINT statement) is executed. If Reply$ has any other value, then the second block (another PRINT statement) is executed. An END IF statement is used to indicate the end of this second block.

Any computer program can be written in terms of three structures: sequential, loop and branch. In later sections, we will examine looping and branching in more detail.

4.3 RELATIONAL OPERATORS

We have already seen how operation of the IF statement depends on a condition that is either true or false. This condition is called a *logical expression*.

Simple Logical Expressions

A logical expression consists of two variables or values connected by a *relational operator*. For example,

```
Sum = 7
```

is a logical expression, where Sum is a numeric variable, the equal sign is a relational operator, and 7 is a constant. This is not an assignment statement because the first word is not LET.

Note that the equal sign (=) when used as a relational operator, has a different meaning than the same character used as an assignment operator (see Chapter 3). The context will always tell you how the equal sign is being used and there should be no confusion about its meaning.

This logical expression, Sum = 7, is true if the variable Sum has a value of 7. We can also say that the logical expression itself has a value of true. If Sum has a value other than 7, then the logical expression is false (or has a value of false).

We have previously introduced the idea of a variable having a value. Now we introduce the idea of a logical expression having a value. Note that this value can only be true or false; it cannot be anything else. Thus the expression itself, Sum = 7, has a value of true if Sum has a value of seven.

The six relational operators are:

= equal
<> not equal
< less than
<= less than or equal
> greater than
>= greater than or equal

Let's look at some examples of IF statements, such as

```
IF Limit >= 0 then PRINT Limit
```

The logical expression is true if Limit has a zero or positive value and the value of Limit will be displayed. If the logical expression, Limit >= 0, is false, the next program statement will be executed.

Here is an example using a string variable:

```
IF Ans$ <> "OK" then LET Value = 0
```

Note that as before, a string constant must be enclosed in quotation marks. The logical expression is true if Ans$ has a value other than "OK".

Most string comparisons involve the equal or not equal operator. It is possible to use the other relational operators with string variables and constants, but an explanation of how these comparisons are made will be deferred until Chapter 11.

Compound Logical Expressions

So far we have discussed IF statements with only a single logical expression. It is possible to join together two or more logical expressions by using the keywords AND or OR. The result is called a *compound logical expression*. For example,

```
IF (A = 5) and (B = 7) then PRINT (A + B)
```

Parentheses are not required, but are added for clarification. This statement will print the sum of A and B if the variable A has a value of 5 and the variable B has a value of 7. The keyword AND requires that both logical expressions be true for the compound expression to be true. If either logical expression is false, or if both are false, then the compound expression is false.

Here is another example:

```
IF (A < 2) or (A > 9) then PRINT "Error in A"
```

This statement will print the error message if A is less than 2 or if A is greater than 9. The keyword OR requires that either one or the other logical expression be true (or that both be true) for the compound expression to be true. If both logical expressions are false, then the compound expression is false.

A Truth Table

The properties of compound logical expressions are shown in Figure 4-1, which is sometimes called a *truth table*.

X and Y are any two logical expressions. T means true and F means false. For example, if X is false and Y is true, then the expression (X and Y) is false, while the expression (X or Y) is true.

It is possible to combine more than two logical expressions into a compound expression. Such complicated compound expressions are seldom needed in True BASIC because of the availability of the SELECT CASE statement (see Section 4.7).

X	Y	X and Y	X or Y
T	T	T	T
T	F	F	T
F	T	F	T
F	F	F	F

Figure 4-1 A logical truth table.

It is also possible to reverse the value of a logical expression by using the keyword NOT. For example, if

```
X = 3
```

is true, then

```
NOT(X = 3)
```

is false.

Note that the expression, not (X = 3), is identical in value to the expression, X <> 3.

4.4 LOOPING—THE DO LOOP

The DO loop provides the most general looping structure in True BASIC. Either the DO or the LOOP statement may be modified to control the duration of a loop. The modifiers are WHILE and UNTIL, and each must be followed by a logical expression.

The WHILE and UNTIL Tests

A DO WHILE or LOOP WHILE statement causes the loop to repeat while the logical expression is true. Examples are

```
DO while Sum < 10
LOOP while Flag = 1
```

A DO UNTIL or LOOP UNTIL statement causes the loop to repeat until the logical expression is true. Examples are

```
DO until Sum >= 10
LOOP until Count = 7
```

Here is an example program using a DO loop:

```
! Example Program 4-4.
! Display a line, version 1.

LET Line$ = "This is a sample line of text."
DO
   PRINT Line$
   INPUT prompt "Display again (Y/N)? ": More$
LOOP until More$ = "N"
END
```

Note that the value of Line$ will be displayed at least once before the value of More$ is checked at the bottom of the loop.

The DO WHILE and DO UNTIL statements check the logical expression at the top of the loop, before it is executed the first time and each subsequent time. The LOOP WHILE and LOOP UNTIL statements check the expression at the bottom of the loop, before the loop is repeated.

Good programming practice suggests that a test phrase (such as WHILE or UNTIL) should be placed either at the top of the loop, after the DO statement, or at the bottom of the loop, after the LOOP statement, but not at both places. This practice follows the principle that there should be only one exit from a loop.

Here are two more sample programs that accomplish essentially the same task as the first program, but use different programming structures. The first example uses a WHILE test instead of an UNTIL test:

```
! Example Program 4-5.
! Display a line, version 2.

LET Line$ = "This is a sample line of text."
DO
   PRINT Line$
   INPUT prompt "Display again (Y/N)? ": More$
LOOP while More$ = "Y"
END
```

Here is another version of the same program, using an UNTIL test after the DO statement:

```
! Example Program 4-6.
! Display a line, version 3.

LET Line$ = "This is a sample line of text."
INPUT prompt "Display line (Y/N)? ": More$
DO until More$ = "N"
   PRINT Line$
   INPUT prompt "Display again (Y/N)? ": More$
LOOP
END
```

In this case, the first request for input is placed outside the loop, and the value of More$ is checked at the beginning of the loop. If the value is ''N'', Line$ will never be displayed. If the value is ''Y'', the line is displayed and another request for input, inside the loop, is executed.

The EXIT DO Statement

Our final example has a direct exit from within the loop:

```
! Example program 4-7.
! Display a line, version 4.

LET Line$ = "This is a sample line of text."
DO
   PRINT Line$
   INPUT prompt "Display again (Y/N)? ": More$
   IF More$ = "N" then EXIT DO
LOOP
END
```

The IF statement tests a condition, More$ = ''N'', and if the condition is true, the EXIT DO statement exits the loop (transfers control to the statement following the LOOP statement).

In general, the EXIT DO test does not produce as readable and easily understood a program as does the WHILE or UNTIL test. The reason for this lack of clarity is that a loop exit occurs in the middle of the loop, whereas we normally look for a loop exit at the end or the beginning of the loop. We recommend that you use the EXIT DO statement only when there is no other simple choice.

Sometimes a programming mistake is made and a loop repeats itself over and over. The program never stops—the loop just keeps repeating. This type of loop is called an *infinite loop*. If you suspect that your program is caught in an infinite loop, you can interrupt it by pressing the Interrupt key (the Ctrl Break key).

4.5 LOOPING—THE FOR LOOP

The FOR and NEXT Statements

There are many occasions when you wish to repeat a loop a fixed number of times. Two companion statements, the FOR statement and the NEXT statement, are used for this purpose. For example, if you wish to sum the integers from 1 through 10, you might write a loop such as

```
! Example Program 4-8.
! Sum of the first ten digits.

LET Sum = 0
FOR Index = 1 to 10
    LET Sum = Sum + Index
NEXT Index
PRINT "Sum of first ten digits is"; Sum
END
```

The variable Index is called the index variable. At the top of the loop, it is given the initial limit value of one. After this value has been added to the variable Sum, the NEXT statement returns control to the top of the loop. The index variable Index is automatically incremented by one to a value of 2 and looping continues. When Index reaches the value of 11, the FOR statement notes that this value exceeds the final limit value of 10 and looping stops, with control transferring to the statement following the NEXT statement.

Note that the variable Sum is initialized to a value of zero. Even though True BASIC automatically initializes every variable, it is good programming practice to initialize variables in the program. Anyone reading the program will be reminded that Sum has been initialized

The STEP Modifier

The foregoing example is a simple FOR-NEXT loop and illustrates the most common use of FOR and NEXT statements. A more general FOR statement is defined as

```
FOR I = A to B step C
```

The initial and final limits, A and B, may be numeric variables, constants, or expressions. The step C may also be a numeric variable, constant, or expression and may be positive or negative. As shown in Example Program 4-8, if no step is specified, a step of +1 is assumed.

After you have executed a FOR-NEXT loop, the value of the index variable will usually be different from the value of the final limit. You should not use this value for subsequent calculations or decisions, because it may vary depending on the limit values and step value used in the FOR-NEXT loop.

If the step is positive and the initial limit is greater than the final limit, the loop is never executed and the index variable retains the value of the initial limit.

Look at this variation of our previous example:

```
! Example Program 4-9.
! Loop with step greater than one.

LET Sum = 0
LET First = 1
FOR Index = First to 10 step 4
    LET Sum = Sum + Index
NEXT Index
PRINT "Sum ="; Sum
END
```

The variable Index takes on the successive values of 1, 5, and 9. The next value of Index is 13, and because this exceeds the final limit, the loop is terminated. Thus the final value of Sum is 15. Go through the example yourself and verify these numbers.

Looping with a Negative Step

Another example uses a negative step:

```
! Example Program 4-10.
! Loop with negative step.

LET Total = 0
LET Jump = -2
FOR Count = 4 to -4 step Jump
    LET Total = Total + Count
NEXT Count
PRINT "Sum ="; Total
END
```

Note that the initial limit (4) must be greater than the final limit (-4) for the loop to work properly with a negative step (-2). You should verify that the final value of Total is zero.

The EXIT FOR Statement

There are times when you may want to stop a FOR-NEXT loop before the index variable has reached the final limit. An EXIT FOR test is available for this purpose and is used to establish an early exit from the loop.

The following program asks a user to enter ten numbers, one at a time, and displays the inverse of each number after it has been entered. The number zero is not a valid entry because you cannot divide by zero. If a zero is entered, the EXIT FOR statement causes the program to stop.

```
! Example Program 4-11.
! Enter ten numbers and display their inverse.
! Stop if any number is zero.

FOR Count = 1 to 10
    INPUT prompt "Number? ": Number
    IF Number = 0 then EXIT FOR
    PRINT "Inverse is"; 1/Number
NEXT Count
END
```

You might say that the EXIT FOR test allows an emergency exit from a FOR-NEXT loop that would normally be expected to go to completion. It should not be used for normal termination of a FOR-NEXT loop.

4.6 BRANCHING—THE IF BRANCH

The most versatile branching structure in True BASIC is the IF branch. We have already described (in Section 4.2) the two-way branch structure using IF and ELSE statements. The syntax of this structure is as follows:

```
IF logical expression THEN
   first block of statements
ELSE
   second block of statements
END IF
```

Each block of statements consists of one or more statement lines. The "logical expression" is the type we discussed in Section 4.3, either a simple expression or a compound expression. The first block is executed if the logical expression is true and control then jumps to the END IF statement.

The ELSE statement and its associated block of statements (the second block) is executed if the logical expression is false. This statement and its second block of statements are optional. The following syntax is used when the ELSE statement is omitted:

```
IF logical expression THEN
   a block of one or more statements
END IF
```

The ELSE and END IF statements must be on lines by themselves unless the IF-THEN-ELSE structure is written as a single statement (see the following example). **Note that END IF must be two words, the space is significant.** An END IF statement is always required with the block IF structure.

Here is an example:

```
! Example Program 4-12.
! A normal two-way branch.

INPUT prompt "Value of A? ": A
INPUT prompt "Value of B? ": B
IF (A = 0) or (B = 0) then
   PRINT "Either A or B is zero."
```

```
ELSE
   PRINT "The value of A/B is"; A/B
   PRINT "The value of B/A is"; B/A
END IF
END
```

A simple version of the IF-THEN-ELSE structure is the single statement:

```
IF Ans = 17 then PRINT "Correct" else PRINT "Wrong"
```

In this case, the entire statement must be written on a single line. As before, the ELSE clause is optional and another example without that clause is

```
IF Reply$ = "Y" then PRINT Value
```

Note that an END IF statement is not required.

The ELSEIF Statement

There is an extended version of the IF-THEN-ELSE structure that permits multiple branching, using the additional statement ELSEIF (or ELSE IF, either form is acceptable).

In the next example, a menu is displayed and the user is asked to choose one of the options. Depending on the choice, a line of different characters is displayed. If a number is entered that is not displayed on the menu, the user is told that the choice is invalid.

```
! Example Program 4-13.
! Use of the ELSEIF statement.

PRINT "Command Menu"
PRINT
PRINT "1...display line of stars"
PRINT "2...display line of periods"
PRINT "3...display line of pluses"
PRINT
INPUT prompt "Your choice? ": Choice

IF Choice = 1 then
   FOR I = 1 to 70
       PRINT "*";
   NEXT I
ELSEIF Choice = 2 then
   FOR I = 1 to 70
       PRINT ".";
   NEXT I
ELSEIF Choice = 3 then
   FOR I = 1 to 70
       PRINT "+";
   NEXT I
ELSE
   PRINT "Invalid choice."
END IF
END
```

Note the use of trailing semicolons in the statements that print the special characters. These semicolons keep all characters on the same line.

4.7 BRANCHING—THE SELECT CASE BRANCH

Another type of branching is the multibranch SELECT CASE structure. This structure allows one of several branches or actions to be selected. The basis of selection can be broader than the simple true or false condition of the IF-THEN-ELSE structure.

The SELECT CASE Statement

The general form of the SELECT CASE structure is

```
SELECT CASE expression
CASE test1, test2
     first block of statements
CASE test3
     second block of statements
CASE test4, test5, test6
     third block of statements
CASE ELSE
     another block of statements
END SELECT
```

The "expression" in the first line may be any expression or variable, string or numeric. If the expression is of type string, all the tests must be string tests; if numeric, all tests must be numeric. If a test is satisfied, the block of statements associated with that test is executed and control jumps to the statement after END SELECT. If no test is satisfied, the block of statements after CASE ELSE is executed.

The CASE ELSE statement and its block of statements is optional. You will get a run-time error, however, if none of the tests is satisfied and there is no CASE ELSE statement. We recommend that you always include this statement in a SELECT CASE structure.

Here is the previous example, written using the SELECT CASE structure:

```
! Example Program 4-14.
! Use of the SELECT CASE statement.

PRINT "Command Menu"
PRINT
PRINT "1...display line of stars"
PRINT "2...display line of periods"
PRINT "3...display line of pluses"
PRINT
INPUT prompt "Your choice? ": Choice

SELECT CASE Choice
CASE 1
     FOR I = 1 to 70
          PRINT "*";
```

```
        NEXT I
CASE 2
        FOR I = 1 to 70
            PRINT ".";
        NEXT I
CASE 3
        FOR I = 1 to 70
            PRINT "+";
        NEXT I
CASE else
        PRINT "Invalid choice."
END SELECT
END
```

The CASE Tests

Tests can be of three types. A test can be a constant value, either string or numeric, that the expression must match. If the expression is a numeric variable named Choice, a CASE statement with two tests might be

```
CASE 7, -5
```

and would be satisfied if Choice has a value of 7 or -5

```
SELECT CASE Choice
CASE 7, -5
        PRINT "Choice has value of 7 or -5."
END SELECT
```

A test can be a range of values, in the form ''low value TO high value'', that the expression must match. Using the same expression as before, a CASE statement might be

```
CASE 14 to 21
```

and would be satisfied if Choice has a value between 14 and 21 inclusive.

```
SELECT CASE Choice
CASE 7, -5
        PRINT "Choice has value of 7 or -5."
CASE 14 to 21
        PRINT "Choice has value between 14 and 21."
END SELECT
```

A test can be a logical comparison, in the form ''IS op value'', which the expression must satisfy. The symbol ''op'' means one of the logical operators. Again using the variable Choice, a CASE statement might be

```
CASE is > 175
```

and would be satisfied if Choice has a value greater than 175.

```
SELECT CASE Choice
CASE 7, -5
     PRINT "Choice has value of 7 or -5."
CASE 14 to 21
     PRINT "Choice has value between 14 and 21."
CASE is > 175
     PRINT "Choice has value greater than 175."
END SELECT
```

Note that variables and expressions cannot be used in a CASE test.

Here is another sample program using the SELECT CASE structure:

```
! Example Program 4-15.
! Result of reading a thermometer.

INPUT prompt "Reading? ": Temperature

SELECT CASE Temperature

CASE is < 98.5
     PRINT "Temperature is subnormal."

CASE 98.5 to 98.7
     PRINT "Normal temperature."

CASE is > 98.7
     PRINT "You have a fever."

END SELECT
END
```

Note the physical appearance of Example Program 4-15 and compare it to Example Program 4-14. Which program do you think is easier to read? Blank lines can often improve the clarity and appearance of a computer program.

The following sample program uses a string expression:

```
! Example Program 4-16.
! Answer to a question.

INPUT prompt "Your answer? ": Ans$

SELECT CASE Ans$

CASE "Y", "y"
     PRINT "The answer is YES."

CASE "N", "n"
     PRINT "The answer is NO."

CASE else
     PRINT "Answer Y or N."

END SELECT
END
```

The tests in a SELECT CASE structure must be written in such a manner that the expression can choose only one block of statements to execute. If tests in two different CASE statements satisfy the expression, the program will become confused. If this situation might occur in your program, use the IF-THEN-ELSEIF structure instead of the SELECT CASE structure.

4.8 MORE ON READING VALUES

We introduced the READ and DATA statements in Chapter 3. At that time, we explained that if you tried to read more values than were available in the DATA statements, your program would stop and display an error message.

The END DATA and MORE DATA Tests

We can now show you how to use the IF statement to determine if there are any more data values. The two tests are MORE DATA and END DATA. The logical expression MORE DATA is true as long as there are unread data values and becomes false when there are no more data to read. The expression END DATA becomes true after the program has read the last data value; otherwise, it is false.

Here is an example using the END DATA test:

```
! Example Program 4-17.
! List names in the DATA statement.

PRINT "List of names:"
DO until end data
   READ Name$
   PRINT Name$
LOOP

DATA John, Betty, Mary, Tom, Penelope
END
```

This program reads values until the end of the last DATA statement, reading names from the DATA statement and displaying these names on the screen.

Counting and Summing Numbers

Another example program computes the average value of a sequence of numbers in DATA statements. A check is made at the beginning of the loop to see if there are any more data that have not yet been read from the DATA statements. If all data values have been read, the loop stops.

The variable Sum is used to accumulate the sum of all data values. Within the loop, a counter variable named Count is incremented each time a new data value is read, and this value is added to the variable Sum.

```
! Example Program 4-18.
! Average numbers in the DATA statement.

LET Count = 0
LET Sum = 0
DO while more data
   READ Number
   LET Sum = Sum + Number
   LET Count = Count + 1
LOOP
PRINT "Average is"; Sum/Count

DATA 1,5,3,4,2,3,7,8,9,2,5,1,9
END
```

Note that both Count and Sum are initialized before the loop starts. After the loop ends, an average value is computed, dividing Sum by Count. This program displays the answer

```
Average is 4.53846
```

Finding Minimum and Maximum Values

Another useful program selects the smallest and largest values from a sequence of values. We shall use numbers and define the largest value as the most positive number, the smallest value as the most negative number.

Here is the program:

```
! Example Program 4-19.
! Find the largest and smallest values.

LET Largest = -Maxnum
LET Smallest = Maxnum
DO while more data
   READ Number
   IF Number > Largest then LET Largest = Number
   IF Number < Smallest then LET Smallest = Number
LOOP
PRINT "Largest value is"; Largest
PRINT "Smallest value is "; Smallest

DATA 12,-3,231,-5,-505,223,147,199,0,58
END
```

Maxnum is a system variable containing the largest possible number recognized by the computer. The variable Largest is set initially to the smallest possible number (negative Maxnum). After a number has been read within the loop, its value is compared with the current value of Largest. If this new number is larger than Largest, it is assigned to Largest and replaces the current value. By starting off with the smallest possible number in Largest, we ensure that any larger number read from the data statement will be assigned to the variable Largest.

Similarly, the variable Smallest is set initially to the largest possible number. If a number is read that is smaller than Smallest, it is assigned to Smallest and replaces the current value.

This choice of initial values for Largest and Smallest ensures that the largest and smallest values will be found. The program displays the answers

```
Largest value is 231
Smallest value is -505
```

The RESTORE Statement

Sometimes you want to read a set of data values more than once. The statement RESTORE resets the system so the next item read will be the first value in the first DATA statement. We say that there is an imaginary *data pointer* that points to or indicates the next data value to be read. The effect of RESTORE is to reposition this pointer at the first item in the first DATA statement.

We illustrate this process in an example program that displays the appropriate zip code when the name of a city is entered. A table of city names and zip codes is placed into DATA statements. The user is asked to type in a city name.

The program searches through the data table for the city name. If the name is found, it is displayed. A dummy city named ZZZ is the last city name in the table. If the search reaches this name, a message tells the user that the search was not successful.

The process of entering a name and searching the table is placed in a loop. At the beginning of the search, the RESTORE statement sets the data pointer to the beginning of the first DATA statement. If the user presses the Enter key in response to a request for a city name, the program stops.

```
! Example Program 4-20.
! Use of the RESTORE statement.
! Display zip code for a given city name.

PRINT "Capitalize first letter of the city name."
PRINT "Press the Enter key to stop."

LINE INPUT prompt "City name...": Name$
DO until Name$ = ""
   RESTORE
   DO while more data
      READ City$, Zip$
      IF Name$ = City$ then EXIT DO
   LOOP

   IF City$ = "ZZZ" then
      PRINT "This name is not in the list."
   ELSE
      PRINT "Zip code for "; City$; " is "; Zip$
   END IF
   LINE INPUT prompt "City name...": Name$
LOOP

DATA Churchville, 21028, Claiborne, 21624
DATA Clarksburg, 20734, Clear Spring, 21722
DATA Clements, 20624, Clinton, 20735
DATA ZZZ, 0
END
```

If the user enters a city name of Clarksburg, the program will display the message

```
Zip code for Clarksburg is 20734
```

A program designed for practical use would have many more DATA statements containing a much larger table of city names and zip codes.

IMPORTANT POINTS

Any computer program can be written in terms of three structures: sequential, loop, and branch.

Avoid using the EXIT DO phrase to exit a loop if a WHILE or UNTIL phrase can be used instead.

When leaving a FOR-NEXT loop, the value of the index variable is not necessarily the same as the value of the final limit.

Use the Ctrl Break key to interrupt an infinite loop.

The END IF statement must be two words, the space is significant.

SELF-TEST QUESTIONS

1. Which keyword is used to mark (a) the beginning of a loop, and b) the end of a loop?
2. In a program containing an IF statement with two branches, which keyword is used to mark (a) the beginning of the first branch, and (b) the beginning of the second branch?
3. What are the values (true or false) of the following logical expressions?
   a) 1 = 1
   b) 2 > 7
   c) "AA" <> "AB"
   d) 2 < 7
4. If X = 1 and Y = 2, what are the values of the following logical expressions?
   a) X + 1 = Y
   b) X = Y + 1
   c) Y <> 2 * X
   d) not (X = Y)
   e) (X = 3) or (Y > 1)
   f) (X <> Y + 1) and (X + 1 = Y)
5. Does the statement

```
LOOP until X = 0
```

   check for further looping at (a) the top of the loop, or (b) the bottom of the loop?
6. If you have a choice of writing a loop using the DO WHILE statement or the EXIT DO statement as a test for exiting the loop, which statement is preferable?
7. How do you stop a program that is executing an infinite loop?
8. If a STEP value is not specified in a FOR statement, (a) what step size is assumed, and (b) is it positive or negative?
9. If the step size is positive, how many times does a FOR-NEXT loop execute if the lower limit is (a) equal to the upper limit, or (b) greater than the upper limit?
10. Given the FOR-NEXT loop

```
FOR I = 1 to 5 step 3
NEXT I
```

   what is the value of I after the loop has finished executing?
11. How many times will the following FOR-NEXT loop execute?

```
FOR Count = 1 to 5 step -1
    PRINT Count
NEXT Count
```

12. Is the ELSE keyword always required in an IF statement?
13. Are both END IF and ENDIF valid statements?
14. Are both ELSE IF and ELSEIF valid statements?

15. What letter is displayed by the following program if a user just presses the Enter key in response to the prompt?

```
LINE INPUT prompt "Your choice? ": Reply$
IF Reply$ = "" then PRINT "A" else PRINT "B"
END
```

16. A CASE structure starts with the statement

```
SELECT CASE Result
```

If Result has a value of 5, what is the logical value (true or false) of the following CASE tests?

a) CASE 1, 3, 6
b) CASE 1 to 6
c) CASE is > 1
d) CASE is < 5

17. If a program contains READ and DATA statements, what is the logical value, before the first READ statement is executed, of (a) the expression MORE DATA, and (b) the expression END DATA?
18. A program reads a sequence of numbers from DATA statements. What information does it have to calculate and store to compute the average value of the numbers in the sequence?
19. A variable Store is used to hold the largest number in a sequence. What initial value should be assigned to Store at the beginning of the program?
20. If variable Store is used to hold the smallest number in a sequence, what initial value should be assigned to it?
21. What does the RESTORE statement do?

PRACTICE PROGRAMS

1. Use the FOR statement with a negative step to display the integers from 10 down to 1 in a single line.
2. Use a loop statement to display all the even integers between 1 and 20 on a single line.
3. Ask a user to enter 15 numbers and then display the largest number and the smallest number, with appropriate labels.

   Test your program using the following numbers:

   2, 7, −13, 8, 19, 5, −3, 15, −6, 21, −2, 0, 13, 4, 9

4. Ask a user to enter a sequence of positive numbers from the keyboard. Enter a negative number to stop the data entry process. Display the average value of the positive numbers.

   Test your program using the following numbers:

   2, 15, 6, 103, 13, 26, 78, 4, 125, −1

5. Repeat Practice Program 4, but read all the numbers from one or more DATA statements. A negative number is not needed in this case.

   Test your program using the following DATA statement:

```
DATA 35,76,180,2,99,54,39,62,101,3,45
```

6. Ask a user to enter a number between 1 and 9. If the number is not in this range, display the message ''Your number must be between 1 and 9'', loop back, and let the user try again. Otherwise, display the message ''Successful entry'' and halt the program.

   Test your program using the numbers 0, 1, 9, and −9.

7. Display a string of 70 asterisks and then the prompt ''More (Y/N)?'' on a separate line. Wait for the user to enter a character. If the character is ''N'', halt the program. Otherwise, display the asterisks again on a new line and then the prompt.

   Test your program using the characters ''Y'', ''n'', and ''N''.

8. Rewrite Practice Program 7 with more careful checking of input. Allow a user to enter only one of the characters ''Y'', ''y'', ''N'', or ''n''. If any other character is entered, display an error message and ask the user to try again. Hint: Use the SELECT CASE statement.

   Test your program using the characters ''Y'', ''y'', ''z'', ''n'', and ''N''.

9. The Fibonacci series is a mathematical number series. In this series, the next term is the sum of the previous two terms in the series. For example, if the first term is 1 and the second term is 1; then the third term is (1 + 1) or 2, and the fourth term is (1 + 2) or 3.

   Ask a user to enter the number of terms (or numbers) in the series and then display the values of all the terms. Assume a value of 1 for each of the first two terms.

   Test your program using a Fibonacci series of 2, 5, and 13 terms.

10. The examination grades for a class are stored in one or more DATA statements. Calculate and display the two highest grades in the class.

    Test your program using the following DATA statement:

```
DATA 70,63,92,100,80,92,85,91,78,88,82,90
```

11. A shipping department is preparing an order of items (footballs or transistor radios or what have you) for shipment. Their large packing cases hold 100 items, medium cases hold 20 items, small cases hold 5 items, and single cases hold 1 item.

    Ask a user to enter the number of items to be shipped and display a table showing how many cases are needed of each size.

    Sample output for shipping 1257 items is

```
CASE                NUMBER
----                ------
large                 12
medium                 2
small                  3
single                 2
```

    Test your program using 1257, 356, and 5 items.

12. Data statements contain the selling prices of used automobiles sold during the week by an automobile dealership. These prices include the sales tax.

    Assume a sales tax of 3 percent on the first $1,000 of the price and 2 percent on everything over $1,000. Calculate and display the total sales tax liability for the week.

    Test your program when it contains the two following DATA statements:

```
DATA 6434,1985,7910,12163,785,4350
DATA 4750,2335,1890,3995,1030,1017
```

5 Standard Functions and Program Development

5.1 INTRODUCTION

True BASIC contains many useful functions in its set of standard functions. We define the term "standard function" and discuss specific functions of several different types—arithmetic, trigonometric, string, conversion, keyboard, and so forth.

We have now introduced enough of the True BASIC language to allow significant programs to be written. We present the recommended procedure for designing a computer program. As an example, we develop and explain a program that averages student grades.

5.2 DEFINITION OF STANDARD FUNCTIONS

What is a *standard function?* In BASIC, it is a named identifier to which is *passed* one or more values, in the form of constants, variables or expressions. The function performs some calculation or manipulation and *returns* a new string or numeric value that is assigned to the function name. For example, the function SQR(9) is passed a value of 9 and returns a value of 3, the square root of 9.

Every version of BASIC has standard or built-in functions, but True BASIC has an especially large and comprehensive set. We will discuss many of the more useful functions and refer you to Appendix G for a complete list.

As another example, let's look at the function that calculates the number of characters stored in a string variable, called the length of the string. Assume that you have a string variable named Phrase$. The string value stored in Phrase$ is passed to the function LEN, which performs a calculation and returns the length of the string, as in the statement

```
LET Length = len(Phrase$)
```

The numeric variable Length is assigned the length of the string stored in the variable Phrase$. If variable Phrase$ has the value TEST FLIGHT, then Length will be assigned a value of 11 (remember that a space is a valid character).

The expression in parentheses is called a *parameter* of the function. This particular function has only one parameter, the string variable Phrase$. In general, functions may have several parameters, and they may be either string or numeric, either constants, variables, or expressions. The function also has a value and in our example, this value is assigned to the numeric variable Length. The value of a function (that is, the value returned by a function) may be either string or numeric. If a function returns a string value, the last character in its name must be a dollar sign ($).

Functions may be used, like variables, in many different BASIC statements. Here are two more examples that use the LEN function:

```
PRINT len(Name$)
LET Indent = (80 - len(Heading$)) / 2
```

5.3 ARITHMETIC FUNCTIONS

The arithmetic functions are numeric functions that perform certain fundamental arithmetic calculations.

The ABS Function

The absolute value function is ABS(X), and it has a numeric value. It converts a negative numeric parameter to a positive number. Examples are

```
abs(-5) is 5
abs(12) is 12
```

The INT, ROUND, and TRUNCATE Functions

These three functions modify numeric variables or constants. The integer function is INT(X), and it has a numeric value. It returns the greatest integer less than or equal to X. Examples are

```
int(100) is 100
int(125.9) is 125
int(125.1) is 125
int(-17.5) is -18
```

Note the last example—the value -18 is the greatest integer less than -17.5.

The function to round a number is ROUND(X,N), and it has a numeric value. It returns the value of X rounded to N digits after the decimal point. If N is not specified, it is assumed to be zero. This is a true rounding function, not a truncating function. Note that any digit 5 or greater in a positive number is rounded up, while any digit less than 5 is rounded down. Trailing zeroes in a number are not displayed.

Be careful with negative numbers, the result is not what you might intuitively expect. Rounding -3.5 yields -3 whereas rounding -3.6 yields -4. Examples are

```
round(3.49) is 3
round(3.49, 1) is 3.5
round(3.94, 1) is 3.9
round(3.95, 1) is 4   (trailing zero not printed)

round(-3.95, 1) is -3.9
round(-3.96) is -4
round(-3.96, 1) is -4 (again no trailing zero)
```

A similar function with a numeric value is TRUNCATE(X,N). Both parameters, X and N, are always required. This function returns a value of X that is truncated or chopped off to N digits after the decimal point. Examples are

```
truncate(3.95, 0) is 3
truncate(3.95, 1) is 3.9
truncate(-3.95, 1) is -3.9
```

Both the last two functions, ROUND and TRUNCATE, display unexpected results if you try to round or truncate a number larger than 9999 with one or more digits after the decimal point. For example,

```
PRINT round(23899.05, 2) displays 23899.
```

The reason for this odd behavior is explained (at least partially) in Appendix E. As a practical solution, use the PRINT USING statement (introduced in Chapter 3) rather than the ROUND function for displaying large decimal numbers.

The SQR Function

The square root function is SQR(X), and it has a numeric value. It returns the square root of the parameter X. Remember that **the square root of a negative number is not defined** and so if the parameter is negative, you will get an error. Examples are

```
sqr(9) is 3
sqr(2) is 1.41421
```

The MOD Function

The function MOD(X,Y) returns a numeric value equal to the remainder when X is divided by Y. The value of Y cannot be zero because **division by zero is not allowed.** Examples are

```
mod(7,3) is 1
mod(127,25) is 2
mod(5.5,2.5) is .5
```

The MOD function is most commonly used with X and Y having integer or whole number values. One use of the MOD function is to determine whether a number is odd or even, as shown in the following example:

```
! Example Program 5-1.
! Test for even or odd number.

INPUT prompt "Enter number: ": Value
IF mod(Value, 2) = 0 then
   PRINT "Number is even."
ELSE
   PRINT "Number is odd."
END IF
END
```

The MIN and MAX Functions

The MAX(X,Y) and MIN(X,Y) functions compare the two numeric parameters and return a value equal to the larger or smaller parameter, respectively. Examples are

```
max(15,0) is 15
min(-7, 5) is -7
```

Here is the last example program from Chapter 4, rewritten to use the MAX and MIN functions:

```
! Example Program 5-2.
! Find the largest and smallest values.

LET Largest = -Maxnum
LET Smallest = Maxnum
DO while more data
   READ Number
   LET Largest = max(Number, Largest)
   LET Smallest = min(Number, Smallest)
LOOP
PRINT "Largest value is"; Largest
PRINT "Smallest value is "; Smallest

DATA 12,-3,231,-5,-505,223,147,199,0,58
END
```

5.4 TRIGONOMETRIC FUNCTIONS

If your understanding of trigonometry is weak, you can skim through this section. We will not use trigonometric functions in most of our examples.

The SIN Function

The function SIN(X) calculates the sine of X and has a numeric value. The parameter X can be expressed in units of either radians or degrees. **The default unit is radians,** but you can change to degrees by including the statement OPTION ANGLE DEGREES in your program. Once this statement has been executed, all subsequent trigonometric functions will expect their parameters to be in degrees. You change back to radians by including the statement OPTION ANGLE RADIANS, and all subsequent functions expect parameters in radians.

The COS, TAN, and ATN Functions

Other trigonometric functions available in True BASIC are COS(X) for cosine of X and TAN(X) for tangent of X. The inverse trigonometric function, ATN(Y), called the arc tangent of Y, is also defined and returns the value of an angle whose tangent is Y.

The DEG and RAD Functions

Two functions are useful for converting between degrees and radians. The function DEG(X) converts X radians to degrees. RAD(X) converts X degrees to radians. Remember that the constant PI is a system constant with a value of 3.14159. . . , up to the maximum system precision.

For example, the program

```
! Example Program 5-3.
! Print some trigonometric function values.

OPTION ANGLE degrees
PRINT "Tangent of 45 degrees is"; tan(45)
OPTION ANGLE radians
PRINT "Convert 45 degrees to radians."
PRINT "Tangent of this angle is"; tan(rad(45))
PRINT "Tangent of PI/4 radians is"; tan(PI/4)
END
```

displays a value of 1 for each of the PRINT statements. Note in the statement "PRINT tan(rad(45))" that the RAD function first converts 45 degrees to radians and then the TAN function finds the tangent of the angle in radians.

5.5 OTHER NUMERIC FUNCTIONS

This section discusses two of the more specialized numeric functions.

The LOG Functions

True BASIC has three logarithmic functions. LOG(X) calculates the natural logarithm of X. LOG2(X) calculates the logarithm of X to the base 2. LOG10(X) calculates the logarithm of X to the base 10.

```
log(10) is 2.30259
log2(10) is 3.32193
log10(10) is 1.
```

If you are not familiar with logarithms, don't worry because we will not use these functions in our example programs.

The RND Function

The random number function is RND, and it returns a random number less than 1 and greater than or equal to 0. When RND is used in a program without a modifying statement, it will always produce the same random number or sequence of random numbers each time the program is run. If the modifying statement RANDOMIZE is executed prior to the use of the RND function, it will return a different random number each time the program is run.

When developing a program that uses the RND function, say, to produce a sequence of random numbers, we recommend that you do not include the RANDOMIZE statement. You will find it easier to locate and correct errors when the same sequence of random numbers is produced each time you run the program. After the program is producing correct results, add a RANDOMIZE statement so that each run produces a different sequence of random numbers.

Here is a sample program that simulates the roll of a pair of dice.

```
! Example Program 5-4.
! Simulate the roll of a pair of dice.

PRINT "Simulating the roll of a pair of dice."
RANDOMIZE
PRINT int(6*rnd + 1), int(6*rnd + 1)
END
```

The expression (6*rnd + 1) produces a number between 1.0 and 6.9999. . . . Note that the function int(6.9999) has a value of 6. The RANDOMIZE statement causes the program to print a different pair of numbers each time it is run. You might try running this program a few times without the RANDOMIZE statement just to see what happens.

5.6 STRING FUNCTIONS

A powerful set of string functions in True BASIC allows string values to be manipulated.

The LEN Function

We have already discussed the LEN function that returns the numeric length of a string:

```
len("Susan Smith") is 11
```

We also discussed the definition and use of substrings in Chapter 3. For example, if the variable Name$ has the value "Susan Smith", then

```
Name$[1:5] is Susan
```

We can use the LEN function to write a substring expression for the last name

```
Name$[7:len(Name$)] is Smith
```

The POS Function

True BASIC has a function named POS that returns the location of a substring within a string. The substring can have one or more characters, and the value of the function returns the character position of the first character in the first occurrence of the substring.

The POS(A$,P$,N) function has a numeric value giving the location of the first character of the pattern string P$ in the string A$. The optional third parameter N specifies the position in A$ where the search will start. If N is not specified, the search starts at the first character of A$. The function returns a value of zero if the pattern cannot be found.

Examples are

```
pos("ABCDE", "C") is 3
pos("ABCAB", "B") is 2
pos("abcde", "A") is 0
```

Here is an example where the starting position is specified:

```
pos("ABCAB", "B", 3) is 5
```

Note that the function returns a number representing the position of the second "B" in the string, not the first "B", because the search starts after the first "B" at the third character.

Remember that **a blank space is a valid character in a string.** If we have a person's full name (first name and last name) in a string variable Reply$, we can use the following program to extract the first name:

```
! Example Program 5-5.
! Look for first space in Reply$
! and display the first name.

LINE INPUT prompt "Enter your full name: ": Reply$
LET Space = pos(Reply$, " ")
IF Space > 0 then
   PRINT "Hello, "; Reply$[1:Space-1]
ELSE
   PRINT "You seem to have no first name!"
END IF
END
```

A LINE INPUT statement is used so that a name containing a comma, such as John Jones, Jr., can be entered. The variable Space will be assigned the position of the first space in the string Reply$. If this value is zero, there is no space in Reply$ and we assume that the entry was not valid. Otherwise, the first name starts at the first character in Reply$ and goes to the character at position (Space-1), the character just before the space.

Returning to our example where the variable Name$ contains the value ''Susan Smith'', we can now write the first name as

```
Name$[1 : pos(Name$, " ") - 1]
```

and the last name

```
Name$[pos(Name$, " ") + 1 : len(Name$)]
```

As long as the string Name$ contains only two names, separated by a space, the first substring always contains the first name and the second substring contains the last name.

The UCASE$ and LCASE$ Functions

The string function UCASE$(A$) converts any lowercase letters in A$ to uppercase letters. LCASE$(A$) does just the opposite, changing uppercase letters to lowercase. No other characters in A$ are affected.

Examples are

```
ucase$("Bill Jones, Jr.") is BILL JONES, JR.
lcase$("Bill Jones, Jr.") is bill jones, jr.
```

The LCASE$ or UCASE$ function is often used when you wish to compare two strings for equality, without regard for whether the characters are lowercase or uppercase. Here is a program that asks a user to enter a name and compares the name with names in a list.

The entered name is stored in the variable Name$ and is changed to uppercase. As each name is read from the list, it is converted to uppercase and is compared to Name$. Thus both strings have all alphabetic characters converted to uppercase before a comparison is made.

```
! Example Program 5-6.
! Compare names.

INPUT prompt "Enter your first name: ": Name$
LET Name$ = ucase$(Name$)
LET Found$ = "false"
DO while more data and Found$ = "false"
   READ List$
   IF Name$ = ucase$(List$) then LET Found$ = "true"
LOOP

IF Found$ = "true" then
   PRINT "Your name is on the list."
ELSE
   PRINT "Your name is not on the list."
END IF

DATA John, Mary, Rebecca, June, Peter, Ernst, Bill
END
```

We use the variable Found$ to indicate whether a comparison was successful. We call this type of variable a *flag*. The value of Found is initially set to "false" and is changed to "true" if a comparison is true. We check at the beginning of the loop and exit if there are no more data or if the value of Found$ is "true", meaning that the last comparison was true.

The last part of the program is a branch structure. We print an appropriate message depending on the value of Found$.

The REPEAT$ and TRIM$ Functions

Another string function, REPEAT$(A$, N), returns the string A$ repeated N times. For example, the statement

```
PRINT repeat$("*", 20)
```

displays

```
*********************
```

The string function TRIM$(A$) removes all leading and trailing blanks from the string parameter A$. For example, strings used to store names in files are sometimes padded with blanks to make all name strings the same length. If Name$ contains the string "   Jane Lively" with leading blanks added to increase its length to 20 characters, then the statement

```
PRINT trim$(Name$)
```

removes the leading blanks and displays

```
Jane Lively
```

5.7 CONVERSION FUNCTIONS

These functions return values that have the effect of converting a character to its ASCII value, and vice versa, and also of converting a numeric value to the corresponding string value, and vice versa. We start with a short discussion of binary notation that is needed to explain the ASCII character set.

Binary Notation

Computers use binary arithmetic for storing numbers in memory. The smallest unit in the binary system is the *bit,* which has a value of 0 or 1. A *byte* consists of eight bits and can store an integer or whole number between 0 and 255. In True BASIC, eight bytes of computer memory are used to store the value of a numeric variable in binary form.

The ASCII Character Set

Since computers can store only numbers, some sort of numeric code is needed to store characters. The usual choice is ASCII, short for American Standard Code for Information Interchange. The ASCII character set can represent 128 characters with numeric values from 0 to 127. Each character in a string variable is stored in ASCII code in a byte of memory. Appendix F contains a table of the ASCII characters with their numeric values.

Examples are

ASCII value of "A" is 65
ASCII value of "a" is 97
ASCII value of "+" is 43
ASCII value of a space is 32

Most IBM PC-compatible computers have an additional 128 characters added to their character set, with numeric code values from 128 to 255. These characters consist of foreign letters, mathematical symbols, musical notes, and so forth. They are also included in the table in Appendix F. Note that all eight bits in a byte are used to represent the expanded set of 256 characters.

The ORD and CHR$ Functions

The ORD(A$) function returns a numeric value equal to the ASCII code of the string A$. A string with only a single character is allowed, and a longer string will produce an error when the program is run.

The CHR$(X) function returns a single-character string value. This value is the ASCII character whose numeric code is X. The variable X must have a value between 0 and 255.

Examples are

```
ord("A") is 65
chr$(66) is B
chr$(90) is Z
```

Here is an example program that uses the ORD function to determine whether an entered character is an uppercase alphabetic character.

```
! Example Program 5-7.
! Check a single character to see
! if it is upper case alphabetic.

DO
   PRINT
   INPUT prompt "Enter a character: ": Char$
   IF len(Char$) > 1 then
      PRINT "Only one character, please."
   END IF
LOOP until len(Char$) = 1

IF ord(Char$) < 65 or ord(Char$) > 90 then
   PRINT "Not an upper case alphabetic character."
ELSE
   PRINT "This is a valid character."
END IF
END
```

The program asks a user to enter a character and refuses to accept more than a single character. It then checks to see whether the ASCII value of the character is within the range of uppercase alphabetic characters and prints an appropriate message.

The VAL and STR$ Functions

The VAL(A$) function returns a numeric value equal to the number represented by the digit characters in A$. A$ may contain digits, a decimal point, plus and minus signs, and the letters E or e. If it contains any other characters, an error will result when the program is run.

The STR$(X) function returns a string whose characters are the same as those in the number X. Examples are

```
val("123") is the number 123
str$(123) is the string "123"
val("-1.2E+5") is the number -120,000
```

Remember that numbers and strings are stored in computer memory using different coding techniques. The number 123 and the string "123" are not the same quantities and are not stored in the same manner.

It is sometimes convenient to enter a number as a string and then convert it to numeric form. If a user is asked to enter a number, but enters some other characters, the program will stop with an error message. A well-designed program should not stop, but rather should tell the user what error has occurred and ask for input again.

Our example is a simple version of a general numeric input program. A number is entered into a string variable named Entry$, and the program checks each character, accepting any digit, the decimal point, the plus and minus signs, and the letters "E" and "e". Any other character is rejected, and the user is asked to enter the entire string again. When a valid entry has been made, it is converted to a number using the VAL function.

```
! Example Program 5-8.
! Check for the entry of a valid number.
! Allow any characters to be entered.

DO
   LINE INPUT prompt "Enter number: ": Entry$
   LET Valid$ = "true"  ! flag for valid number
   FOR I = 1 to len(Entry$)
       LET D$ = Entry$[I:I]
       SELECT CASE D$
       CASE "0" to "9", ".", "+", "-", "E", "e"
       CASE else
            PRINT "Character '"; D$; "' is not allowed."
            LET Valid$ = "false"  ! invalid number
       END SELECT
   NEXT I
LOOP until Valid$ = "true"

LET Number = val(Entry$)
PRINT "Entry is a valid number, equal to "; Number
END
```

We use the CASE statement to accept each valid character. If the character is not valid, the CASE ELSE branch is used to display an error message and set the flag so that another number is requested.

Note that this program as written will accept some strings that are not valid numbers, such as "eee" or "E−E+E", and then the VAL function will fail. You might try to write a better program that will accept only valid numbers. One method is to use error trapping, as discussed in Chapter 6.

5.8 PRINT AND KEYBOARD FUNCTIONS

This section introduces a function used to modify PRINT statements and a logical function used to detect keyboard input. Several new statements, used with input or output operations, are also introduced.

The TAB Function

The TAB(X) print function allows some additional format control in the PRINT statement. It is not a normal function because it does not return a value, but rather changes the location where the next expression in the PRINT statement is displayed. It can only be used in a PRINT statement.

TAB(X) moves the cursor to column X before the next expression is displayed. The lefthand column on the screen is column 1, and the righthand column is usually column 80. Semicolons are used to separate this function from its neighboring expressions.

The statement

```
PRINT "A"; tab(4); "B"; tab(20); "XYZ"
```

will display

```
A  B               XYZ
```

The TAB function is particularly useful when you use PRINT statements to display a table of values.

```
! Example Program 5-9.
! Display a table with column headings.

PRINT "Part Number"; tab(30); "Quantity on Hand"
PRINT
DO while more data
   READ Part, Quantity
   PRINT tab(2); Part; tab(36); Quantity
LOOP
DATA 131516,10,132133,25,136815,11,137442,87
END
```

This program produces the table in Figure 5-1.

Note particularly that the TAB function does not directly control the space between displayed items. Instead, it controls the location of the item immediately following the TAB function, specifying in which column that item will be displayed.

```
Part Number                    Quantity on Hand

  131516                             10
  132133                             25
  136815                             11
  137442                             87
```

Figure 5-1 Table produced by example program 5-9.

The CLEAR, SOUND, and PAUSE Statements

We introduce three simple statements that we will use in example programs. The statement

```
CLEAR
```

clears the screen and makes the entire screen available for displaying program results.

After the program has executed, the normal divided screen of True BASIC is immediately displayed again.

The statement

```
SOUND Freq, Length
```

generates a tone of frequency Freq hertz (cycles per second) and of duration Length seconds.

The statement

```
PAUSE Length
```

suspends program execution for a time of Length seconds.

The KEY INPUT Function

The test phrase KEY INPUT is a logical function, returning a value of true if the user has pressed a key since the last time the program read input from the keyboard. A logical function can only have a value of true or false.

Here is a sample program that shows how the KEY INPUT function works. The screen is cleared, a message is displayed, and it remains displayed while the program waits in a small loop until any key is pressed.

```
! Example Program 5-10.
! Clear the screen and display a message
! until any key is pressed.

CLEAR
PRINT
PRINT tab(20); "Press any key to delete this message"
DO until key input
LOOP
END
```

Another program uses the KEY INPUT function to turn off the computer's buzzer (actually a loudspeaker that produces a tone). These program statements could be used as part of a larger program where the computer is performing some long calculation. When the calculation is finished, the buzzer attracts the user's attention and is turned off by pressing any key.

We generate a tone of frequency 1,000 hertz and duration 0.5 seconds. After generating the tone, we wait 1 second before repeating the loop. The process continues until any key is pressed.

```
! Example Program 5-11.
! Test the KEY INPUT function.

PRINT "Press any key to turn off the sound."
DO until key input
   SOUND 1000, 0.5
   PAUSE 1
LOOP
END
```

The GET KEY Statement

The keyboard input statement

```
GET KEY Variable
```

serves a similar purpose. It waits for a key to be pressed and then assigns a numeric value to *Variable,* corresponding to the ASCII value of the character produced by the key. If the particular key that is pressed does not produce an ASCII character (for example, one of the function keys on an IBM keyboard), a number outside the ASCII range of values is assigned. These numbers for IBM PC-compatible computers are listed in Appendix I.

Here is a simple program that waits until a key is pressed and then prints the ASCII (or other numeric) value of that key:

```
! Example Program 5-12.
! Test the GET KEY statement.

PRINT "Press any key [";
GET KEY Value
PRINT chr$(Value);
PRINT "] its value is"; Value
END
```

If you run Example Program 5-11, you may notice that the character you pressed to stop the sound appears right after the next OK prompt. The KEY INPUT function accepts a character if a printing character key is pressed, and this character is then displayed if a PRINT statement is executed or, if not, as soon as the program ends.

We can correct the problem by using the GET KEY statement to ''gobble up'' this unwanted character and assign it to a dummy variable. Here is a revised and better version of Example Program 5-11:

```
! Example Program 5-13.
! A better KEY INPUT test program.

PRINT "Press any key to turn off the sound."
DO until key input
   SOUND 1000, 0.5
   PAUSE 1
LOOP
GET KEY Dummy
END
```

The character entered to stop the program is stored in the variable Dummy and then the program ends. The value in Dummy will not be displayed.

5.9 DEVELOPMENT OF A COMPUTER PROGRAM

The recommended steps for developing a computer program are to start with a general outline of the program, refine the outline to make it more specific, and only at that point start to write program statements. This is the same method used by good writers when developing a book or article. If you start from a general program outline, you are more likely to avoid logical errors and produce a program whose component parts all work together properly.

We recommend that you write the outline of your program on paper, as a sequence of steps. These outline steps are often called *pseudocode* statements. If any of the steps in your outline are long or complicated, write out a secondary outline of these steps. After carefully reviewing the outline, start writing the program statements that will accomplish the steps you have written down.

We stress the importance of writing the program outline, not just creating it in your mind. If your program is of any size (say, over 20 statements in length), there is too much chance of forgetting some point in the outline if it is not written down.

Pseudocode versus Flowcharts

Many older textbooks on computer programming advise students to draw *flowcharts* rather than write program outlines. A flowchart is a diagram that shows how a computer program works, using boxes and arrows as symbols for such actions as looping, branching, and I/O (input and output) operations. The symbols are joined by lines showing the flow of program control.

Figure 5-2 is an example of a section of a flowchart.

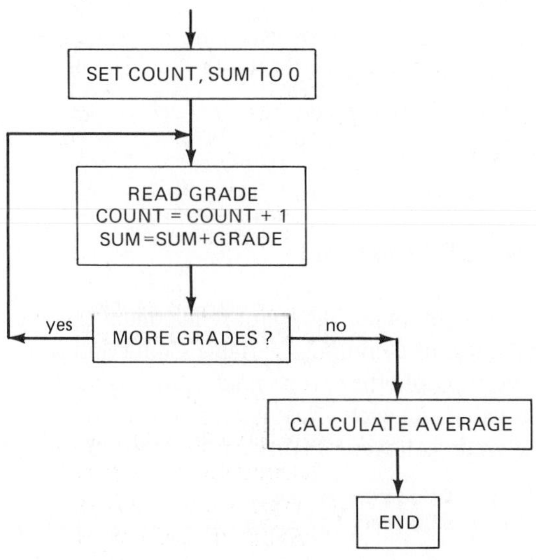

Figure 5-2 Part of a computer program flowchart.

Our experience is that flowcharts are not needed to explain small programs, and they become too complicated and difficult to draw for large programs. In both cases, it is questionable whether the benefit is worth the extra work. It is a fact that in many commercial programming operations, flowcharts are used primarily to document large programs and are drawn after the program has been completed.

On the other hand, we find that program outlines in pseudocode are easy to write (once you understand the problem) and provide invaluable guidance during program development. We strongly recommend their use.

A Program Outline

Let's look at an example of program development. We have a relatively simple problem, to compute the average of a student's grades. These grades are stored in DATA statements. Before computing the average, we would also like to be able to drop the student's lowest grade on a selective basis.

Here is an outline of the program:

```
Initialize the variables for sum and count.
Top of loop.
   Exit loop if there are no more grades.
   Read a grade value into the grade variable.
   Save this grade value if it is the lowest so far.
   Increment the count of grades.
   Add the new grade value to the sum of grades.
Bottom of loop.
Subtract the value of the lowest grade from the sum.
Reduce the count by one.
Calculate the average grade.
Print the average grade.
End the program.
```

First Version of Program

Here is the first version of our program. It calculates the average after dropping the lowest grade. We make use of a counting variable Count and a summing variable Sum. We add a variable Lowest to hold the lowest grade. This variable is initialized to 100, the highest possible grade value. As each grade is read, it is compared to the current value of Lowest and if the new grade is lower (smaller), it is stored in Lowest as the current lowest value.

```
! Example Program 5-14.
! Average student grades and drop the lowest.

LET Count = 0
LET Sum = 0
LET Lowest = 100
DO while more data
   READ Grade
   IF Grade < Lowest then LET Lowest = Grade
   LET Count = Count + 1
   LET Sum = Sum + Grade
LOOP
```

```
LET Count = Count - 1   ! adjust for drop.
LET Sum = Sum - Lowest
LET Average = round(Sum/Count)
PRINT "Average grade is"; Average

DATA 70,95,84,88,100,79,92
END
```

We read the grades from DATA statements, using the MORE DATA test to determine if there are more grades to be read. After all grades have been entered, we adjust the sum by subtracting the lowest grade and reduce the number of grades to be averaged by one. It is then a simple matter to calculate the average by dividing the sum of the grades by the number of grades. We use the ROUND function to convert our answer to the nearest integer. This program displays

```
Average grade is 90
```

Second Version of Program

It is sometimes important for the instructor to be able to specify for each student whether the lowest grade should be dropped. We now write a second version of the program that includes this feature.

```
! Example Program 5-15.
! Average student grades with
! option to drop the lowest.

LET Count = 0
LET Sum = 0
LET Lowest = 100
DO while more data   ! read the grades
   READ Grade
   LET Lowest = min(Grade, Lowest)
   LET Count = Count + 1
   LET Sum = Sum + Grade
LOOP

DO
   INPUT prompt "Drop lowest grade (Y/N)? ": Ans$
   LET Ans$ = ucase$(Ans$[1:1])
   IF Ans$ <> "Y" and Ans$ <> "N" then
      PRINT "Answer yes or no."
   END IF
LOOP until Ans$ = "Y" or Ans$ = "N"

IF Ans$ = "Y" then   ! adjust for drop
   LET Count = Count - 1
   LET Sum = Sum - Lowest
END IF

LET Average = round(Sum/Count)
PRINT "Average grade is"; Average

DATA 70,95,84,88,100,79,92
END
```

The lowest grade is selected using the MIN function while the grades are read, and this grade is stored in the variable Lowest. A loop asks the user if the lowest grade should be dropped. The answer must be a word beginning with Y or N, in uppercase or lowercase. Any other answer is considered incorrect, and the question is asked again. This is good programming practice because it reduces the possibility of the program misunderstanding a user's response. If the answer is ''yes'', the lowest grade is dropped.

IMPORTANT POINTS

You cannot take the square root of a negative number.

Division by zero is not allowed in any arithmetic expression.

The radian is the default unit of angular measure in trigonometric functions.

A blank space is a valid character in a string.

You should write out a program outline before starting to write program statements.

If you use the KEY INPUT function to stop a program, follow it with a statement such as GET KEY Dummy to remove the entered character.

SELF-TEST QUESTIONS

1. What is (a) the parameter, and (b) the value of the function SQR(9)?
2. What is the value of ABS(– 12)?
3. What is the value of each of the following functions?
   a) round(7.32)
   b) truncate(7.32, 0)
   c) round(12.85, 1)
   d) truncate(12.85, 1)
4. Under what conditions might you get unexpected results from the ROUND function?
5. What happens when you ask the computer to calculate SQR(– 9)?
6. What is the value of MOD(Num, 2) if the variable Num contains (a) an even number, or (b) an odd number?
7. What is the value of MAX(100,101)?
8. Which is the default unit for measuring angles, the degree or the radian?
9. What statement is used to specify that angles will be measured (a) in radians, and (b) in degrees?
10. What statement should be included in a program to prevent the RND function from always producing the same sequence of random numbers?
11. What is the value of LEN(''Good try'')?
12. Assume that you have a string variable Line$ with a value such as ''10,5,Duke'', where the first number is games won, the second is games lost, and the third is the name of the team. How do you calculate the value of a variable X representing the position of the first comma?

13. Using a string with the format in Question 12, how do you calculate the value of a variable Y representing the position of the second comma? You can assume that the value of X has already been calculated.
14. Assuming you have calculated the value of Y in Question 13, write a substring of Line$ that contains the team name.
15. If the variable Reply$ contains the answer to a prompt, how do you construct a substring containing only the first letter, in uppercase, of the value of Reply$?
16. What logical expression can you use to compare the values of Name1$ and Name2$, where the names are considered equal if they contain the same sequence of letters, either lowercase or uppercase?
17. What logical expression can you use to compare the values of Name1$ and Name2$, disregarding leading and trailing blanks?
18. If the value of ORD(''A'') is 65, what is the value of CHR$(65)?
19. In computer usage, what is (a) a bit, and (b) a byte?
20. A number is entered into a string variable Num$. How do you convert the value of Num$ to a numeric value and assign it to a variable Num?
21. Why might a program be designed so that numbers are entered into string variables rather than into numeric variables?
22. Can the TAB function be used in any statement other than the PRINT statement? If so, which statement?
23. What are the allowed values of the function KEY INPUT?
24. What value is assigned to the variable KeyValue in the statement

```
GET KEY KeyValue
```

when the shift key is held down and the ''A'' key is pressed?
25. What is the first thing you should do before you start writing a computer program?

PRACTICE PROGRAMS

1. Ask a user for a positive or negative number and display it rounded to the nearest integer. If 11.5 is entered, 12 should be displayed. If −6.7 is entered, −7 should be displayed.
   Test your program using the numbers 11.5, −6.7, 3.95, 9.11, and −3.95.
2. Ask a user to enter a date in the MM-DD-YY format. The month and the day may be specified by single digits, that is, by 1-5-85 rather than by 01-05-85. Separate the numbers representing the month, day, and year, and display each number on the screen with an appropriate label. Remember that the system variables Date and Date$ are reserved words.
   Test your program using the dates 11-15-85, 12-08-86, 11-7-83, 2-27-81, and 3-1-09.
3. Ask a user to enter a date in the MM-DD-YY format (see note in Practice Program 2). Display the date in a format with the month named, that is, May 25, 1981. Assume the date is in the twentieth century. The month names must be read from DATA statements.
   Test your program using the same dates as in Practice Program 2.

4. Ask a user to enter a time period expressed in seconds and display the same time period in hours, minutes, and seconds. Remember that the system variables Time and Time$ are reserved words. Consider using the MOD function.
   Test your program using times of 136, 9192, and 18456 seconds.
5. Ask a user to enter a number from the keyboard. If the number is zero, display the word ZERO; if it is positive, display the word POSITIVE; if it is negative, display the word NEGATIVE.
   Test your program using the numbers 12, −2, 0, and 199.
6. Ask a user to enter a number between 1 and 5 inclusive. Your program should allow the user to enter any sequence of characters. Check the input, and if it is longer than one character, is not numeric, or is not in the proper range, display an error message that describes the specific error. If the input is not correct, ask the user to try again.
   Test your program using the numbers 1, 0, 8, and 4, also the characters Z, #3, and A1A.
7. A palindrome is a sequence of characters that reads the same backward and forward. Punctuation marks and spaces are ignored. No distinction is made between lowercase and uppercase letters. Example: Name no one man. Ask the user to enter a string and determine if this string is a palindrome.
   Test your program using the following string values:

   Hannah
   winchester
   Madam, I'm Adam
   The time has come the Walrus said

8. Ask a user to enter a string containing only uppercase letters. Examine the value of each key as it is pressed. Display each uppercase letter as it is entered and ignore anything else. Pressing the Enter key terminates the input process. Assign the entered string of uppercase letters to a string variable named Entry$.
   Test your program using the following string values:

   SUBROUTINE
   123ABC
   New York
   HDK-468

The last three programs are somewhat longer and more difficult than the previous programs.

9. Ask a user to enter a dollar amount that may contain a dollar sign and one or more commas. For example, the entry might be $12,575.50. Assume that the entry will not be in exponential notation. Ignore (i.e., pass over) any characters that are not digits or a decimal point or a plus or minus sign. The program should ask the user to try again if the number contains more than one decimal point or more than one plus or minus sign. Store the number in a numeric variable named Amount and display it on the screen.
   Test your program using the following values:

   $12,575.50
   +125
   + −555
   123. . .456

10. The TAB function can be used for displaying and printing simple graphs, provided that you plot the graph on its side with the X axis vertical and the Y axis horizontal. Any character may be used for plotting points, but we recommend the asterisk (*). Use the dash (—) to mark the Y axis and the vertical bar (|) to mark the X axis.

Display a graph of the function $Y = 2^X$ for values of X ranging from -4 to 4 in steps of 0.5. The values of Y will be between 0 and 16.

11. A user enters an address on one line in the format

CITY, STATE ZIP

where STATE is a two-letter abbreviation and ZIP is a five-digit number. CITY may contain one or more words (i.e., Chicago, New York). Your program should check whether the entered value for ZIP is a five-digit number and the value for STATE is a two-letter string. If an error is made in input, the program should loop and let the user try again.

Extract the zip code and assign it to a numeric variable named Zip. Display this zip code value with an appropriate label.

Test your program using the following string values:

San Francisco, CA 94101
Boston, MA 021095
Worcester, 99 01601
West Menlo Park, CAL 95691
Adams, OR 9781A

6 Finding and Correcting Errors

6.1 INTRODUCTION

A large fraction of the time spent developing a computer program is devoted to finding and eliminating errors. We discuss several techniques for helping a programmer find errors. In discussing one of these techniques, we need to explain the use of function keys on the IBM PC-compatible keyboard. We also discuss a program structure for trapping and handling errors.

In addition to learning how to find errors, it is important to learn how to write programs that contain few errors. We present a recommended procedure for writing computer programs that are likely to run correctly the first time they are executed.

6.2 PLAYING COMPUTER

Our goal is to write programs that contain no errors. It is probably an impossible goal to attain, but we need to learn how to reduce the number of errors to a minimum. At the same time, we must develop skill in finding errors and then removing them from our programs. This process is called *debugging*.

One of the best methods for finding errors is to read through a computer program, pretending that you are the computer. You make all the calculations and decisions that would normally be made by the computer. Many simple errors will be revealed.

This method is easy to understand and to apply, but it can be tedious. You will find it most useful for examining small sections of a program. You will make better progress if you write down intermediate results on paper, in a systematic format. If complicated arithmetic calculations are involved, the process can be slow and you should use a hand calculator.

In spite of the limitations, we recommend that you try this method first. It is a natural way to find errors if a program is not working properly.

6.3 TEMPORARY PRINT STATEMENTS

Beginning programmers often say "I know that the value of variable X at this point in the program is 15.2, but when I make a calculation using X and print the results, they are wrong." Our response is "How do you know that the value of X is 15.2?"

One way to answer the question is to put a temporary PRINT statement into your program and see what the value of X actually is at the point of calculation. It is surprising how often it will be different from what you thought it should be.

It is not unusual to insert half a dozen temporary PRINT statements in a program before finding an error. Sometimes it is helpful to include a label in the PRINT statement to help identify its location.

For example,

```
PRINT "In report section: X ="; X
```

identifies the variable being displayed and the program section where it has this value. A single PRINT statement can be used to print out the values of several different variables. For example,

```
PRINT "After first search: I,Sum = ";I; Sum
```

You must, of course, remember to delete the temporary PRINT statements after you have found the error.

In many cases, these two techniques, playing computer and inserting temporary PRINT statements, are sufficient to identify programming errors.

6.4 THE OTHER FUNCTION KEYS

Before discussing the next method for finding errors, we need to learn about the F4 function key that is used to mark text. Remember that we have already discussed three of the function keys, the F1 key, and the F2 key, which move the cursor between the command window and the program window, and the F10 key, which is the Help key. We now discuss all the remaining function keys, F3 through F7 and F9. The F8 key is not used in True BASIC.

The Find Key

The *F3 key* is the Find key, used to find words or sequences of characters in your program. When you move the cursor to the program window and press this key, the prompt "Find:" is displayed in the command window. If you are trying to find a particular word, type in that word and press the Enter key. The cursor will move to the first occurrence of the word in your program. If you want to search for the next occurrence of the word, just press the F3 key and then the Enter key again. If the word you specify cannot be found, the message "Not found." will be displayed.

Search always starts from the position of the cursor in the program window when you pressed F3. If you want to start searching at the beginning of your program, move the cursor there by pressing the Home key before pressing the F3 key. This search for words is insensitive to uppercase or lowercase. If you ask to find the word *BOX,* both *BOX* and *box* will be found.

If you want to find a sequence of characters rather than a complete word, you must enclose the sequence in quotation marks. Thus if you ask to find the sequence "*box*", the words *box* and *boxer* will both be found. The word *BOX,* however, will not be found because when characters are enclosed in quotation marks, the search is sensitive to uppercase or lowercase.

The Mark Key

The *F4 key* is used to mark blocks of text that later will be moved, copied, or deleted. A marked block consists of one or more program lines. Place the cursor over the line tag of the first line to be included in the marked block and press the F4 key. Then move the cursor to the last line to be included in the marked block and press the F4 key again. You will notice that the line tags of all lines in the marked block are now displayed in reverse mode. To mark a single line, just press the F4 key once while the cursor is over the line tag of that line.

Only one block of program lines can be marked at a time. If you have marked the wrong block or change your mind, you can erase the marking on the block by pressing the F4 key again. You can then use the same key to mark another block. Experiment with the F4 key until you are familiar with the way it works.

The Delete and Move Keys

A marked block of text can be deleted by pressing the *Del* key when the cursor is on the line tag of one of the marked lines. A marked block can be moved to a new position in your program, being inserted right after another program line. Place the cursor on the line tag of this line where the block is to be inserted and press the *F6 key*. The marked block will be deleted from its old location and inserted in the new location.

The Copy Key

The *F5 key* copies a marked block from its current location and inserts it in a new position. It works just like the F6 key except the marked block is not deleted from its old location. You will probably make greater use of the F6 key for moving marked blocks than of the F5 key for copying marked blocks.

The Undelete Key

Another useful function key is the *F7 key,* which serves as the "undelete" key. If you have just deleted a character or a line or a block of lines, you can recover it by pressing the F7 key. Only the last item deleted can be recovered, all previously deleted items are lost. Thus if you use the Del key to delete several characters one by one, only the last character deleted will be restored. You will find the F7 key most useful for restoring program lines that you delete by mistake.

The Run Key

The *F9 key* is used to execute or run a program, producing the same results as the RUN command. If you press the F9 key when the cursor is in the program window, it will move automatically to the command window and the program will be executed. This key is a convenient alternative to the RUN command.

As we mentioned earlier, a list of all function keys for IBM PC-compatible computers is in Appendix B.

6.5 STOP AND CONTINUE PROGRAM EXECUTION

Returning now to our discussion of how to find program errors, we examine two special True BASIC commands, BREAK and CONTINUE. This pair of commands provides a way to stop an executing program, examine variables and change their values, and then continue execution from that point in the program. The command BREAK tells the computer program to stop execution at the first line of a marked section of the program. This marked section can be, and often is, a single program line. The command CONTINUE tells the program to continue execution from that point.

The BREAK Command

Use the F4 key to mark a program line. With a line marked, go to the command window and enter the command BREAK. You will notice that a small triangle appears next to the line tag, indicating that a breakpoint has been set at that line. Now press the F9 key or type the command RUN and the program will start executing. It will halt with the cursor in the program window when the breakpoint line is reached. Use the F2 key to move back to the command window.

Examining and Changing Variable Values

With the program halted, you can examine the value of any variable by using PRINT in the direct or immediate mode as a command. Direct mode means that you enter the statement on the command window in response to the BASIC prompt. Here is an example, where the prompt **OK** is displayed by the computer and the following command is entered by the user.

```
OK. PRINT X, A$
```

The values of variables X and A$ will be displayed on the screen. You can also change the value of any variable by using the assignment statement in the direct mode as a command. For example,

```
OK. LET X = -16
```

A separate command is used to change the value of each variable. **You may not enter a new program statement or modify an old statement while the program is stopped.**

The CONTINUE Command

When you have finished examining your program and possibly changing the values of some variables, enter the CONTINUE command, and the program will resume execution.

A breakpoint is removed by entering the command BREAK a second time. If you have more than one breakpoint in your program, the breakpoint you wish to remove must be marked. After removing a breakpoint, the line can be released from "marked" status by pressing the F4 key.

Using a breakpoint is a little more complicated than using a temporary PRINT statement, but this new technique can give you more information. You should become familiar with both debugging methods.

We recommend a systematic approach to debugging programs. First, read through your program carefully and see if you can spot an obvious error. Another person will often find errors in your program that you have not noticed. As you read your program, you will automatically start to "play computer" and ask yourself what the values of different variables should be.

If you still have errors, then start inserting PRINT statements or breakpoints. Don't hesitate to use lots of PRINT statements or breakpoints to find an elusive error.

The art of program debugging can only be learned by experience. It can be time consuming and frustrating, but if you persist, you should be able to find and eliminate most program errors.

6.6 CALCULATION ERRORS

Most calculation errors are due to incorrect programs, but some are due to limitations of the computer or the language. These latter errors are hard to find and require some understanding of how your computer works. We will discuss two examples.

Limited Space for Storing Numbers

The first type of error occurs because of limited storage space for numeric variables. Referring to our earlier terminology, the mailbox for storing numeric variables can hold only a certain number of digits. Additional digits are lost.

True BASIC stores its numbers in an eight-byte format on an IBM PC-compatible computer, providing a precision of about 14 digits. That precision is sufficient for most applications. There are occasions, however, when you need greater precision. Here is a sample program to show the type of problem that can arise when you manipulate numbers with too many digits:

```
! Example Program 6-1.
! Test the handling of many digits.

INPUT prompt "Enter large number X...": X
PRINT "Value of (X + 1) - X is"; (X+1)-X
PRINT "Value of (X - X) + 1 is"; (X-X)+1
END
```

As you might expect, problems start to arise when the number of digits in the value you enter approaches the numeric variable precision. When you enter the value 5e15 for the variable X, you get the correct value of one for each answer. When you enter the value 5e16, the first PRINT statement displays an incorrect value of zero. The second PRINT statement displays the correct value of one.

Converting Between Binary and Decimal Numbers

The second type of error occurs because computers use binary arithmetic for manipulating numbers, while people write programs that use decimal arithmetic. This means that the computer must make conversions between binary and decimal representations of numbers.

In binary arithmetic as in decimal arithmetic, certain fractions can only be represented by nonterminating sequences of digits. A familiar example in decimal arithmetic is the value of 0.333. . . (a nonterminating sequence of the digit 3) for the fraction $1/3$. If the sequence is terminated, it is not exactly equal to the fraction. For example, the sequence 0.33333 is not equal to the fraction $1/3$.

The fraction $1/10000$ or 0.0001 is represented in binary arithmetic as a nonterminating sequence of binary digits. If the sequence is terminated, as it must be if the number is stored and manipulated in the computer, it is no longer exactly equal to the fraction $1/10000$.

This type of error causes problems when an equality is used to make a program decision. Here is an example:

```
! Example Program 6-2.
! Failure of an equality test.

LET X =  999
PRINT X;
DO until X = 1
   LET X = X + .0001
   PRINT X;
LOOP
END
```

The problem with this program is that the value of X is never exactly equal to one, even though the PRINT statement displays a value of one. Thus the loop will continue indefinitely. The problem can be corrected, in this example, by testing whether the value of X differs by only a small amount (small compared to the increment of .0001) from one. Here is a program that works:

```
! Example Program 6-3.
! A successful equality test.

LET X = .999
PRINT X;
DO until abs(X - 1) < 1e-15
   LET X = X + .0001
   PRINT X;
LOOP
END
```

The conclusion to draw from these examples is to **avoid using an equality with numeric values as a condition in an IF statement.**

These and similar types of errors will occur in computer programs written in almost any language. Try the sample programs yourself on your computer. Simple test programs, such as the ones we have listed, can be written to determine how True BASIC will behave on your particular computer. With a little care, you can write computer programs that avoid these types of errors.

6.7 ERROR TRAPPING AND HANDLING

Program errors can be divided into several general classes. Compile errors (also called syntax errors) are errors in statement syntax, generated when your program is being compiled. These errors are identified immediately, and you can use the editor to correct your program, and then compile the program again.

Logic errors are the result of mistakes in logic when the program was designed or written. The program may run perfectly but produce meaningless results. These errors are hard to find and can be corrected only by thoroughly testing the program.

Run-time errors occur while the program is executing. These errors may be caused by logic errors or by other mistakes when writing the program. They are usually fatal and cause the program to stop. Computer programmers say the program has "crashed". True BASIC provides a facility for *trapping* these run-time errors, allowing the user to make corrections and continue executing the program.

The syntax for trapping errors is as follows:

```
WHEN EXCEPTION IN
     protected block
USE
     exception handler block
END WHEN
```

The Protected Block of Statements

EXCEPTION is the ANS BASIC word for an error, but True BASIC allows the word ERROR to be used in place of the standard word EXCEPTION. The protected block can be any sequence of statements in the main program unit or in a subprogram unit. It cannot include a subprogram definition statement such as SUB (parameters) or FUNCTION (parameters) (these statements are discussed in Chapter 7). In most applications, the protected block is a short sequence of statements.

The Error Handler Block

The exception or error handler block is another sequence of statements that is executed only if there is a run-time error in the protected block. Under normal circumstances, the program skips over the error handler block and executes the first statement after the END WHEN statement.

The EXTYPE and EXTEXT$ Functions

Two system functions are particularly useful in the error handler block. The numeric function EXTYPE returns an error number when a run-time error occurs. These numbers are listed in Appendix H. The value of EXTYPE can be used to make a decision in the error handler block.

The string function EXTEXT$ returns the specific error message (also listed in Appendix H). When error trapping is in operation, this message is not printed automatically. The value of EXTEXT$ (the error message string) can be displayed or used in any other manner in the error handler block.

Here is a sample program using error trapping:

```
! Example Program 6-4.
! Calculate the square root of a number.

LET NoError$ = "false"
DO
   LINE INPUT prompt "Enter number: ": Value$

   WHEN error in ! protected block
        LET Number = val(Value$)
        LET Result = sqr(Number)
        PRINT "Square root of "; Value$; " is"; Result
        LET NoError$ = "true"

   USE ! error handler block
       IF extype = 3005 or extype = 4001 then
          PRINT "Error: "; extext$
       ELSE
          PRINT "Unexpected error: "; extext$
       END IF
       PRINT "Please try again."
   END WHEN

LOOP until NoError$ = "true"
END
```

Note the use of the LINE INPUT statement to accept any sequence of characters, with checking for a proper number taking place when the VAL function is invoked. Error 3005 is taking the square root of a negative number. Error 4001 is using the VAL function on a string that is not a proper number. In either case, the appropriate error message is printed. If another, unexpected run-time error occurs, a general error message is printed.

We introduce the concept of a *logical flag* in this program. A logical flag can have one of only two possible values, true or false. We use the string variable NoError$ as a flag and assign it a value of "false" before entering the main loop. If the program successfully converts the string Value$ to a number and calculates the square root, a value of "true" is assigned to NoError$. The flag permits an exit from the loop when a valid number has been entered and its square root displayed.

Error trapping is an example of good defensive programming. You should anticipate the possibility of run-time errors and develop plans to handle them when they occur. Nothing is more discouraging to the user of an application program than to have the program suddenly stop and display an error message that is not understood.

6.8 HINTS FOR WRITING CORRECT PROGRAMS

Most of our discussion in this chapter has been about methods for finding and correcting program errors. An equally important topic is how to write programs that have no errors in the first place.

When we say that a program is error-free, we mean that extensive testing has revealed no errors. There is no way of knowing, however, that every single error has been found and corrected. Unfortunately, some errors are never found until the program has been used by many different people in many different applications.

Throughout the book we stress **logical program design, development of a program in small modules, and use of clear structures for looping and branching.** Keep these points in mind as we discuss some hints for writing better programs.

Understand the Problem

You cannot write a program to solve a problem until you completely understand the problem. This is an obvious statement, but a lot of people start programming before they understand clearly what the program must do. Keep asking questions or investigate further until you do understand the problem.

Plan First, Program Later

A common mistake made by beginning programmers is to start writing their programs too soon. This doesn't mean to do nothing until just before the program is due, but it does mean to do a lot of thinking and planning before writing your first program statement. Here are two steps you should take:

First, you must decide how you will solve the problem. The method of solution is called an *algorithm*. You want an efficient algorithm that will solve the problem accurately and quickly. You learn algorithms by reading books and articles, by looking at other programs and by discussing methods of solution with experienced programmers.

Second, you must **write an outline of your program.** An outline can be written as one or more descriptive paragraphs, or in the more traditional outline form. Try to divide your problem solution into separate tasks and then outline a solution for each task. When you learn about the subprogram capabilities of True BASIC in Chapter 7, you will be able to organize your program into a collection of program units. The more detailed your outline, the easier it will be to write the computer program.

Only when you have taken these two steps are you ready to start writing the program itself.

Write Simple Programs

Use all the tools you have available to write a program that is easy to read and understand. Use variable names that are as descriptive as possible. Use indentation to identify the statements in a branch or a loop. Use comments to explain the logical action of the program, not what an individual statement does.

Avoid program structures that are tricky or hard to understand. There is usually no justification for writing programs that are difficult to understand to make them more efficient. Remember that computer memory is becoming less expensive and computers are becoming faster. Programs should be written to minimize the time required for maintenance rather than to minimize the amount of memory used or the execution time.

Most important, write your program as a series of small modules, as independent from one another as possible. No module should be larger than a single page. We will show you in Chapter 7 how to write a module as an external subroutine or function. We recommend that you use this technique.

Thoroughly test each module before adding it to your program. Small modules tend to be easier than large programs to write and debug. If each module is free of errors, the resulting program should also be error-free.

Test and Debug Carefully

If you are careful in writing your program, it should contain few errors. Test your program for as many conditions as possible that might cause an error. Look carefully at extreme conditions, such as the largest and smallest values of key variables. Ask someone else to run your program and see if they can make it fail.

A common type of error is called the ''off by one bug''. This is the error that occurs, for example, when you are counting and the sum turns out to be one less or one greater than it should be. Look carefully at your logic and you should be able to find the mistake.

Your ability to write error-free programs will improve quickly if you follow these suggestions. There will be times, however, when in spite of your best efforts, you cannot get a program to work. You should then go back and examine your program outline. If you are not satisfied with it, you may save time by starting over again. It is difficult to write a good program from a bad outline.

IMPORTANT POINTS

Use lots of temporary PRINT statements to help locate program errors.

Never modify a program statement or add a new statement when a breakpoint is executed.

Avoid using an equality with numeric values as a condition in an IF statement.

You must **understand** the problem before writing a program to **solve** the problem.

Always write down a program outline before starting to write program statements.

Develop your program as a series of small, simple modules that have been thoroughly tested.

Don't use ''tricky'' or complicated logic to make a program shorter or more efficient.

SELF-TEST QUESTIONS

1. What is meant by the term ''debugging''?
2. What is the method of ''playing computer''?
3. What statement can you insert into a program to display the value of a variable?
4. Which function key is used (a) to start marking part of your program, and (b) to stop marking?
5. Which function key removes the marking from a block of marked text?
6. What is the easiest way to delete a block of several program lines?
7. What is the function (a) of the F5 key, and (b) of the F6 key?
8. If you delete a line by mistake, which key do you press to recover that line?

9. When program execution has been stopped by entering the BREAK command, can you (a) change the value of a program variable, (b) insert a new program statement, or (c) delete an existing statement?
10. After a program has been stopped with the BREAK command, what command do you enter to restart execution?
11. What problem may occur when you use an expression like X = 5 in a program to test whether a process (such as a loop) should be stopped? How can you avoid the problem?
12. When an error occurs in a protected block of program statements, control transfers to the error handler block. Which statements are used to denote (a) the beginning and (b) the end of the error handler block?
13. If an error occurs, what general type of expression is assigned to EXTEXT$ and to EXTYPE?
14. What is an algorithm? Can you develop an algorithm for a problem if you do not understand the problem?
15. Why is a written program outline preferable to a mental outline?
16. Why is it important to write programs that are clear and easy to understand?

PRACTICE PROGRAMS

1. You are asked to calculate the roots of the equation

$$AX^2 + BX + C = 0$$

Recall that the roots are given by the expressions

$$X_1 = \frac{-B + \sqrt{B^2 - 4AC}}{2A}$$

$$X_2 = \frac{-B - \sqrt{B^2 - 4AC}}{2A}$$

You write the following program:

```
! Program with a logical error.

INPUT prompt "Value of A? ": A
INPUT prompt "Value of B? ": B
INPUT prompt "Value of C? ": C
LET X1 = (-B + sqr(B*B - 4*A*C)) / (2*A)
LET X2 = (-B - sqr(B*B - 4*A*C)) / (2*A)
PRINT "The roots are"; X1; "and"; X2
END
```

A user enters a value of 3 for A, 2 for B, and 2 for C. The program responds with a run-time error. What is wrong? Write a corrected program that will handle this set of values.

2. Practice Programs 2 and 3 in Chapter 5 ask a user to enter a date in MM-DD-YY format. The month and the day may be specified by single digits; that is, by 1-5-85 rather than by 01-05-85. Assume 29 days in February.

Write a program that requests such a date and then checks the validity of the entry. If a user enters an invalid date, the program should loop back and allow the date to be entered again.

Test your program using the values

13-20-85
2-30-81
11-31-88
1-17-77

3. If you have not already done so, write Practice Program 1 with a protected block for the root calculations and an error handler block. Use the same numeric entries to test your program.
4. A user is asked to enter two numbers, A and B, and the quotient A/B is displayed. Place the calculation of A/B in a protected block and use an error handler block to report if division by zero is attempted. If an error occurs, display the text of an appropriate error message. All error-trapping and error-handling statements should be within a loop so that the user can enter new values if an error is detected.

   Test your program using the following number pairs:

   13.5, 7.7
   0, 33.2
   125, 0
   25, 5

5. Write a program similar to Example Program 5-8 that uses a protected block and an error handler block to warn a user if an entry is not a valid number.

   Test your program using the values

   125.99
   11,234.50
   13.2E−3
   13.2E+ −3
   +e+e+e
   −55

6. This exercise is designed to give you practice with the function keys. Using Example Program 5-15, perform the following operations:

   a) Move the cursor to the top of the program in the program window and use the F3 key to find all occurrences of the word Ans$. Change each occurrence of Ans$ to the word Reply$.

   b) Look up the command CHANGE and use it to change all occurrences of Reply$ back to Ans$.

   c) Delete the line **LET Count = Count − 1.** Use the F5 key to make a copy of the line **LET Count = Count + 1** and insert it where you deleted the first line. Change the plus sign to a minus sign.

   d) Move the program fragment

```
LET Average = round(Sum/Count)
PRINT "Average grade is"; Average
```

   and insert it after the first DO loop. Mark and delete the second DO loop and the following IF block.

   e) Mark and delete the three REMARK lines at the beginning of the program. Use the F7 key to restore this deletion.

7 Writing Programs Using Subprograms

7.1 INTRODUCTION

Modern computer languages allow a program to be designed as a series of independent subprogram units. We will discuss two such units that are available in True BASIC—the external function and the external subroutine.

Subprogram parameters allow information to be passed to external subprogram units and, in the case of external subroutines, to be returned back to the original program. Local variables provide isolation between the main program and subprograms, and between individual subprograms. Libraries of subprograms can be constructed, saved on disk, and subsequently incorporated into new True BASIC programs.

7.2 PROGRAM UNITS

As a program becomes larger, several benefits result from dividing it into modules or units. These modules are called *program units* and are further identified as the *main program* and *subprograms*. The main program (or one of the subprograms) can *call* or use other subprograms as it carries out its task and is then identified as the *calling* program unit.

There are several benefits to be derived from writing modular programs.

Well-designed Programs: Programs designed as a collection of modules are easier to write and debug, easier to read and understand, and easier to maintain and modify. This type of design is called *modular program design*—dividing a large program into smaller modules or program units.

For example, suppose that we want to write a program to develop a class room schedule. This is not an easy problem to solve, and we have not yet discussed all the techniques required to write such a program. We can, however, analyze the problem and see how it can be divided into subtasks.

Task: Develop a classroom schedule.

Subtask A: Enter list of classes with time and size of each class. Enter list of classrooms with size of each room.

Subtask B: Sort classes by hour of the day. For each hour, sort classes by descending size. Sort classrooms by descending size.

Subtask C: For each hour, assign class to room, starting with the largest size class. Note any class that cannot be assigned.

Subtask D: Print list of classes not assigned to rooms. Print list of rooms showing hours not assigned.

Whereas the task is complex and stated in general terms, each subtask is more specific and thus easier to understand. There may be a further division of one of the listed subtasks; for example, a general sorting module might be a separate sub-subtask within subtask B. After more experience, you will be able to write a program based on such a modular design.

Isolation: Isolation implies that each program unit is separate and distinct from the other units. Complete isolation means that a variable in one program unit is completely different from a variable with the same name in another program unit. Changes in the value of a variable are confined to a single program unit.

The importance of isolation is that a change in a variable value in one program unit can never cause an unexpected change in another program unit. Lack of program unit isolation can be a major and hard-to-find source of errors in large programs.

In practice, complete isolation may not be possible when we want to return or pass back information from a called program unit to the calling program unit. The goal of complete isolation is still desirable, however, and to the extent that this goal can be achieved, the chance of errors will be reduced.

Subprogram Libraries: Libraries of well-designed and error-free subprogram units can be created and used in several different programs. A subprogram that does a particular job, and does it well, does not have to written over and over again. It can be placed in a library and used in any new program that is written. These library functions and subroutines serve as language extensions to True BASIC and are discussed at the end of this chapter.

In view of these benefits, we will use modular program design in most of the large example programs in this and subsequent chapters. The possible program units are

The main program
External functions
External subroutines
External pictures

The main program is the type of True BASIC program that we have developed in previous chapters, always ending with an END statement. Statements in the main program must name and identify all the external subprogram units.

External functions and subroutines will be discussed in the next two sections. They are usually written after the main program's END statement, although they may be invoked from separate libraries.

External pictures are mentioned here for completeness, but are not discussed until Chapter 12.

7.3 EXTERNAL FUNCTIONS

We have already defined a standard function in Chapter 5. A similar definition describes an external function unit. It is a separate block of program statements that is identified by name. It can have values passed to it as parameters from the calling program unit. The external function unit performs some calculation or manipulation and returns a string or numeric value that is assigned to the function name. An example might be a function to calculate the cube root of a number.

The external function is invoked or called when its name is used in an expression. **A value must be assigned to the function name before control returns to the calling program unit.** When we refer to a function in this section, we mean an external function.

For example, we might have a function named Volume that calculates the volume of a box. When we call or invoke this function, we have to pass to it the values of a particular box's length, width, and height. To display the volume of a box of length 10 inches, width 5 inches, and height 3 inches, we use the statement

```
PRINT Volume (10, 5, 3)
```

The external function unit itself consists of the statements

```
EXTERNAL FUNCTION Volume (L, W, H)
    LET Volume = L * W * H
END FUNCTION
```

where the function named Volume is assigned a value equal to the volume of the box.

Function Unit Heading

The first statement in a function unit must be

```
EXTERNAL FUNCTION Name (Parameters)
```

where *Name* is the function name and *Parameters* is a list of variable names, separated by commas. The function name must follow the same rules that apply to variable names (see Chapter 3). The function value may be either numeric or string, and if the function has a string value, the function name must end with a dollar sign.

In our example, this statement is

```
EXTERNAL FUNCTION Volume (L, W, H)
```

and the parameters are the variables L, W, and H.

Function Parameters

The parameters are variables, separated from one another by commas, and are of type string or numeric. These variables are called *local variables,* meaning that they are known and can be used only within the function unit itself. Values are assigned or *passed* to these parameter variables when the function is called. This method of passing information through parameters is called *pass by value* and the parameters are called *value parameters*. These parameters are also sometimes referred to as *one-way parameters*.

The concept of local variables is important because it provides isolation between an external function and other program units. In addition to the parameter variables, any other variable introduced and used in the function unit is a local variable.

Consider the case of a main program with a variable named Reply$ and an external function with a variable named Reply$. These two variables have the same name, but they refer to different mailboxes or memory locations. Thus a value assigned to Reply$ in the function is placed in one mailbox, while the value of Reply$ in the main program is contained in another mailbox. The two variables may have the same name, but they are really completely different variables.

As an analogy, post office box 572 in the main post office contains entirely different letters than post office box 572 in a branch post office, although they both have the same name or identifying number.

Other FUNCTION Statements

The last statement in a function unit must be

```
END FUNCTION
```

The unit from which the function is called (usually the main program) must have a declaration statement containing the function name. One declaration statement may contain several function names, and there may be more than one declaration statement. The syntax is

```
DECLARE FUNCTION Name1, Name2...
```

Finally, there must be a specific assignment statement (a LET statement) in the function unit that assigns a value to the function name. This value may be either a number or a string, depending on the function type. The value must be assigned before the END FUNCTION statement is executed.

Our complete example program looks like this:

```
! Example Program 7-1.
! Using an external function.

DECLARE FUNCTION Volume
PRINT Volume(10, 5, 3)
END

EXTERNAL FUNCTION Volume (L, W, H)
    LET Volume = L * W * H
END FUNCTION
```

and displays the value 150.

It is possible to exit a function at points other than the end, using the phrase

```
EXIT FUNCTION
```

but an error will occur if the function has not been assigned a value before exiting.

When a function is called, the values passed to it can be the values of variables or constants or expressions, as in this example:

```
! Example Program 7-2.
! Using an external function.

DECLARE FUNCTION Volume
LET L = 10
PRINT Volume(L, L/2, 3)
END

EXTERNAL FUNCTION Volume (Length, Width, Height)
    LET Volume = Length * Width * Height
END FUNCTION
```

The function call in the statement PRINT Volume(L, L/2, 3) obtains its first parameter value from the variable "L", its second value from the expression "L/2", and its third value from the constant "3".

Our next example uses a function to calculate the factorial value of a positive number entered from the keyboard. For example, the factorial value of 5, denoted 5! by mathematicians, is equal to 1*2*3*4*5, or 120. By definition, zero factorial equals 1. This program prompts the user to enter a number from the keyboard, checks if the number is negative, and if it is, displays an error message and stops.

```
! Example Program 7-3.
! Calculate a factorial number.

DECLARE FUNCTION Factorial
INPUT prompt "Enter number: ": Number
IF Number < 0 then
   PRINT "Number must be positive."
ELSE
   PRINT "Factorial of"; Number;
   PRINT "is"; Factorial(Number)
END IF
END

EXTERNAL FUNCTION Factorial (X)
    ! Calculate the factorial of X.
    LET Result = 1
    FOR I = 1 to X
        LET Result = Result * I
    NEXT I
    LET Factorial = Result
END FUNCTION
```

If the number is positive or zero, the function Factorial is called by the PRINT statement. The factorial value is calculated in the function and is returned to the main program. If X has a value of zero, the FOR-NEXT loop is never executed and a value of one is assigned to Factorial. Note that the value of the number, stored in the variable Number in the main program, is passed to the variable X in the function.

Another example uses string functions. A palindrome is a sentence or sequence of letters that reads the same backward and forward. To test a palindrome, all letters must be converted to the same case (say, uppercase) and all nonalphabetic characters (including spaces or blanks) must be removed from the sentence.

The main program asks the user to enter a string of characters from the keyboard. The standard function UCASE$ is called to convert all letters to uppercase. The user-defined function Remove$ is called to remove all nonalphabetic characters. Finally, the user-defined function Reverse$ is called to write a new string that is the reverse of the original string.

```
! Example Program 7-4.
! Find a palindrome.

DECLARE FUNCTION Remove$, Reverse$
LINE INPUT prompt "Enter string: ": String$
LET String$ = ucase$(String$)
LET String$ = Remove$(String$)
LET Compare$ = Reverse$(String$)
IF String$ = Compare$ then
   PRINT "String is a palindrome."
ELSE
   PRINT "String is not a palindrome."
END IF
END

EXTERNAL FUNCTION Remove$ (A$)
    ! Remove nonalphabetic characters.
    LET B$ = ""   ! a null string
    FOR I = 1 to len(A$)
        IF A$[I:I] >= "A" and A$[I:I] <= "Z" then
           LET B$ = B$ & A$[I:I]
        END IF
    NEXT I
    LET Remove$ = B$
END FUNCTION

EXTERNAL FUNCTION Reverse$ (A$)
    ! Reverse a string.
    LET B$=""
    FOR I = len(A$) to 1 step -1
        LET B$ = B$ & A$[I:I]
    NEXT I
    LET Reverse$ = B$
END FUNCTION
```

Note how the string B$ is initially assigned a null value in each function. The selected characters are then added to B$, one by one. The two strings, String$ and Compare$, are compared, and if they are the same, the original string is a palindrome. Try this program yourself with the well-known palindrome ''Madam, I'm Adam''.

More on Writing and Using Functions

True BASIC allows you to use the word DEF in place of the standard word FUNCTION in a function heading. We believe that FUNCTION is more descriptive and will use it in this book. The word EXTERNAL is optional in the first line of a function block as long as the function block follows the main program END statement.

Functions may be nested, meaning that one function may call another function. The calling function must have a DECLARE statement naming the called function.

Each time a function is called, all local parameter variables have values passed to them. Other local variables are reinitialized, numeric variables to zero and string variables to the null string.

This example illustrates the error of expecting a local variable to hold its value between function calls. A sum will not be accumulated in the variable Sum because it is reset to zero each time the function is called.

```
! Example Program 7-5.
! *** THIS IS NOT A VALID PROGRAM ***
! Display the sum of numbers entered from keyboard.

DECLARE FUNCTION Add
PRINT "Enter zero to stop input."
INPUT prompt "Number? ": Number
DO until Number = 0
   LET Result = Add(Number)
   INPUT prompt "Number? ": Number
LOOP
PRINT "The sum is"; Result
END

EXTERNAL FUNCTION Add (N)
    LET Sum = Sum + N
    LET Add = Sum
END FUNCTION
```

The local variable Sum is reset to zero each time Add is called and so contains only the last value of the parameter N. The program does not display the expected result.

7.4 EXTERNAL SUBROUTINES

In contrast to a function, we can define the general purpose of a subroutine as performing some task or carrying out some action, such as printing a standard business form.

Subroutine Unit Heading

Like functions, external subroutines are separate blocks of program statements. They are identified by name, and the first statement in a subroutine program unit must be

```
EXTERNAL SUB Name (Parameters)
```

Unlike a function, **no value is associated with a subroutine name.** Thus a subroutine name cannot represent a string value, and the dollar sign character is not allowed. The name is used only to identify the subroutine and never has any value assigned to it. In True BASIC, the word EXTERNAL may be omitted.

The parameters in a subroutine heading are local variable names, separated from one another by commas. These parameters are different from the value parameters of a function. We will discuss their behavior in detail in the next section. Any other variables used in the subroutine are also local variables.

The last statement in a subroutine block must be

```
END SUB
```

and other exit points may be identified by the phrase

```
EXIT SUB
```

A subroutine that displays a string parameter named Value$ on the screen, centered between the left and right margins, is

```
EXTERNAL SUB Center (Value$, Width)
    PRINT tab((Width - len(Value$))/2); Value$
END SUB
```

The parameter Width is the width of the screen in columns.

Calling a Subroutine

A subroutine is called from another program unit by the statement

```
CALL Name (Parameters)
```

Parameters in the CALL statement may be variables, constants, or expressions. They must agree in number and type (numeric or string) with the parameter list in the subroutine unit heading. The calling program unit may be the main program, a function, or another subroutine.

Using our example subroutine, the call statement might be

```
CALL Center ("Analysis of 1983 Earnings", 80)
```

It creates the following display:

```
                    Analysis of 1983 Earnings
```

Subroutine Parameters

A major difference between functions and subroutines is the way that information is passed through parameters. In the CALL statement, parameter variable names refer to specific mailboxes or memory locations. In the SUB statement, parameter variable names are local names for these same mailboxes. Thus if a change is made in the value of one of the local parameter variables in a subroutine, the value of the corresponding variable in the calling program is also changed.

Using our previous analogy, our post office box may be known officially as box 572, but when we forget the key and ask the postmaster for our mail, we usually refer to it as John Adam's box. The public knows this box as 572, but the postmaster knows it as John Adam's box. Obviously, the contents of box 572 and John Adam's box are the same.

Passing information in this manner does not provide complete isolation between the subroutine and the calling program unit because both parameter variable names refer to the same mailbox and the value it contains. On the other hand, this type of parameter does allow information to be passed back to the calling unit because the value in the mailbox is accessible to the calling unit. This method of passing information through parameters is called *pass by reference* and the parameters are called *variable parameters* or *reference parameters*. These parameters are also sometimes referred to as *two-way parameters*.

Here is a simple program that uses a subroutine to halve a numeric parameter. The program contains lots of PRINT statements that show a user just what is going on at various points in the program. We suggest that you run this program if you are uncertain about just how variable parameters behave in subroutines.

```
! Example Program 7-6.
! Display values of certain variables.

INPUT prompt "Type in a number...": In
PRINT "Before calling subroutine, In ="; In
CALL Halved (In)
PRINT "After returning from subroutine, In ="; In
END

EXTERNAL SUB Halved (New)
    PRINT "Start of subroutine named Halved"
    PRINT "Within the subroutine, New ="; New
    LET New = New / 2
    PRINT "After division, New ="; New
END SUB
```

The preceding example is a good illustration of how you can use lots of PRINT statements to see what is happening inside a program.

If any parameters in the CALL statement are constants or expressions, their values are assigned to temporary variables when the CALL statement is executed. These variables can then be referenced by the corresponding parameter variables in the subroutine and the values used in the subroutine. The temporary variables are deleted, however, and the information in them is lost when control returns to the calling program. **Values cannot be passed back to the calling program through temporary variables.** In effect, constant and expression parameters in subroutines behave just like value parameters.

For example, the statement

```
CALL Blank (Num, Sum - 1, List$)
```

can result in the subroutine changing the values of Num and List$ in the calling program, but not the value of Sum. Sum is part of an expression, Sum − 1, and the value of the expression is assigned to a temporary variable that is subsequently deleted.

If you want a variable used as a parameter to behave like an expression, surround it with parentheses. In the statement

```
CALL Blank ((Num), Sum -1, (List$))
```

all parameters behave like one-way or value parameters and values are not passed back to the calling program. This technique does provide complete isolation between the subroutine and the calling program.

Look at these two example programs. In the first program, the parameter behaves as a value parameter.

```
! Example Program 7-7.
! Subroutine with value parameter.

LET Number = 5
PRINT "Before calling subroutine, Number ="; Number
CALL New ((Number))   ! note double parentheses
PRINT "After calling subroutine, Number ="; Number
END

EXTERNAL SUB New (X)
    LET X = 10
END SUB
```

This program displays the value 5, because the new parameter value 10 is not passed back to the main program. Note that the variable Number is surrounded by an additional pair of parentheses and thus is assigned to a temporary variable. On the other hand, the second program demonstrates the use of a variable parameter.

```
! Example Program 7-8.
! Subroutine with variable parameter.

LET Number = 5
PRINT "Before calling subroutine, Number ="; Number
CALL New (Number)
PRINT "After calling subroutine, Number ="; Number
END

EXTERNAL SUB New (X)
    LET X = 10
END SUB
```

A value of 10 is displayed by the program because this value is passed back to the main program from the subroutine. The variables Number and X both refer to the same memory location.

Substrings used as parameters are considered expressions and thus cannot be changed. For example,

```
CALL Blank (12, Sum, List$[2:5])
```

allows only the value of Sum in the calling program to be changed because 12 is a value and List$[2:5] is an expression.

All variables in a subroutine are local variables and, except for parameter variables, are reinitialized each time the subroutine is called.

Here is an example of a program that asks the user to enter a report title from the keyboard. It clears the screen and then calls a subroutine named Box that displays the centered title inside a box of asterisks or stars. Our previous subroutine example, named Center, is used to center each line of the boxed title on the screen. The variable X is a return variable that is set to a value greater than zero if the title in its box of asterisks will not fit between the margins.

```
! Example Program 7-9.
! Get title and display in box of stars.

PRINT "Press any key to clear screen after display."
LINE INPUT prompt "Enter title: ": Title$
LET X = 0   ! return variable
CALL Box (Title$, X)
IF X > 0 then PRINT "Title is too long."
END

EXTERNAL SUB Box (String$, Ret)
    ! Display the title in a box.
    ASK margin Width
    IF len(String$) > (Width - 4) then
       LET Ret = len(String$) - (Width - 4)   ! too long
    ELSE
       CLEAR  ! clear the screen
       LET Stars$ = repeat$("*", len(String$) + 4)
       LET TitleLine$ = "* " & String$ & " *"
       CALL Center (Stars$, Width)
       CALL Center (TitleLine$, Width)
       CALL Center (Stars$, Width)
       GET KEY Dummy   ! pause until a key is pressed
    END IF
END SUB

EXTERNAL SUB Center (Value$, Width)
    ! Print a centered string.
    PRINT tab((Width - len(Value$))/2); Value$
END SUB
```

Subroutine Box uses the ASK MARGIN statement that assigns the value of the right margin to the variable Width. The width of the screen, reduced by 4 to account for the star and space at each end of the title, is compared with the length of the title string. If the string is too long, the return variable is set to the number of characters by which the name exceeds the available space and the subroutine is exited. If the length is acceptable, subroutine Center is called to print a row of asterisks, the specified name with an asterisk and space at each end, and another row of asterisks.

The CLEAR statement is used to clear the screen, and the REPEAT$ function to create a row of asterisks. Note that after the title has been written, we use a GET KEY statement with a dummy variable. This statement requires a user to press any key in order to execute the END statement and return to the normal True BASIC divided screen. If we did not have this statement in our program, the title would appear only briefly on the screen and then disappear as the END statement was executed.

The output of Example Program 7-9 looks like this when the title "Analysis of 1983 Earnings" is entered:

```
******************************
* Analysis of 1983 Earnings *
******************************
```

Remember that **each program unit can declare its own local variables.** Even if the same variable name is used in two different program units, it represents two different variables (two different mailboxes).

7.5 LIBRARIES AND INTERNAL SUBPROGRAMS

External functions and subroutines can be kept in special files called *libraries*. A library file is not a program that can be run, but rather a collection of functions and subroutines that can be made available to any program.

A library file must start with the word

```
EXTERNAL
```

on a line by itself as the first statement. This statement identifies the file as a library file, not a True BASIC program. The remainder of the file is a sequence of external functions and subroutines.

Here is an example of a library file containing some useful functions and subroutines for handling strings:

```
! Example Library 7-10.
! String subprogram units.
EXTERNAL

FUNCTION Ans$(Question$)
    ! Check Y/N answer.
    DO
        PRINT Question$;
        LINE INPUT prompt "": Reply$
        LET Reply$ = ucase$(Reply$[1:1])
        SELECT CASE Reply$
        CASE "Y", "N"
             LET Ans$ = Reply$
             LET Finished$ = "true"
        CASE else
             PRINT "Answer YES or NO."
             PRINT
             LET Finished$ = "false"
        END SELECT
    LOOP until Finished$ = "true"
END FUNCTION
```

```
FUNCTION More$(Question$)
    ! Check Y/N/Q answer.
    DO
        PRINT Question$;
        LINE INPUT prompt "": Reply$
        LET Reply$ = ucase$(Reply$[1:1])
        SELECT CASE Reply$
        CASE "Y", "N", "Q"
             LET More$ = Reply$
             LET Finished$ = "true"
        CASE else
             PRINT "Answer YES, NO or QUIT."
             PRINT
             LET Finished$ = "false"
        END SELECT
    LOOP until Finished$ = "true"
END FUNCTION

FUNCTION Reverse$ (String$)
    ! Reverse characters in a string.
    LET Temp$ = ""   ! null string
    FOR Index = len(String$) to 1 step -1
        LET Temp$ = Temp$ & String$[Index:Index]
    NEXT Index
    LET Reverse$ = Temp$
END FUNCTION

SUB Center (String$)
    ! Print a centered string.
    ASK margin Width
    LET Space = (Width - len(String$))/2
    PRINT tab(Space); String$
END SUB

SUB Outline (String$)
    ! Print string in box.
    ASK margin Width
    LET Space = (Width - len(String$))/2
    PRINT tab(Space - 2); "+";
    PRINT repeat$("-", len(String$) + 2);
    PRINT "+"
    PRINT tab (Space - 2); "| "; String$; " |"
    PRINT tab(Space - 2); "+";
    PRINT repeat$("-", len(String$) + 2);
    PRINT "+"
END SUB

SUB Vertical (String$, Column)
    ! Print a vertical string.
    FOR I = 1 to len(String$)
        PRINT tab(Column); String$[I:I]
    NEXT I
END SUB
```

Note that we have omitted the word EXTERNAL in the headings for functions and subroutines. This word is required in ANS BASIC, but may be omitted in True BASIC. Even if the word EXTERNAL is omitted, any subprogram defined after the main program END statement or in a library file is still considered an external subprogram.

After a library file is written, it must be saved as a disk file. The library file may be given any legal MS-DOS file name. We recommend that you use a name containing the letters LIB to identify a library file and to distinguish it from a True BASIC program.

Let's assume we have saved our example library file under the name STRGLIB.TRU. If this file is on a disk in drive B, we can use it in a program by including the statement

```
LIBRARY "B:STRGLIB.TRU"
```

as one of the first statements in our program. If we want to access the function Reverse$, for example, we must include the statement

```
DECLARE FUNCTION Reverse$
```

The library statement must be placed ahead of any reference to a subprogram in that library. A program may contain more than one library statement and each library statement may refer to one or more library files, with their individual file names in quotation marks and separated by commas.

A library function must be declared before it can be used. A library subroutine is called by a CALL statement in the program. Two subprogram units in your program cannot have the same name, whether they are located in a library attached to the program or written as part of the program itself.

Here is an example of a short program using the library of string subprograms:

```
! Example Program 7-11.
! A simplified palindrome program.

! You may need to change the disk
! drive letter (B:) in the library name.
LIBRARY "B:STRGLIB.TRU"
DECLARE FUNCTION Reverse$
LINE INPUT prompt "Enter a string: ": Name$
LET Pal$ = Reverse$ (Name$)
IF Pal$ = Name$ then
   PRINT "String is a palindrome."
ELSE
   PRINT "String is not a palindrome."
END IF
END
```

Several library files are currently distributed with the True BASIC system, and other library files will undoubtedly become available in the future. For example, the file FNMLIB.TRU contains several mathematical and statistical functions, while the file MENULIB.TRU contains subroutines useful for writing a program menu system.

Single-Line DEF Statement

Both ANS BASIC and True BASIC allow the definition of a single-line function using the word DEF. This function is one form of the internal function (discussed next). We usually prefer external functions because of the isolation they provide between program units. There are times, however, when the single-line function is useful.

Consider a financial program that often needs to calculate the future value of a principal sum where the interest is compounded annually and added to the principal. A statement such as

```
DEF FutureValue (P, I, N) = P * ((1 + I/100)^N)
```

defines a function that calculates the future value of P dollars invested for N years at an interest rate of I percent. This defining statement must be placed early in the program, before the function FutureValue is used.

At some later point in the program, the statement

```
PRINT FutureValue(10000, 11.5, 7)
```

displays the value 21291, the future value of the initial sum of 10000 dollars.

Internal Functions and Subroutines

Functions and subroutines may be written within the main program unit, before the END statement, and then they are called internal functions or internal subroutines. They share one of the advantages of external subprograms: the ability to create a modular program that is easier to understand. As you might assume, the word EXTERNAL is never used with internal subprograms.

The most serious disadvantage of internal subprograms is that they do not maintain the desired isolation between subprogram variables and main program variables. **Values of variables declared in an internal subprogram are known throughout the main program unit, including all its internal subprograms.** Thus the change of a variable value in one subprogram will affect all variables with the same name in any other internal subprogram and in the main program. To avoid interaction between subprogram variables, we normally use only external functions and subroutines in the programs we write.

IMPORTANT POINTS

Each program unit in True BASIC—main program, external function, external subroutine, external picture—may have its own local variables.

All external functions used in a program unit must be declared in one or more DECLARE statements.

A value must be assigned to the function name before control returns to the calling program unit.

Function parameters are value or one-way parameters.

No value is associated with a subroutine name.

Subroutine parameters are variable or two-way parameters.

Values cannot be passed back through temporary variables from an external subroutine to the calling program.

A library file must start with the statement EXTERNAL on a line by itself.

Variables declared in internal functions and subroutines are known throughout the main program.

SELF-TEST QUESTIONS

1. What is an advantage of writing a program as a sequence of small modules?
2. What is meant by the concept of isolation between program units?
3. Can the dollar sign character be included as part of (a) a subroutine name, or (b) a function name?
4. Does an external function unit require an assignment statement to assign a value to the function name?
5. What is meant by a local variable in a program unit?
6. If a local variable named Number in an external subroutine unit is assigned a value of 5, what will be the value of the same variable, Number, when the subroutine is called again?
7. (a) Is a value assigned to a subroutine name when the subroutine is called? (b) Is a value assigned when control returns to the calling program?
8. If an external function named First$ is to call another external function named Second$, what declaration statement must be included in the first function?
9. Are the following words palindromes?

   a) WILLIAM
   b) HANNAH
   c) BABY

10. What is the factorial value of 4 (in mathematical notation, what is the value of 4!)?
11. If a main program unit has a variable named One and an external function declares a variable named One, do these two variables refer to the same or different memory locations?
12. What is meant by the term "pass by value"?
13. What statement must be the last statement in (a) an external function unit, and (b) an external subroutine unit?
14. What word does True BASIC allow you to use as a substitute for the word FUNCTION?
15. Is the word EXTERNAL optional or required in the heading statement of a subroutine unit that follows the main program END statement?
16. What statement is used to call an external subroutine?
17. If a main program CALL statement has a parameter variable named Two and the called external subroutine has a corresponding parameter variable named Two, do these two variables refer to the same or different memory locations?
18. What is meant by the term "pass by reference"?
19. Can values be passed to an external subroutine through (a) variable parameters, (b) constant parameters, or (c) expression parameters?
20. Can values be returned to a calling program unit from an external subroutine through (a) variable parameters, (b) constant parameters, or (c) expression parameters?

21. What statement must be the first statement in a True BASIC library file?
22. If a program contains an internal function, are variables declared in the function (a) local to the function or (b) known to the entire main program?

PRACTICE PROGRAMS

These problems ask you to write subprograms. To show how each subprogram works, you must also write a short main program unit for each problem that tests the subprogram. For example, you might write a subroutine called Swap in Practice Program 1, and test this subroutine using a short program such as

```
! Test Practice Program 1.
LET A = 5
LET B = 10
PRINT "Before swap, A ="; A; "and B ="; B
CALL Swap (A, B)
PRINT "After swap, A ="; A; "and B ="; B
END
```

1. Write a subroutine to exchange or swap two numbers that are passed as parameters. Test your subroutine using the numbers 0 and 1.
2. Write a subroutine to swap two strings that are passed as parameters. Test your subroutine using the strings "TRUE" and "FALSE".
3. Write a function PRED$ that returns the predecessor (in the ASCII table) of a character parameter. If the parameter string is longer than one character, the function returns the predecessor of the first character.

   Test your function using the string values "C", "A", "@", and "qed".
4. Write a function SUCC$ that returns the successor (in the ASCII table) of a character parameter. If the parameter string is longer than one character, the function returns the successor of the first character.

   Test your function using the string values "C", "z", "*", and "ABC".
5. Write a subroutine to display N characters of type C$ on the screen. Both N and C$ are parameters.

   Test your subroutine using the pairs of values:

   20, "*"
   50, "-"
   10, "x"
6. Write a function CUBE that returns the cube of its numeric parameter. Test your function using the numbers 2, 5, and 132.
7. Write a function DECIMAL that returns the decimal part of its numeric parameter. Test your function using the numbers 12.75, 35, 3.3333333, and −1.001.
8. Write a subroutine to clear the entire screen and fill it with an 80-by-24 grid of dots. Such a subroutine might be used in a computer graphics program.
9. Write a function that returns the volume of a sphere whose radius is passed as a parameter. Test your function using radii of 5, 10, and 2.32 units.

10. Write a function that returns the English word corresponding to its single-digit numeric parameter, that is, TWO for parameter 2, SEVEN for 7, and so forth.

Test your function using the digits 0, 9, and 5.

11. Write a function TODAY$ that returns the current date in MM-DD-YY format. This problem assumes that your computer has a built-in clock or that you entered the correct date when you turned on the system. Review the date and time functions in Appendix G.

12. Write a function that compares two string parameters, returning one if they are equal and zero if not equal.

Test your function using the pairs of string values

"abc", "xyz"
"aaa", "aaa"
"abc", "abcdef"
"abc", "ABC"

13. Write a function that returns the number of words in a string. Assume there is a word (no initial blank) at the beginning of the string and a word (no final blank) at the end of the string. Any other sequence of one or more characters surrounded by blanks is defined as a word. Assume only one blank between words.

Test your function using the phrases

This is a test string.
Will you dance? Will you dance? Will you dance?

14. Write a function that returns the number of times that a character appears in a string. For example, the function should show that the character "T" appears four times in the string "THIS IS THE STRAIGHT WAY". Both the string and the character are parameters.

Test your function using the string values

"T" in "THIS IS THE STRAIGHT WAY"
"X" in "Use the Xerox machine"
"*" in "!************"

15. Write a function that returns the average word length in a string parameter. Use the function developed in Practice Program 13.

Test your function using the sentences

Dependents must furnish evidence of eligibility.
Now is the time for all good men to fight or flee.

16. Write your own version of a VAL function that includes error trapping and returns a value of Maxnum if you try to convert a nonnumeric string. This specification means that your function cannot be used to convert the string equivalent of Maxnum—not a serious limitation.

Test your function using the numbers 25.2, A1A, −133, 210-55-8787, $12,033.75, and #9.

8 Arrays for Lists and Tables

8.1 INTRODUCTION

Lists and tables are examples of arrays—a new type of variable that we introduce in this chapter. We explain how to establish the size of an array. We discuss the concept of an index number used to identify a specific item in an array.

Two application programs using arrays are presented. The first program develops and maintains a room occupancy list for a motel. The second program uses a mileage table to calculate the distance between two cities.

8.2 ARRAYS WITH ONE DIMENSION

We have discussed how a variable can be thought of as a mailbox in which a value may be placed. As you now know, the mailbox is actually a memory location. There are times when it is convenient to be able to refer to a group of mailboxes rather than to a single mailbox, such as when a group of mailboxes contains a collection of similar quantities. The group can be designated by a single name, and each mailbox within the group can be identified by a number or *index*. This group of mailboxes or memory locations is called an *array variable*.

Let's look at some examples of array variables. The index is a number and is enclosed in parentheses. The variable Day$ represents the days of the week, and each mailbox in the array can be assigned the name of a day:

Day$(1) is day 1 (mailbox 1) and is assigned a value of Sunday.
Day$(4) is day 4 (mailbox 4) and is assigned a value of Wednesday.

The variable Room represents the rooms in a motel:

Room(10) is mailbox 10 and is assigned the number of occupants in room 10.
Room(35) is mailbox 35 and is assigned the number of occupants in room 35.

The individual mailboxes are called *elements* of the array, and the maximum number of elements in the array is called the *size* of the array. Each element is identified by a numeric index that usually starts at one for the first element and goes up to the size of the array. In this section, we discuss arrays with only one index and call these arrays *one-dimensional arrays*.

The rules for naming an array variable are the same as those for naming a simple variable (the kind of variable we have discussed in earlier chapters). An individual element is identified by the array name followed by an index number enclosed in parentheses. Arrays whose elements contain string values are called string arrays and the last character in the array name must be a dollar sign. Numeric arrays have elements containing numeric values.

Referring to our examples, Day$(1) is the first element of the array Day$. When Day$ is used in a program, element Day$(1) is assigned a value of Sunday. Room(35) is the thirty-fifth element of the array Room. In a later example program, each array element will be assigned a numeric value equal to the number of occupants of the corresponding room.

Dimensioning an Array

Before using an array in a BASIC program, you must tell the computer its size. This is done with the DIM statement. **An array can be declared only once in a DIM statement. The same DIM statement cannot be executed more than once.** This means, for example, that a DIM statement should not be placed in a loop where it would be executed on each pass through the loop.

DIM statements are usually placed together near the beginning of a program. An example DIM statement is

```
DIM Day$(7)
```

indicating that the array Day$ has 7 elements, each of which can hold a string value. Another example is

```
DIM Room(70)
```

which indicates that there are 70 elements (corresponding to rooms in the motel). Note that the size of the array (the value in parentheses) must be an integer value and a constant. **It cannot be a variable or an expression.**

This restriction on the DIM statement is an important point and should be carefully noted. A variable **cannot** be used to dimension an array. The DIM statement also initializes an array, assigning the value zero to each element of a numeric array and the null string to each element of a string array.

Array Bounds

The smallest or most negative value of the index is called the *lower bound* of the array. The default value of the lower bound is one. The largest or most positive value of the index is called the *upper bound* and has a default value equal to the size of the array. Thus the array Room, as dimensioned, has a lower bound of one and an upper bound of 70.

True BASIC allows both the lower bound and the upper bound to be specified in the DIM statement. The Room array can be dimensioned as

```
DIM Room(1 to 70)
```

or as

```
DIM Room(1:70)
```

The lower bound does not necessarily have to be one, as shown in these examples:

```
DIM Census(1950 to 1999)
DIM Yield(-32 to 212)
```

The lower and upper bounds must be integer values in the range of −1E9 to +1E9. Variables or expressions are not allowed. The upper bound of an array may be changed while the program is running, as explained in Section 8.6. The system functions LBOUND(N) and UBOUND(N) return the values of the lower and upper bounds of the array named N. The system function SIZE(N) returns the number of elements in the array named N.

For example, referring to the foregoing DIM statements,

```
lbound(Census) has a value of 1950.
ubound(Yield) has a value of 212.
size(Yield) has a value of 245.
```

Array Indexing

The elements of an array variable can be used in a True BASIC program in most of the same ways that simple variables are used. They can be assigned values, used in expressions, and displayed on the screen. An array element cannot be used as the index variable in a FOR statement; that is, the statement

```
FOR A(2) = 1 to 5   !*** NOT VALID ***
```

is not a valid statement.

Here is an example that does not do much, but does illustrate how array elements can be manipulated.

```
! Example Program 8-1.
! Use of a simple array.

DIM Strength(20)
LET Strength(5) = 134.72
LET Working = Strength(5) / 2
PRINT Working
END
```

The array named Strength is dimensioned to be large enough to hold 20 numeric values. A value of 134.72 is assigned to the fifth element of the array, element Strength(5). Note that the number in parentheses in the DIM statement is the size of the array, while in the LET statement it is an index referring to a particular element in the array. The element Strength(5) can be manipulated in expressions just like a simple variable. This program displays the value 67.36.

The index can be a numeric constant, as in the previous example, or it can be a numeric variable. For example,

```
! Example Program 8-2.
! Use of a variable index.

DIM Structure(5)
FOR Index = 1 to 5
    PRINT Structure(Index);
NEXT Index
PRINT

LET Index = 2
LET Structure(Index) = 33
FOR Index = 1 to 5
    PRINT Structure(Index);
NEXT Index
PRINT
END
```

Because individual array elements can be designated by index and the size of the array is known, arrays are often manipulated with FOR-NEXT loops. After the array Structure is dimensioned and initialized, this sequence of array values will be displayed:

```
0  0  0  0  0
```

A specific value is then assigned to the element whose index is 2, and a new display shows this sequence of values:

```
0  33  0  0  0
```

Here is an example of how to initialize each element of an array to a value of 10.

```
! Example Program 8-3.
! Initialize array elements
! to the same constant value.

DIM Quantity(50)
FOR I = 1 to 50
    LET Quantity(I) = 10
NEXT I
END
```

Another example assigns values to the array Day$ and then displays the day of the week corresponding to a number entered by a user.

```
! Example Program 8-4.
! Use an array representing days of the week.

DIM Day$(7)
FOR I = 1 to 7
    READ Day$(I)
NEXT I
DATA Sunday, Monday, Tuesday, Wednesday
DATA Thursday, Friday, Saturday

PRINT "Enter a number between 1 and 7."
PRINT "The corresponding day of the week"
PRINT "will be displayed.  Enter zero to stop."
PRINT
INPUT prompt "Day number? ": Number
DO until Number = 0
   PRINT "Day number"; Number; "is "; Day$(Number)
   INPUT prompt "Day number? ": Number
LOOP
END
```

If a user enters the number 2, the program will display

```
Day number 2 is Monday
```

An Array as a List

We often think of a one-dimensional array as a list or, more specifically, an indexed list. A list can have either string elements or numeric elements. The maximum size or length of the list is declared in a DIM statement. We can refer directly to any element of the list by using its index number or position in the list.

Using Part of an Array

There are times when we want to use an array for storing information, but do not know how many items we will need to store. As already noted, **the size of an array cannot be a variable.** If the maximum number of items to be stored can be determined, however, we can set the size of the array to this value. The array can then be used for storing a number of items up to this maximum, keeping track of the actual number of items stored with a counter.

Here is an example of this technique, creating a list of names in a partially filled array. After all names have been entered, the number of names is displayed, and the names are listed on the screen for verification.

```
! Example Program 8-5.
! Store up to 100 names in an array.
! Enter a single period to stop.

DIM Names$(100)
PRINT "Enter up to 100 names, one name per line."
PRINT "Enter a single period to stop the process."
LET Count = 0

DO until Count >= 100
   LINE INPUT prompt "Name? ": Reply$
   IF Reply$ = "." then EXIT DO
   LET Count = Count + 1
   LET Names$(Count) = Reply$
LOOP

PRINT
PRINT Count; "names entered."
PRINT "Here is the list:"
PRINT
FOR I = 1 to Count
    PRINT Names$(I)
NEXT I
END
```

The array Names$ is dimensioned to hold up to 100 names. Each name is entered into a variable named Reply$. If the name is a single period, the entry process stops. If not, the counter Count is incremented, and the name is placed in the array Names$. After all names have been entered, a simple loop uses the final value of Count to display the stored names.

Note that the main loop in this program has two possible exit points—the EXIT DO statement and the LOOP statement. Many advocates of structured programming prefer that a loop have only a single exit point. Here is another version of the same program with the loop written in a different and more structured way:

```
! Example Program 8-6.
! Store up to 100 names in an array.
! Enter a single period to stop.

DIM Names$(100)
PRINT "Enter up to 100 names, one name per line."
PRINT "Enter a single period to stop the process."
LET Count = 0

LINE INPUT prompt "Name? ": Reply$
DO until Count >= 100 or Reply$ = "."
   LET Count = Count + 1
   LET Names$(Count) = Reply$
   LINE INPUT prompt "Name? ": Reply$
LOOP

PRINT
PRINT Count; "names entered."
PRINT "Here is the list:"
PRINT
FOR I = 1 to Count
    PRINT Names$(I)
NEXT I
END
```

Both conditions for exiting the loop are now attached to the DO statement. Another LINE INPUT statement is needed outside the loop to assign the initial name to the variable Reply$.

We normally prefer well-structured programs, but this program might be considered an exception. In our opinion, the structure of the second version is no easier to understand and does not end as nicely when the limit of 100 names is reached (name 101 is requested, but not assigned to the array). We believe, however, that either version of the program is perfectly acceptable.

Arrays as Subprogram Parameters

Arrays containing either number or string values may be used as parameter variables for functions and subroutines. Passing an array to a subroutine means that the array is given two names—the name used in the calling program and the name used in the subroutine. Only one copy of the array exists in memory, and the values of every array element can be accessed by either program unit.

Passing an array to a function means that the values of all the array elements are copied into the corresponding elements of a local array. If the array is large, many memory locations will be needed to store this second copy of the array. Limited memory may become a problem with some small computers.

In the subprogram parameter list, an array parameter must be identified by dummy parentheses so it can be distinguished from a simple variable parameter. Here is an example using a list of names as an array parameter. The array is passed to a subroutine that converts each name to uppercase:

```
! Example Program 8-7.
! Convert all names in a list to upper case.

DIM Name$(5)
FOR Index = 1 to 5
    READ Name$(Index)
NEXT Index
CALL Capital (Name$)
FOR Index = 1 to 5
    PRINT Name$(Index)
NEXT Index

DATA John, Rob, Ginny, Peter, Sally
END

EXTERNAL SUB Capital (List$())
    ! Change characters in string to uppercase.
    FOR I = 1 to ubound(List$)
        LET List$(I) = ucase$(List$(I))
    NEXT I
END SUB
```

The names List$ and Name$ are both names for the same array and thus the converted uppercase values can be printed by the main program. The array is dimensioned in the calling program and so does not have to be dimensioned again (in fact, cannot be dimensioned again) in the subroutine. The notation List$() indicates to the subroutine that this parameter is a one-dimensional array.

We use the function UBOUND to calculate the upper bound of the array List$ in the subroutine. This practice makes the subroutine more general, and it can now be used to convert the elements of any one-dimensional string array to uppercase.

8.3 EXAMPLE PROGRAM USING A LIST

Planning the Program

Our task is to design a computer program that stores information about motel room occupancy. The motel has 70 rooms, and we want to indicate whether or not each room is occupied. If the room is occupied, we would like to know the number of occupants. This program will be run by the desk clerk during afternoon and evening hours as travelers come in off the highway. We decide to store the room occupancy information in an array and choose an array named Room.

Our program must be able to store information on room occupancy, to find the next vacant room, to ask for the number of new occupants in this room, and to display the total number of guests staying in the motel.

Note that our program is not as versatile as we might wish, because we store information in an array in memory and when the computer is turned off, the information will be lost. In the next chapter, you will be shown how to store this type of information on a disk in a more permanent fashion. The program as written, however, will provide useful occupancy information to a desk clerk if used as designed.

Here is an outline of the program.

Initialize the room array.

Top of main loop:

a) Find next vacant room and assign occupants; if no vacant room, stop the loop.

b) Display new occupancy total.

c) Check whether to continue or quit.

Bottom of main loop:

End program.

Writing the Program

One section of the program will declare the size of the array and initialize its elements.

```
DIM Room(70)
FOR I = 1 to 70
    LET Room(I) = 0
NEXT I
```

We will use the room number as the array index and the following section finds the next vacant room and asks for the number of occupants. Note that the array Room is just a list of room occupancy—the first number in the list is the number of occupants of room 1, the second number is the occupants in room 2, and so forth. The section is written as a subroutine and the array Room and the room number Number are passed to it as parameters.

```
EXTERNAL SUB Assign (Room(), Number)
    ! Find and assign the next vacant room.
    DO
       IF Room(Number) <> 0 then
          LET Number = Number + 1
       END IF
    LOOP until Room(Number) = 0
    PRINT "Room"; Number; "is vacant."
    INPUT prompt "How many occupants? ": Room(Number)
END SUB
```

The next section gives the total number of occupants in the motel. We use the familiar summing technique with the sum stored in variable Sum. Sum does not need to be a parameter because printing is done in the subroutine.

```
EXTERNAL SUB Occupancy (Room())
    ! Calculate total room occupancy.
    LET Sum = 0
    FOR I = 1 to ubound(Room)
        LET Sum = Sum + Room(I)
    NEXT I
    PRINT "Total occupancy is"; Sum
END SUB
```

We also have to provide a way for the user to exit the loop and stop the program. Another subroutine asks if the user wishes to continue and the reply is converted to a single uppercase character. If the user enters "QUIT" or "quit" or just "q", the program will interpret it as a signal to stop. This signal is passed back to the calling program through the variable More$.

Checking input in this way is an example of careful programming to protect and help the user, a program characteristic sometimes called *user-friendly*. We urge you to design your programs in this manner.

```
EXTERNAL SUB Check (More$)
    ! See if user wants to stop the program.
    PRINT "Type Q to stop the program."
    PRINT "Press ENTER key to continue."
    LINE INPUT More$
    LET More$ = ucase$(More$[1:1])
END SUB
```

Now let's put everything together in a working program. Remember that this program and the computer must run continuously, so most of the program consists of one big loop.

```
! Example Program 8-8.
! Motel occupancy record program.

! Initialize the occupancy list.
DIM Room(70)
FOR I = 1 to 70
  LET Room(I) = 0
NEXT I

LET Count = 1     ! room number counter
LET More$ = ""    ! flag to continue

! Main program, call the appropriate subroutines.
DO until Count = ubound(Room) or More$ = "Q"
   CALL Assign (Room, Count)
   CALL Occupancy (Room)
   CALL Check (More$)
LOOP
IF Count = ubound(Room) then
   PRINT "There are no vacant rooms."
END IF
END  ! of main program

EXTERNAL SUB Assign (Room(), Number)
    ! Find and assign the next vacant room.
    DO
       IF Room(Number) <> 0 then
          LET Number = Number + 1
       END IF
    LOOP until Room(Number) = 0
    PRINT "Room"; Number; "is vacant."
    INPUT prompt "How many occupants? ": Room(Number)
END SUB
```

```
EXTERNAL SUB Occupancy (Room())
    ! Get total occupancy.
    LET Sum = 0
    FOR I = 1 to ubound(Room)
        LET Sum = Sum + Room(I)
    NEXT I
    PRINT "Total occupancy is"; Sum
    PRINT
END SUB

EXTERNAL SUB Check (More$)
    ! See if user wants to stop the program.
    PRINT "Type Q to stop the program."
    PRINT "Press ENTER key to continue."
    LINE INPUT More$
    LET More$ = ucase$(More$[1:1])
END SUB
```

The main structure of this program is a loop, and we assemble our program from several small sections or modules. Just as an article is more readable if separated into paragraphs, a computer program is more easily understood if separated into modules. We use subroutines for three of the modules and place a descriptive comment at the beginning of each subroutine. Within each program unit, we use indentation to set off the body of each loop and branch. It is important that you use these techniques as you write your own programs—it is a way to develop good programming style.

8.4 ARRAYS WITH TWO DIMENSIONS

The arrays we have discussed in previous sections have a single index and are called one-dimensional arrays. An example is the familiar list. We can also have arrays with two or more indices and these are called *multidimensional arrays*.

An example of a two-dimensional array is a table that has several rows and several columns. The location of an element in the table is specified by two indices, one index specifying the row number and the other specifying the column number. We will restrict our discussion to two-dimensional arrays, although True BASIC supports arrays with more than two dimensions. **Note that a one-dimensional array and a two-dimensional array in the same program cannot have the same name.**

Two-Dimensional Array Notation

A two-dimensional array containing string values is named Salesman$. Figure 8-1 shows how the array might look (with labels and numbers added to identify rows and columns).

The element in the third row and first column is designated as Salesman$(3,1) and has a value of ''Gary Despio''. It is common convention for the first index to refer to the row number and the second index to refer to the column number. If you visualize the array as a table, the horizontal lines of element values are called rows, and the vertical lines are called columns.

Tables are often organized in this manner, with each column referring to a different type of information and each row referring to a different person or item. For example, the element Salesman$(3,1) in column 1 refers to a salesman's name, Salesman$(3,2) in column 2 refers to a salesman's city, and Salesman$(3,3) in column 3 refers to a salesman's telephone number.

Column	1	2	3
Row			
1	John Adams	Chicago	312-202-5674
2	Bill Cullins	New York	212-405-1298
3	Gary Despio	Atlanta	404-813-8824
4	Bill Morris	Miami	305-222-5141
5	Jack Williams	Boston	617-267-0351

Figure 8-1 Table of sales information.

Dimensioning Two-Dimensional Arrays

Arrays with two dimensions are declared with the DIM statement, in a manner similar to one-dimensional arrays. For example,

```
DIM Salesman$(100,3)
```

declares an array with 100 rows and 3 columns. This array can hold 300 string values. There is now a size associated with each dimension. The size of the first dimension, given by SIZE(Salesman$, 1), is 100, and the size of the second dimension, given by SIZE(Salesman$, 2), is 3.

Remember that a string array is initialized just like any other string variable, with a null string assigned to each element. As with one-dimensional arrays, it is not necessary that every element be assigned another value, and in our example, information has been assigned to only the first five rows.

Two-Dimensional Arrays as Tables

An example of a two-dimensional numeric array is the table, often found on road maps, showing distances between cities. Let's use the variable Distance to represent this table. If you want to find the distance between Boston and New York, you go down the left margin until you find the row labeled Boston and then across that row until you find the column labeled New York. Where this row and column intersect, you find the distance in miles. If Boston is the label for row 2 and New York the label for column 6, then the distance between these two cities is given by the value of the element Distance(2,6). In the next section, we will discuss a program to create and use such a table.

Nested FOR-NEXT Loops

Two-dimensional arrays can be initialized with nested FOR-NEXT loops. Here is an example that uses this structure to assign a value of zero to each element of an array.

```
! Example Program 8-9.
! Initialize a two-dimensional array.

DIM Grid(12,30)
FOR I = 1 to 12
    FOR J = 1 to 30
        LET Grid(I,J) = 0
    NEXT J
NEXT I
END
```

Note that for each value of I in the outer loop, the variable J runs through its set of values from 1 to 30 in the inner loop. If you think of the variable I as the row number, then each element in the Ith row is set to zero. This process is repeated for each row (or value of I) from 1 to 12. We say that this program assigns values to the array elements by rows.

Note also that the outer I loop must completely surround and contain the inner J loop. If the two NEXT statements are reversed, the loops overlap and the program will not work. **Nested FOR-NEXT loops cannot overlap.** Indentation helps to show how the inner J loop nests within the outer I loop.

As another example, we write a program to read numbers from DATA statements into a two-dimensional array and then display the array. We use a small array with three rows and five columns so it will fit easily on the screen. We put five values in each DATA statement and read values into the array by row. This program demonstrates the use of FOR-NEXT loops for reading two-dimensional arrays and for printing these arrays in a formatted display.

Here is the program:

```
! Example Program 8-10.
! Program to fill and display an array.

DIM Table(3,5)

! Fill array from data statements.
FOR Row = 1 to 3
    FOR Column = 1 to 5
        READ Table(Row, Column)
    NEXT Column
NEXT Row

! Display the array
FOR Row = 1 to 3
    FOR Column = 1 to 5
        PRINT Table(Row, Column);
    NEXT Column
    PRINT
NEXT Row

DATA 3,5,7,3,8,4,1,0,3,4,5,2,7,5,3
END
```

The READ statement uses a DATA statement located at the end of the program. Note that the process of assigning values to the elements is equivalent to initializing the array.

In the display module, the semicolon at the end of the first PRINT statement causes all values in a row to be displayed on the same line (this won't work if there are too many columns to fit on the screen). The second PRINT statement moves the cursor to the next line on the screen after a row of values has been displayed.

This program produces the following display:

```
3  5  7  3  8
4  1  0  3  4
5  2  7  5  3
```

Two-Dimensional Arrays as Parameters

Two-dimensional arrays can also be used as parameters for subroutines and functions. The subprogram heading must indicate that the parameter is a two-dimensional array by inserting a comma between the dummy parentheses. Examples are

```
EXTERNAL FUNCTION Trace (X(,))
EXTERNAL SUB Rotate (One(), Two(), R(,))
```

In the last example, arrays One and Two are one dimensional, while array R is two dimensional.

The functions UBOUND and LBOUND can still be used, but they now require two parameters. The first parameter is the name of the array; the second parameter is the number of the dimension.

For example,

```
ubound(Trace, 1) is for the first dimension.
ubound(Trace, 2) is for the second dimension.
```

The function SIZE also requires two parameters, the first parameter being the array name, and returns the size of the dimension specified by the second parameter.

```
size(Trace, 1) is the size of the first dimension.
size(Trace, 2) is the size of the second dimension.
```

Our next example passes the values of a two-dimensional array to a function that calculates the *trace* of an array. The trace is a mathematical value that can be calculated for an array of numeric values when the number of rows equals the number of columns. It is equal to the sum of all elements that have the same index for row and column.

For example, in the array

1	3	6
2	7	8
9	2	4

the trace is 1 + 7 + 4 and equals 12.

Here is the example:

```
! Example Program 8-11.
! Read an array and calculate its trace.

DIM A(3,3)
DECLARE FUNCTION Trace
PRINT "The array is"
FOR I = 1 to ubound(A,1)
    FOR J = 1 to ubound(A,2)
        READ A(I,J)
        PRINT A(I,J);
    NEXT J
    PRINT
NEXT I
PRINT "Its trace is"; Trace (A)

DATA 1,3,6,2,7,8,9,2,4
END

EXTERNAL FUNCTION Trace (X(,))
    ! Calculate the trace.
    LET Sum = 0
    FOR K = 1 to ubound(X,1)
        LET Sum = Sum + X(K,K)
    NEXT K
    LET Trace = Sum
END FUNCTION
```

In this case, the trace equals the sum of X(1,1), X(2,2) and X(3,3). Note the notation X(,) in the heading statement of the function, which tells the function that X is a two-dimensional array. The array X in the function unit is a local copy of the array A in the main program unit. As before, the array is dimensioned in the calling program. Note the upper limit of the FOR statement in the function Trace. In this case, we can use either ubound(X,1) or ubound(X,2) because the two dimensions of X are the same size.

8.5 EXAMPLE PROGRAM USING A TABLE

We now return to an earlier example, the mileage table showing the distance between cities. Our example program contains the following sections:

Read a list of cities.

Read a mileage table of distances between cities.

Ask the user to enter the names of two cities.

Look up and display the distance between cities.

End the program.

We will read the list of cities and table of distances from DATA statements, although after we learn about files in the next chapter, we can write a more flexible program that reads this information from data files. We will write subroutines for reading the list of cities (a one-dimensional array) and the table of distances (a two-dimensional array).

Here is a straightforward subroutine to read the list of cities. The list array is passed to the subroutine as a parameter.

```
EXTERNAL SUB ReadList (List$())
    ! Read the list of cities.
    FOR I = 1 to ubound(List$)
        READ List$(I)
    NEXT I

    DATA ATLANTA, BOSTON, CHICAGO, DETROIT
    DATA MIAMI, NEW YORK, WASHINGTON
END SUB
```

Another subroutine reads the mileage table and assigns the values to a two-dimensional array named Distance. In our example, this information will be placed in an array with seven rows and seven columns. Let's look carefully at the information contained in this table.

The table must have the same number of rows and columns because each row represents one of the cities in the list and each column represents one of the cities in the same list. We use the same order of city names for both the rows and columns.

The list of cities we have chosen is shown in Figure 8-2, and the distance table is in Figure 8-3.

Note that the distance between two cities with the same name is zero; that is, Distance(1,1) is zero, Distance(2,2) is zero, and so forth. All these zeroes lie along what we call the principal diagonal, the diagonal running from the upper left corner of the table to the lower right corner. In general, all elements of the type Distance(I,I) must equal zero.

Note further that the elements lying below the principal diagonal contain the same information as those lying above this diagonal. For example, element Distance(1,2) represents the distance between cities 1 and 2 (in our case, ATLANTA and BOSTON).

1	ATLANTA
2	BOSTON
3	CHICAGO
4	DETROIT
5	MIAMI
6	NEW YORK
7	WASHINGTON

Figure 8-2 List of cities.

	1	2	3	4	5	6	7
1	0	1065	675	715	665	850	605
2	1065	0	965	710	1515	215	445
3	675	965	0	270	1335	790	695
4	715	710	270	0	1370	620	520
5	665	1515	1335	1370	0	1300	1080
6	850	215	790	620	1300	0	230
7	605	445	695	520	1080	230	0

Figure 8-3 Table of distances between cities.

Distance(2,1) represents the distance between cities 2 and 1. These distances should, of course, be the same and they are—1065 miles. In general terms, any element Distance(I,J) must equal the corresponding element Distance (J,I).

This discussion helps to explain the subroutine used to read the table of distances. We first set all elements along the principal diagonal equal to zero. We then read in the 21 elements lying above the principal diagonal and, as we read each value, assign it also to the corresponding element lying below the principal diagonal.

Here is the subroutine to read the table of distances.

```
EXTERNAL SUB ReadTable (Table(,))
    ! Read the table of distances.
    FOR I = 1 to ubound(Table, 1)
        LET Table(I,I) = 0
    NEXT I

    FOR I = 1 to (ubound(Table, 1) - 1)
        FOR J = (I + 1) to ubound(Table, 2)
            READ Table(I, J)
            LET Table(J, I) = Table(I, J)
        NEXT J
    NEXT I

    DATA 1065, 675, 715, 665, 850, 605
    DATA 965, 710, 1515, 215, 445
    DATA 270, 1335, 790, 695
    DATA 1370, 620, 520
    DATA 1300, 1080
    DATA 230
END SUB
```

Note particularly the FOR-NEXT loops used to read the DATA statements. We read only rows 1 through 6 because these rows include all elements lying above the principal diagonal. Thus I ranges from 1 to 6 or in more general notation, from 1 to (ubound(Table, 1) − 1).

In row 1 we start reading at column 2, in row 2 at column 3, and so forth. That is, we start reading values in row I at column (I + 1). Thus J (the column number) ranges from (I + 1) to 7 or in more general notation, from (I + 1) to ubound(Table, 2).

One disadvantage of using an array to hold the distance values is that we waste over half the storage space in the array. This might become a problem with very large tables, but we use comparatively little memory space in our example. A compensating advantage is that a two-dimensional array is probably the simplest and easiest structure to use for the table of distances and produces a simple and easy-to-understand program.

A function is used to calculate the numerical position of any city in the list of cities. We need this information to calculate the indices of the appropriate distance table element. The name of the city is passed to the function as parameter Name$, along with the array List$ containing the list of cities. The position of this city in the list is assigned to the function Location.

```
EXTERNAL FUNCTION Location (Name$, List$())
    ! Find location of a city in the city list.
    LET CityNum = 0
    LET Count = 1
    DO
       IF Name$ = List$(Count) then
          LET CityNum = Count
       END IF
       LET Count = Count + 1
    LOOP until CityNum > 0 or Count > ubound(List$)
    LET Location = CityNum
END FUNCTION
```

Note that if a city name cannot be found in the list, a value of zero is returned by the function.

Finally, all the modules are put together in a complete program. The name of the first city is First$, and its location in the city list is First. The second city is Second$, and its location is Second. The distance between these two cities is simply the array element Distance(First, Second).

```
! Example Program 8-12.
! Calculate the distance between two cities.

DECLARE FUNCTION Location
DIM City$(7), Distance(7,7)
CALL ReadList (City$)
CALL ReadTable (Distance)

INPUT prompt "Name of first city? ": First$
LET First = Location (ucase$(First$), City$)
INPUT prompt "Name of second city? ": Second$
LET Second = Location (ucase$(Second$), City$)

IF First = 0 or Second = 0 then
   PRINT "One of the city names is not in the list."
ELSE
   PRINT "Distance between "; First$; " and ";
   PRINT Second$; " is"; Distance (First, Second);
   PRINT "miles."
END IF
END
```

```
EXTERNAL SUB ReadList (List$())
    ! Read the list of cities.
    FOR I = 1 to ubound(List$)
        READ List$(I)
    NEXT I

    DATA ATLANTA, BOSTON, CHICAGO, DETROIT
    DATA MIAMI, NEW YORK, WASHINGTON
END SUB

EXTERNAL SUB ReadTable (Table(,))
    ! Read the table of distances.
    FOR I = 1 to ubound(Table, 1)
        LET Table(I,I) = 0
    NEXT I

    FOR I = 1 to (ubound(Table, 1) - 1)
        FOR J = (I + 1) to ubound(Table, 2)
            READ Table(I, J)
            LET Table(J, I) = Table(I, J)
        NEXT J
    NEXT I

    DATA 1065, 675, 715, 665, 850, 605
    DATA 965, 710, 1515, 215, 445
    DATA 270, 1335, 790, 695
    DATA 1370, 620, 520
    DATA 1300, 1080
    DATA 230
END SUB

EXTERNAL FUNCTION Location (Name$, List$())
    ! Find location of a city in the city list.
    LET CityNum = 0
    LET Count = 1
    DO
       IF Name$ = List$(Count) then
          LET CityNum = Count
       END IF
       LET Count = Count + 1
    LOOP until CityNum > 0 or Count > ubound(List$)
    LET Location = CityNum
END FUNCTION
```

A user is asked to enter the name of two cities. If both cities are in the city list, the distance between them is displayed. If not, an error message appears on the screen.

8.6 REDIMENSIONING ARRAYS—THE ZER AND NUL$ VALUES

The DIM statement establishes the size of an array, usually by specifying the upper bound of each dimension. If the array is too large, we have discussed how only part of the array can be used (see Example Program 8-5). If the array is too small, we cannot write a new

DIM statement with larger upper bounds. A further restriction of the DIM statement is that the upper bounds specifying array size must be numeric constants, not variables or expressions.

There is a statement, however, that allows us to initialize an existing array and change its size at the same time. This statement is one of the MAT statements that will be discussed in greater detail in Chapter 13. The word MAT is an abbreviation of *matrix,* another name for an array. The MAT assignment statement, used with the standard array ZER or the standard array NUL$, reinitializes and redimensions an existing array. All the elements of the ZER array have a value of zero, while the NUL$ array has elements that are null strings.

The syntax of this redimensioning statement is

```
MAT Array = ZER(Size)
```

or

```
MAT Array$ = NUL$(Size)
```

The variable names Array and Array$ denote arrays that have already been dimensioned with a DIM statement. The identifier *Size* denotes one or more constants, variables, or expressions that specify the new upper bounds of the array. **Redimensioning changes the value of the upper bound only, not the lower bound. Redimensioning cannot change the number of dimensions.** The new upper-bound values may be larger or smaller than the original upper-bound values.

For example, assume that an array has been dimensioned with the statement

```
DIM Ratio(5,4)
```

Here are some example statements that change the size of Ratio and reinitalize its elements to zero:

```
MAT Ratio = zer(2, 2)
MAT Ratio = zer(1 to N, 2)
MAT Ratio = zer(3 + abs(Y), X)
```

In the first example, Ratio is redimensioned to an array with two rows and two columns. This array is called a square array because it has the same number of rows and columns. In the second example, Ratio is redimensioned to an array with N rows and two columns. Note that the lower bound of both dimensions remains at 1.

The third example is more complex. An arithmetic expression, 3 + abs(Y), is evaluated and its integer value is the new number of rows. The integer value of N is the new number of columns.

It is often convenient to dimension an array originally to a nominal size, say, a value of 1 for each dimension and then redimension it when the size of each dimension is known. Here is an example program that asks a user to specify the size of a square array and then enter the element values.

```
! Example Program 8-13.
! Dimension and fill a square array.

DIM Table(1,1)
INPUT prompt "Size of the square array? ": N
MAT Table = zer(N,N)
FOR I = 1 to N
    FOR J = 1 to N
        PRINT "Element("; str$(I); ","; str$(J); ")";
        INPUT Table(I,J)
    NEXT J
NEXT I

PRINT
PRINT "Here is the array:"
FOR I = 1 to N
    FOR J = 1 to N
        PRINT Table(I,J);
    NEXT J
    PRINT
NEXT I
END
```

Another example program allows a user to specify the maximum number of items that can be stored in an array and then redimensions the array. Here is Example Program 8-5 rewritten to allow the size of array Names$ to be changed.

```
! Example Program 8-14.
! Store names in an array.
! Enter a single period to stop.

DIM Names$(100)
PRINT "The array has room for";ubound(Names$);"names."
PRINT "Maximum number of names you plan to enter";
INPUT N
MAT Names$ = nul$(N)

PRINT
PRINT "Enter up to"; N; "names, one name per line."
PRINT "Enter a single period to stop the process."
LET Count = 0
DO until Count >= N
   LINE INPUT prompt "Name? ": Reply$
   IF Reply$ = "." then EXIT DO
   LET Count = Count + 1
   LET Names$(Count) = Reply$
LOOP

PRINT
PRINT Count; "names entered."
PRINT "Here is the list:"
PRINT
FOR I = 1 to Count
    PRINT Names$(I)
NEXT I
END
```

Note especially that redimensioning an array also reinitializes the array. If you have already entered information into an array, you cannot easily redimension the array without erasing entered information.

IMPORTANT POINTS

An array can be declared only once in a DIM statement.

The same DIM statement cannot be executed more than once.

The size of an array cannot be a variable or an expression.

Nested FOR-NEXT loops cannot overlap.

In a subprogram parameter list, an array parameter must be identified by dummy parentheses

Use the UBOUND function instead of a constant for the upper bound of an array in a subprogram.

A one-dimensional array and a two-dimensional array in the same program cannot have the same name.

Redimensioning changes the value of the upper bound only, not the lower bound.

Redimensioning cannot change the number of dimensions.

SELF-TEST QUESTIONS

1. What is (a) an array, (b) an array element, (c) the dimension of an array, and (d) the size of an array dimension?
2. If an array is dimensioned with the statement DIM Name$(50), can a value be assigned (a) to the element Name$(0), or (b) to the element Name$(50)?
3. If a variable N has an integer value of 7, is the statement DIM Bound(N) a legal statement? If not, why not?
4. If an array is dimensioned with DIM Value(−5:5), how many elements are contained in the array?
5. If an array is dimensioned with DIM Structure(5) and all its elements are assigned positive values, is the statement FOR I = 0 TO Structure(3) a legal statement? If not, why not?
6. Which of the following dimension statements are allowed?
   - **a)** DIM Array(15)
   - **b)** DIM Array(1,15)
   - **c)** DIM Array(1;15)
   - **d)** DIM Array(1-15)
   - **e)** DIM Array(1 to 15)
   - **f)** DIM Array(1 through 15)

7. If an array is dimensioned with DIM List$(100), what is (a) the value of UBOUND(List$), and (b) the value of LBOUND(List$)?
8. If a one-dimensional array named Structure is passed as a parameter to an external subroutine named Analyse, what is the proper form of (a) the subroutine call statement, and (b) the subroutine unit heading statement?
9. If an array is dimensioned in the main program unit and passed as a parameter to an external function, should it be dimensioned again in the function unit?
10. What, if anything, is wrong with the following program?

```
FOR I = 1 to 5
    DIM Num(5)
    LET Num(I) = 0
NEXT I
END
```

11. A subroutine heading statement is written as EXTERNAL SUB Capital(List$(,)). (a) Is the statement syntax correct? (b) The array List$ has how many dimensions?
12. (a) What function returns the upper-bound value of the second dimension of the two-dimensional array Result? (b) What function returns the lower-bound value of the same dimension?
13. What is meant by the principal diagonal of an array?
14. What, if anything, is special about the values of the two indices of elements along the principal diagonal of an array?
15. An array representing a table is dimensioned DIM Table(5,3). This table contains (a) how many columns, and (b) how many rows?
16. What, if anything, is wrong with the following program?

```
DIM Table(5,3)
FOR I = 1 to 5
    FOR J = 1 to 3
        LET Table(I,J) = 0
    NEXT I
NEXT J
END
```

17. The following program is supposed to display the array Mileage as a table with rows and columns.

```
DIM Mileage(5,5)
FOR I = 1 to 5
    FOR J = 1 to 5
        PRINT Mileage(I,J);
    NEXT J
NEXT I
END
```

Will it display the table with 5 rows and 5 columns? If not, how would you correct the program to make it work properly?

18. If a program contains the statement

```
DIM Mileage(5,5), List$(50)
```

what, if anything, is wrong with the following statements?

a) MAT Mileage = nul$(7,7)
b) MAT Mileage = zer(5)
c) MAT List$ = nul$(1:100)
d) MAT List$ = zer(1:10)
e) MAT List$ = nul$(10:100)

PRACTICE PROGRAMS

1. A matrix is a one-dimensional or two-dimensional array of numbers. A square matrix has the same number of rows and columns. The principal diagonal of a square matrix goes from the upper left corner to the lower right corner. The identity matrix is a square matrix with elements along the principal diagonal having a value of 1, and the other elements having a value of 0. For example,

1	0	0	0
0	1	0	0
0	0	1	0
0	0	0	1

Using FOR statements, create and display an identity matrix with ten rows and columns (a 10-by-10 matrix).

2. A transposed matrix is a square matrix (see Practice Program 1) whose rows and columns have been interchanged. Thus old row 1 becomes new column 1, old row 2 becomes new column 2, and so forth. Read the elements of a 6-by-6 matrix from DATA statements, transpose the matrix, and display the transposed matrix. Do not use the MAT statements discussed in Chapter 13.

Test your program using the following DATA statements:

```
DATA 1,5,3,6,7,2
DATA 7,1,4,9,2,3
DATA 9,0,2,1,6,3
DATA 0,1,3,2,7,5
DATA 6,4,7,3,8,9
DATA 4,6,2,2,3,1
```

3. Enter ten names from the keyboard, using an indexed variable to store the names as they are entered. After the tenth name has been entered, display the list of names in reverse order.

Test your program using the following names:

Simpson
Johnson
Clemons
Thornton
Newcomb
Tuttle
Maury
Cocke
Jefferson
Washington

4. Enter a sentence from the keyboard. Place the alphabetic characters in the sentence into an array, converting any uppercase characters to lowercase. Pass over any nonalphabetic characters, including spaces and punctuation marks. Display the array in reverse order.
   Test your program using the sentence

   He said ''Hello! How are you?'', and I smiled.

5. Read eight part names and associated prices from DATA statements and place these values in a two-dimensional array with 100 rows and 2 columns. Names are placed in column 1 and prices in column 2. Search the array for the name of the highest-priced part and the lowest-priced part. Display these two part names and prices with appropriate labels.
   Test your program using the values:

hammer	13.45
pliers	8.60
saw	21.40
wrench	19.95
ruler	1.85
punch	4.50
screwdriver	3.75
crowbar	12.50

You may assume that the data arrays in the following problems have no more than 100 rows.

6. A primitive way to encode a short message is to substitute a number for each word. Write a function to do the encoding. The value of the function will be the code number when a word is passed to it as a string parameter. The function is passed an array parameter containing values that have been read from DATA statements that look like this:

```
DATA HOME, 1, FAMILY, 2, HELP, 3
```

   where 1 is the code for HOME, 2 for FAMILY, and so forth.
   Your DATA statements should contain pairs of words and numbers, as shown here. Return a value of zero if a word is not found in the DATA statements.

HOME, 1	FAMILY, 2	HELP, 3
MONEY, 4	TRAVEL, 5	COMES, 6
DANGER, 7	NORTH, 8	WEST, 9
SEND, 10	EAST, 11	SOUTH, 12
TO, 13	FROM, 14	THE, 15
COME, 16	STOP, 17	END, 18
CAR, 19	TRAIN, 20	MESSAGE, 21
SENT, 22	RECEIVED, 23	TROUBLE, 24

   Use this function in a program designed to display a sequence of code numbers for a sentence entered from the keyboard. Your message is limited to one sentence and to the words contained in your DATA statements. Do not include any punctuation marks in the sentence.
   Test your program by encoding the message

   SEND MONEY STOP FAMILY SENT HOME STOP DANGER TO EAST END

7. Using the same DATA statements as in Practice Program 6, write another function that will return a word when a number parameter is passed to it. The function will return a null string value if the parameter is not a valid number.

   Use this function in a program to display an English sentence for a sequence of code numbers entered from the keyboard. Enter the code numbers one by one. A value of zero tells the program that all code numbers have been entered and thus zero cannot be one of your code numbers.

   Test your program by decoding the message

   4 22 17 3 6 18

8. Information on common stocks is contained in several DATA statements. The stock symbol, highest price for the year, lowest price for the year, and current price are listed for each stock.

   Read the DATA statements into a two-dimensional array and display the information in a table with column headings of SYMBOL, HIGH, LOW, CURRENT.

```
DATA RCA,44,34.75,43.12
DATA RIHL,4,1.5,3.75
DATA RY,32,27.5,27.75
DATA SHRM,10.5,6,10
DATA SWS,33,29.5,30.5
DATA SOCR,10.75,6.75,8.75
DATA SMLS,10.25,5.5,6
DATA SEEQ,7.5,2.5,2.75
DATA SLON,9,4,7.25
DATA SY,56.75,39.25,51
```

   Calculate the relative position of the current price of each stock within the range between its lowest and highest price for the year. The term "relative position" is best explained by an example. Consider two stocks:

SYMBOL	HIGH	LOW	CURRENT
A	100	10	15
B	20	10	15

   Each stock has a current price that is $5.00 higher than its low price. For stock A, this represents a relative position of (5/(100 − 10)) or .055. Expressed in percentage, stock A has risen 5.5 percent from its low. For stock B, the relative position is (5/(20 − 10)) or .5, representing a 50 percent rise from its low.

   Display, with appropriate labels, the symbol of the stock with the highest relative position and that with the lowest relative position.

9 Storing Information in Text Files

9.1 INTRODUCTION

Disk files provide a relatively permanent way to store information in a computer system. We discuss how to name and open text files from True BASIC programs, how to write information on files, and how to read information from files. We examine some of the limitations of text files.

Files of data are used widely in business for storing company records such as payrolls, inventories, mailing lists, and so forth. We design and develop a simple database program that creates and uses a telephone directory file containing customer names and telephone numbers.

9.2 SEQUENTIAL TEXT FILES

You may remember that we defined a file in Chapter 2 as a collection of characters or other information, usually stored on a computer disk. Up to this point, our files have contained BASIC program statements. We have talked about saving our programs in files on the disk.

There is no reason, however, to restrict files to BASIC programs. Any kind of information may be placed in a file. You are familiar with the concept of reading or inputting values from the keyboard and writing or printing values on the screen. These values may be numbers or strings. In a similar manner, we can write values on a disk file and read values from a disk file. Thus some files may contain values or *data,* while other files contain *programs.*

In this chapter, we will discuss only files containing characters. These files are called *text files.* They are further identified as *sequential text files,* meaning that the information they contain can only be read sequentially, from beginning to end.

A sequential file has its information stored sequentially, one item after another. In our case, each item consists of a separate line of text. This means that two nonprinting characters, the carriage return (ASCII value 13) and the line feed (ASCII value 10), are used together to separate one data item from another. This pair of characters, carriage return and line feed, is called a *line delimiter.*

Thus our type of simple, sequential text file has *lines* or items of information consisting of ASCII characters, these lines are stored sequentially, and they are separated from one another by line delimiters. A line may contain numeric characters and represent a numeric value, or it may contain any characters and represent a string value.

There is no other structure inherent in the file itself—it is nothing more than a sequence of lines of text (ASCII) characters. Here is a list showing the contents of a short text file containing names:

Mark C. Kitchin	Mary G. Sandridge
Judy Wright	H. B. Napier
G. Helen Lee	Roger Shingle
Frederic Taylor	William A. Sampson III
J. Andrew Koontz	Joseph P. Smith

Here is another list showing the contents of a text file containing numbers:

22903	22932
22945	22931
22932	22191
24521	23230
23607	24219

A BASIC program can write information on a sequential file, or it can read information from the file. Writing on a newly created file starts at the beginning of the file. Writing can also start at the end of an existing file, adding new information to that which already exists. Reading from a file always starts at the beginning and continues as long as requested by the program or until the end of file is reached.

These descriptions of writing and reading may seem obvious, but they are crucial to understanding the nature of sequential files. **You cannot start reading somewhere in the middle of a sequential file, only at the beginning. You cannot go to the beginning or the middle of an existing sequential file and write new information.** If you try to do so, you will get an error message.

Let's examine the writing process in more detail. It is useful to imagine a *file pointer* that indicates or "points to" the position in the file where the next character will be written. If you have opened the file for writing, but have not yet written anything on it, the pointer indicates the beginning of the file. When you write one character on the file, the pointer moves to a position immediately after that character, indicating where the next character will be written. At the same time, this position is denoted as the current end of file. When you write the next character, the pointer moves ahead again, and its new position now becomes the end of file.

Files are identified by their names. We discussed MS-DOS file names in Chapter 2, and you will remember that file names can be only eight characters long, plus an optional suffix consisting of a period and three characters. The characters usually are letters or digits, although certain other characters are allowed in MS-DOS. We recommend that you use only letter or digit characters. **Spaces or blank characters are not allowed in file names.** Here are some examples of valid file names:

CHAPT15.DOC might be a document file.
PAYROLL.DAT might be a data file.
SORT.TRU might be a True BASIC program file.

A floppy disk may be organized with more than one file directory, with each directory containing several files. In this case, you must specify the directory name as well as the file name when referring to a file. In general, you access a file by specifying its path name; a combination of the disk drive name, the directory name, and the file name. For example, the file named TEST.DAT, located in directory CH09 on the disk in drive B, is designated by the pathname

```
B:\CH09\TEST.DAT
```

Note that backslash (\) characters are used to separate the disk drive name from the directory name, and the directory name from the file name.

If a disk has only one directory, it is not necessary to specify a directory name. The backslash separator between the disk drive name and the file name may also be omitted. If the disk in our previous example contains only a single directory, the correct path name for file TEST.DAT is

```
B:TEST.DAT
```

More information about disk directories can be found in the MS-DOS (or PC-DOS) manual.

In True BASIC, programs are stored as lines of ASCII characters in sequential text files. The computer does not care whether the information stored in a file is a program or data or a document. The user, however, does need to distinguish files containing one type of information from files containing another type, and thus descriptive suffixes can be helpful.

9.3 WRITING TEXT FILES

Opening a File for Writing

To use a file in a BASIC program, it must first be opened. The process of opening a file makes that file available for use and associates a *file number* or channel number with the MS-DOS file name. A BASIC program can neither write information on a file nor read information from a file until the file has been opened.

Every file used in a BASIC program must be identified by a file number. Thus the main part of the statement to open a file is

```
OPEN #N: name Pathname$
```

where N is a numeric variable or constant representing the file number and *Pathname$* is a string variable, expression, or constant representing the path name. In many cases, the path name will just be the file name. Once the file has been opened, it is known from then on in the program as file number N, not as a file identified by *Pathname$*.

The file number must be an integer between 1 and 1,000. File #0 is reserved for the keyboard and screen—this file or channel is always open. If N has a noninteger value, it will be rounded to the nearest integer. You can use a numeric constant like 2, or a numeric expression, instead of a numeric variable. We usually open the first file in a program as file #1, the second as file #2, and so forth, but actually any number up to 1,000 is valid. True BASIC on an IBM PC-compatible allows you to have a maximum of five files open at the same time.

The rest of the OPEN statement consists of one or more optional phrases, separated from each other by commas. These phrases are

```
ACCESS Mode$
CREATE Action$
ORGANIZATION Type$
```

The ACCESS Phrase—Default Value is OUTIN

The identifier *Mode$* following ACCESS is one of the words INPUT, OUTPUT, or OUTIN. It can also be a string variable containing one of these words as its value. INPUT mode means that the file is opened for reading only and information cannot be written on it. OUTPUT means that the file is opened for writing only. OUTIN means that the file is opened for both writing and reading. If the ACCESS phrase is not present, the file is opened by default for both writing and reading. We will generally use this default access mode when writing on a file.

Possible phrases are

access input
access output
access outin

The CREATE Phrase—Default Value is OLD

The identifier *Action$* following CREATE is one of the words NEW, OLD, or NEWOLD. It can also be a string variable containing one of these words as its value. NEW means that you are creating a new file. If a file already exists with the same name, you will get an error message. OLD means that you are using an existing file. If a file with that name does not exist, you will get an error message. NEWOLD means that you are using an old file if it exists or creating a new file if it does not exist. If the CREATE phrase is not present, the OLD action is assumed by default. Note that the NEWOLD action must be specified explicitly if you are uncertain whether or not a file exists.

Possible phrases are

create new
create old
create newold

The ORGANIZATION Phrase—Default Value is TEXT

For a text file, the identifier *Type$* following ORGANIZATION is the word TEXT or a string variable containing that word as its value. If this phrase is omitted, True BASIC checks the organization of an existing file or assumes an organization type of TEXT for a new file as soon as a line of text is written on it. As we will see in Chapter 11, if a record size is specified in the program, the organization will be of type RECORD rather than type TEXT.

Assuming the normal defaults, the usual statement for opening a new text file for writing, where the name of the file has been assigned to the variable FileName$, is

```
OPEN #1: name FileName$, create new
```

We assume in this and subsequent examples that the path name is just a simple file name.

Here are some other examples of statements to open text files for writing:

```
OPEN #1: name "B:MYFILE.DAT", organization text

! Assume N = 2, Reply$ = "HW1.DAT", Use$ = "NEW"
OPEN #N: name Reply$, create Use$

! Assume Fname$ = "A:\WILCOX\RESUME.DOC"
OPEN #3: name Fname$, access output
```

True BASIC handles file names without a suffix in a special way. If you open a new file for writing with the statement

```
OPEN #1: name "LETTER", create new
```

the file will be given the MS-DOS file name of LETTER.TRU. If you don't want the file name to have the .TRU suffix, you must use the statement

```
OPEN #1: name "LETTER.", create new
```

where a trailing period after LETTER suppresses any suffix in the file name.

If you open an old file for further writing (or for reading—see Section 9.4), the statement

```
OPEN #1: name "LETTER", create old
```

produces a run-time error if the file named LETTER.TRU does not exist. The statement

```
OPEN #1: name "LETTER.", create old
```

allows you to open a file, without a suffix, named LETTER.

Setting the File Pointer

When a text file containing text is opened for writing, you can start to write only at the end of the file. You cannot start writing at any other point in the file. The place where you start to write is designated by the file pointer. The appropriate statement for file #1 is

```
SET #1: pointer end
```

If you try to overwrite part of an existing file, you will get an error message. If you have just created a new, empty file, the file pointer will be located at the end of the file (or beginning, they are the same for an empty file).

In True BASIC, an abbreviated version of the statement to set the pointer is

```
RESET #1: end
```

A similar statement moves the file pointer to the beginning of a file #1, using either

```
SET #1: pointer begin
```

or

```
RESET #1: begin
```

Remember that when you first open a file, the file pointer is set to the beginning of the file.

Sometimes when you are working with files, you may need to use a temporary or scratch file to hold information that will be moved later to a permanent file. If you have already written some information on a temporary file, you probably want to erase that information before writing on the file again. The statement

```
ERASE #99
```

erases old information and resets the pointer to the beginning of file #99. **It is good practice to erase a temporary file before writing on it.**

Writing on a File

A modified form of the PRINT statement is used to write information on a file:

```
PRINT #N: Item
```

where the identifier *Item* represents a variable, expression, or constant, either string or numeric. If *Item* is numeric, however, the digits and other characters in the number will still be stored on the file as individual ASCII characters.

You may choose to have more than one variable in your PRINT statement, and if so, the variables should be separated by commas or semicolons:

```
PRINT #N: Item1, Item2, Item3,...
```

Values represented by the identifiers will be formatted on the file in the same way they would be formatted on the display screen. This means that several blanks may be stored on the disk between item values, especially if commas are used as separators.

We recommend that you use the PRINT statement with only a single variable, expression, or constant. Using a single item in the PRINT statement produces a simpler file structure, with each item value on a separate line, and thus makes the file easier to read. This method often saves space on the disk by eliminating the blanks between item values.

The main advantage of using a single item is that its value will be separated from the next value on the file by a carriage return and line feed. We have previously defined this pair of control characters as a line delimiter, and it serves to separate adjacent string values. A set of program statements like

```
LET First$ = "First line of text."
PRINT #1: First$
PRINT #1: "Second line."
PRINT #1: "something"
```

will write a file whose schematic diagram is shown in Figure 9-1.

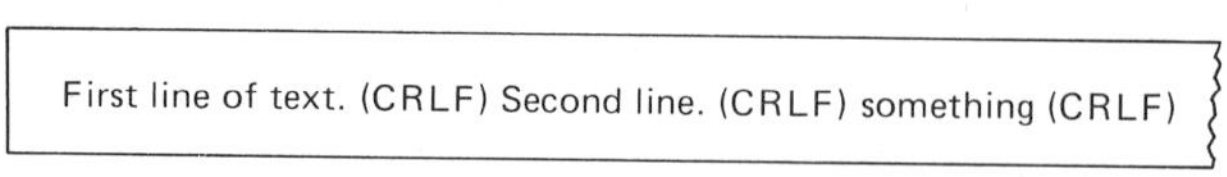

Figure 9-1 Schematic diagram of part of a disk track.

You can think of the schematic diagram as depicting part of a magnetic disk track, showing the characters and delimiters that have been written on that section of the track. The symbol (CRLF) means the pair of characters, carriage return and line feed, used as a line delimiter.

Closing a File

After you have finished writing on a file, you can release the specific file name from the file number by closing the file. The statement to close file #1 is

```
CLOSE #1
```

While it is not strictly necessary to close a file unless you plan to use the file number with another file name, it is good programming practice to do so. Closing a file makes certain that all information you have written on the file has actually been transferred from a section of memory called a file buffer to the disk.

It does no harm and produces no error message to close a file that is already closed. We suggest that you close each file when you are through writing on it.

Programs to Write Files

We look first at a simple and fundamental program to accept information from the keyboard and write it on a text file. This type of program is part of every application program that manipulates text, such as a text editor or word processor. We use a file named TEST.DAT that is located in directory CH09 on the disk in drive B. We select a character (in this case, a period) that would not normally appear as the first and only character on a line of text to signal the end of text entry.

```
! Example Program 9-1.
! Write a new sequential text file.

! You may have to change the disk
! drive letter (B:) in the file name.
OPEN #1: name "B:\CH09\TEST.DAT", create new
PRINT "Type a line of text after each ? prompt."
PRINT "Enter a single period to stop the program."
LINE INPUT Reply$
DO until Reply$ = "."
   PRINT #1: Reply$
   LINE INPUT Reply$
LOOP
CLOSE #1
END
```

A file named TEST.DAT is created in directory CH09 on the disk in drive B and opened with read and write access. The DO loop then prints string values to the file until a single period causes the program to exit the loop. You will get an error if the file already exists, so be sure you delete or "unsave" any file named TEST.DAT before running this program. After exiting the loop, the file is closed and the program ends.

When developing a program that writes on a file, we often first write output on the screen so we can see if everything is working properly. Once we see that the proper lines are being written on the screen, we modify the program to write on a file.

The method we use is simple. We put an exclamation point (!) before every specific file statement, such as OPEN, CLOSE, ERASE, RESET, and so forth, changing these statements to remarks. We change all PRINT #N statements to PRINT #0 statements, directing output to the display screen. Here is the previous program with these changes.

```
! Example Program 9-2.
! Write a new sequential text file.
! Modified for testing during development.

! You may have to change the disk
! drive letter (B:) in file name.
!   OPEN #1: name "B:\CH09\TEST.DAT", create new
PRINT "Type a line of text after each ? prompt."
PRINT "Enter a single period to stop the program."
LINE INPUT Reply$
DO until Reply$ = "."
   PRINT #0: Reply$
   LINE INPUT Reply$
LOOP
!   CLOSE #1
END
```

You can run the modified program to check your logic and to see if the proper results are displayed. Then remove the changes (the added exclamation points) and your program will usually work. If it has any errors, they are probably in one of the statements that you changed.

Remember that you can use the True BASIC editor to view any text file. The command

```
OLD B:\CH09\TEST.DAT
```

displays the file TEST.DAT, located in directory CH09 on the disk in drive B, in the program window.

A slight modification of the first program allows you to write additional information to an existing text file. In this example, we ask the user to specify the file name.

```
! Example Program 9-3.
! Append to an existing text file.

PRINT "Include disk drive letter in file name."
INPUT prompt "Name of file? ": FileName$
PRINT
OPEN #1: name FileName$, create old
RESET #1: end
PRINT "Type a line of text after each ? prompt."
PRINT "Enter a single period to stop the program."
LINE INPUT Reply$
DO until Reply$ = "."
   PRINT #1: Reply$
   LINE INPUT Reply$
LOOP
CLOSE #1
END
```

The user is prompted to enter a file name which is assigned to the variable FileName$. The file is assumed to exist. The program will stop with an error message if the file does not exist. The RESET statement moves the file pointer to the end of the file so that new text is appended to the existing test.

One further variation of our file writing program allows you to rewrite an existing file.

```
! Example Program 9-4.
! Rewrite an existing text file.

PRINT "Include disk drive letter in file name."
INPUT prompt "Name of file? ": FileName$
PRINT
OPEN #1: name FileName$
ERASE #1   ! remove existing contents
PRINT "Type a line of text after each ? prompt."
PRINT "Enter a single period to stop the program."
LINE INPUT Reply$
DO until Reply$ = "."
   PRINT #1: Reply$
   LINE INPUT Reply$
LOOP
CLOSE #1
END
```

The ERASE statement has the effect of deleting all information from a file, making it an empty file. The file pointer is set to the beginning of the file. An error message is displayed if the file has not been opened or if the access mode is INPUT or read only.

Text lines can be formatted on a file in the same way they are formatted on the screen. For example, the statement

```
PRINT #1, using "####": 12
```

will display the number 12 right-justified in a field of four spaces.

Print zone width and right margin (screen width) can be determined and changed using the statements

```
ASK #N: zonewidth Var
ASK #N: margin Var
SET #N: zonewidth Expr
SET #N: margin Expr
```

where N is the file number, *Var* is a numeric variable, and *Expr* is any valid numeric expression.

9.4 READING TEXT FILES

Statements similar to those for writing are used when reading information from sequential text files. The file must be opened for reading by using the OPEN statement. Most of the optional phrases that we discussed in Section 9.3 may be used (of course, the access mode cannot be OUTPUT or write only).

Opening a File for Reading

If a file is to be used for reading only, the OPEN statement might be

```
OPEN #1: name FileName$, access input
```

A file opened in this manner may not be used for writing, only for reading. It must already exist and have information stored in it. If both reading and writing capability are desired and the file may not exist, use the statement

```
OPEN #1: name FileName$, create newold
```

Remember that the default access mode is OUTIN, so both reading and writing are allowed.

If you want to avoid creating a new file when the named file does not exist, use the statement

```
OPEN #1: name FileName$, create old
```

or

```
OPEN #1: name FileName$
```

These forms of the OPEN statement will give you an error message if the named file does not exist. Remember that the default create action is OLD.

When a file is opened with any of the foregoing statements, the file pointer will be at the beginning of the file. **This is the only place where you can start reading a sequential text file.**

Reading from a File

A modified form of the INPUT or LINE INPUT statement is used to read information from a file. **When reading string values from a text file, we recommend the use of the LINE INPUT statement because it will read all characters, including commas, up to the end of the line.** For example,

```
LINE INPUT #1: Line$
```

The identifier Line$ must be a string variable. After reading a line of text, the file pointer moves to the beginning of the next line.

You can also use the LINE INPUT statement with two or more variables. As before, we assume that the file was written with a single string value on each line. The values of sequential lines in the file will be assigned to the variables in the LINE INPUT statement, one line per variable. For example,

```
LINE INPUT #1: Line1$, Line2$, Line3$...
```

If a line in your file contains characters representing a number, you can read the line as a string and convert it to a number with the VAL function. You can also use the INPUT statement (not LINE INPUT) with a numeric variable:

```
INPUT #1: Number
```

A fatal error will result if one of the characters you are converting or reading is not allowed in a numeric expression. You can use the error-handling techniques discussed in Chapter 6 to trap the error.

Closing a file is not necessary when you have finished reading it, unless you want to assign the same file number to another file. It does no harm to close a file that is either open or already closed, and we usually close every file that we are through using.

Programs to Read Files

Another fundamental program reads text information from a file specified by the user and displays it on the screen. This type of program is also part of every application program that manipulates text. We start reading at the beginning of the file and continue until we reach the end of the file.

```
! Example Program 9-5.
! Read a sequential text file.

PRINT "Include disk drive letter in file name."
INPUT prompt "Name of file? ": FileName$
PRINT
OPEN #1: name FileName$, create old
DO until end #1
   LINE INPUT #1: Line$
   PRINT Line$
LOOP
CLOSE #1
END
```

The user is asked to name an existing file and it is opened. If the file does not exist, an error message will be displayed. A new logical function, END #1, is used to check for the end of file #1. It has a value of true if the file pointer has reached the end of the file; otherwise, it has a value of false. It is used as part of a DO UNTIL statement to control the DO loop. After all information on the file has been read, it is closed and the program ends. Note that the CREATE OLD phrase is not really necessary because this is the default create value.

Another logical function is MORE #1, which has a value of true if there is more information in file #1. It can be used in place of the END #1 function to control the DO loop.

```
! Example Program 9-6.
! Read a sequential text file.

PRINT "Include disk drive letter in file name."
INPUT prompt "Name of file? ": FileName$
PRINT
OPEN #1: name FileName$, create newold
DO while more #1
   LINE INPUT #1: Line$
   PRINT Line$
LOOP
CLOSE #1
END
```

This program uses the NEWOLD option to avoid an error message if the file does not exist, although no information will be read in that case because the newly created file is empty.

After writing a program to read a file, you can test it by reading any text file, including a True BASIC program file. Remember that a program file is just a sequential text file.

9.5 FILES AS SUBPROGRAM PARAMETERS

File names can be passed as string values to both functions and subroutines. **File numbers may be passed as parameters to external or internal subroutines, but not to functions.** If a file is opened by name in a subprogram unit, either function or subroutine, it is closed automatically when control returns to the calling unit.

When file numbers are passed to subroutines, a special notation is used. The file number must be a numeric constant, not a numeric variable, and it must be preceded by the symbol "#". For example, the statement

```
CALL Sort (List$, #1)
```

in the calling program unit makes the file designated #1 available to the subroutine Sort. List$ is the name of a one-dimensional array. The heading statement of subroutine Sort might be

```
EXTERNAL SUB Sort (A$(), #9)
```

This heading makes the file identified by #9 in the subroutine the same as the file identified by #1 in the calling program unit. The file number used in the subroutine is completely arbitrary. If the file is opened in the calling program unit, it will remain open in the subroutine and continues to remain open when control returns to the calling unit.

Here is a sample program that writes a line of text to a file, calls a subroutine that reads the line of text from the file, and then returns to the calling program unit:

```
! Example Program 9-7.
! Use the same file in two program units.

! You may need to change the disk
! drive letter (B:) in the file name.
OPEN #1: name "B:\CH09\TEST.DAT", create new
LINE INPUT prompt "Enter test line: ": Line$
PRINT #1: Line$
PRINT "Test line is written to file."
PRINT "Call subroutine, passing file number."
CALL View (#1)
END
```

```
SUB View (#9)
    ! Read a line from the file.
    RESET #9: begin
    PRINT "File pointer reset to beginning."
    INPUT #9: Entry$
    PRINT "Test line is read from file."
    PRINT "Test line: "; Entry$
END SUB
```

A new file named TEST.DAT is opened in the main program unit as file #1, and a string is written to it. This file is then designated as file #9 in the subroutine. The file pointer is moved to the beginning of the file, and the string is read into the variable Entry$ and displayed. Control then returns to the main program unit where the file, again known as #1, is closed.

Note that in this example we use the optional form of the subroutine heading, omitting the word EXTERNAL. The program knows that View is an external subroutine because it is listed after the main program END statement.

The SET MARGIN statement, which we mentioned in Section 9.3, has an important use when writing string values on files. Remember that the default value of MARGIN is 80 columns. Sometimes when writing on files, we need to write strings that are longer than 80 characters. If we leave the margin set at the default value, a long string (over 80 characters) will be written on the file as a series of substrings, each substring less than 80 characters long.

A solution to this problem is to set a wider margin with the SET MARGIN statement. Many word processors produce files with each text paragraph stored as a single long string. Here is an example program that copies text from a word processor (XyWrite) file to a True BASIC text file. We assume that no paragraph contains more than 2,048 characters.

This program uses a subroutine named OpenFile to open files. One parameter of the subroutine is the desired prompt for a file name; another parameter is information on whether the file is old or new. The file number is passed as the third parameter. In this particular example, the output file is opened with a CREATE mode of ''newold'' and its contents erased if the file already exists.

```
! Example Program 9-8.
! Read a text file with long strings
! and copy to another file.

CALL OpenFile ("Input file", "old", #1)
CALL OpenFile ("Output file", "newold", #2)
ERASE #2
SET #2: margin 2048  ! for long strings
DO until end #1
   LINE INPUT #1: Line$
   PRINT #2: Line$
LOOP
CLOSE #1
CLOSE #2
END
```

```
EXTERNAL SUB OpenFile (Prompt$, Mode$, #9)
    ! Prompt for file name and open file.
    LET FileOpened$ = "false"
    DO
       WHEN error in
            PRINT Prompt$;
            LINE INPUT FileName$
            LET X = pos(FileName$, ":")
            IF X = 0 then
               INPUT prompt "On disk in which drive? ": Drive$
               LET FileName$ = Drive$[1:1] & ":" & FileName$
            END IF
            OPEN #9: name FileName$, create Mode$
            LET FileOpened$ = "true"
       USE
            PRINT "Error: "; extext$
            PRINT "Check file name and try again."
            PRINT
       END WHEN
    LOOP until FileOpened$ = "true"
END SUB
```

The subroutine sets the flag FileOpened$ to false, prints the prompt, and tries to open the file using a file name supplied by the user. If the file is successfully opened, the flag is set to true. If not, the error message is displayed, and the user is asked to enter the file name again. The loop continues until a file is opened. A subroutine of this type is useful in any program where a file is opened and we will use it in subsequent programs.

9.6 THE PRINTER AS A FILE

True BASIC allows you to treat an attached printer as a sequential text file. You can write information on a printer, but you cannot, of course, read information from a printer. A printer is identified by the keyword PRINTER and is assigned a file number using the statement

```
OPEN #N: printer
```

If you are using a computer connected to a network that supports printers, network software should be available to transfer information from a disk file to a printer. The procedures we discuss probably will not work with shared printers on a network.

Here is a simple program that prints any text file specified by the user. It uses a subroutine to check whether the text file exists and, if it does not exist, asks the user to try again.

Unfortunately, no error message is displayed if the printer is not turned on. The computer waits for a while and then continues executing the program. All information sent to the printer is lost. If this happens to you, all you can do is interrupt the program by pressing the Ctrl Break key. We include a warning message in our program to remind the user to turn on the printer.

```
! Example Program 9-9.
! Print a text file.

CALL OpenFile ("Name of file", "old", #1)
PRINT "Be sure printer is attached and turned on."
PRINT "Press any key to continue."
GET KEY Dummy
OPEN #2: printer
DO until end #1
   LINE INPUT #1: Line$
   PRINT #2: Line$
LOOP
CLOSE #1
CLOSE #2
END

! Subroutine to open a text file.
EXTERNAL SUB OpenFile (Prompt$, Mode$, #9)
    ! Prompt for file name and open file.
    LET FileOpened$ = "false"
    DO
       WHEN error in
            PRINT Prompt$;
            LINE INPUT FileName$
            LET X = pos(FileName$, ":")
            IF X = 0 then
               INPUT prompt "On disk in which drive? ": Drive$
               LET FileName$ = Drive$[1:1] & ":" & FileName$
            END IF
            OPEN #9: name FileName$, create Mode$
            LET FileOpened$ = "true"
       USE
            PRINT "Error: "; extext$
            PRINT "Check file name and try again."
            PRINT
       END WHEN
    LOOP until FileOpened$ = "true"
END SUB
```

9.7 A SAMPLE DATABASE PROGRAM

As an example of the use of files, we will develop a telephone directory program. This program maintains a file of names and telephone numbers. Such a file is commonly called a *database,* although that term more properly denotes a collection of several related data files.

The telephone directory program is a simple example of one of the most important uses of computers, maintaining information in databases. It is a substantial program, longer and more complex than anything we have written so far.

Our directory file is a text file, and each line contains one item of information. For each directory entry, we have two items of information, a name and a telephone number. The entry is called a *logical record,* and each item is called a *field* of the record. Thus our directory file consists of an indeterminate number of logical records, each record containing two lines.

A menu, which allows the user to select one of several commands, controls the program. Our first step is to decide what commands should be included in the menu. Let's design a program with these five commands:

1 . . . . . create a new directory file
2 . . . . . add information to the file
3 . . . . . list the directory file
4 . . . . . search for a name
5 . . . . . quit

The menu section of the program should display the foregoing information on the screen and ask the user to make a selection. This selection must be a number between 1 and 5. If any other character is entered, the program should reject it and ask the user to make another selection.

A menu-driven program lends itself to *modular design.* We write the program module for each command in the form of an external subroutine and use the CASE statement to select the appropriate module for a specified command. We use comments to label each module and blank lines to separate modules. This extra effort in program design and formatting produces a program that is easy to read and understand. It is good programming practice.

Program Outline

As usual, we start our program design by writing an outline of the main program:

Initialize constants (i.e., screen length).
Ask for file name and open file.
Begin loop.
  Display the command menu.
  Ask for command choice.
  Check validity of command.
  Branch to selected command subroutine.
End loop if command is QUIT.

Main Program Unit

The main program unit first takes care of such preliminary matters as clearing the screen, setting the screen length constant, and opening the telephone directory file. Then within a loop structure, the menu is displayed, the user is asked to make a selection, the user entry is checked for errors, and a CASE statement calls the appropriate command subroutine.

```
! Example Program 9-10.
! Telephone Directory Program.

CLEAR               ! Clear the screen
LET Page = 21       ! Number of lines displayed
LET Ins = 20        ! Tab insert for command menu
CALL OpenFile ("Directory file name", "old", #1)

DO ! top of main loop
   CLEAR
   PRINT tab(Ins); "Command Menu"
   PRINT
   PRINT tab(Ins); "1.....create a new directory file"
   PRINT tab(Ins); "2.....add data to the directory"
   PRINT tab(Ins); "3.....list the directory file"
   PRINT tab(Ins); "4.....search for a name"
   PRINT tab(Ins); "5.....quit"
   PRINT
   PRINT tab(20); "Your selection";
   LINE INPUT Command$

   SELECT CASE Command$
   CASE "1"   ! Create new directory file
        CALL Create (#1)
   CASE "2"   ! Add data to the directory
        CALL Add (#1)
   CASE "3"   ! List the directory file
        CALL List (#1, Page)
   CASE "4"   ! Search for a name
        CALL Search (#1)
   CASE "5"   ! Quit the program
   CASE else
        PRINT tab(Ins); "Enter number between 1 and 5."
        PRINT tab(Ins); "Press any key to continue."
        GET KET Dummy
   END SELECT
LOOP until Command$ = "5"   ! bottom of main loop
CLOSE #1
END
```

As noted in the comments, the first statement clears the screen. A variable named Page is assigned a value representing the maximum number of lines that will be displayed on the screen. The OpenFile subroutine that we have previously developed is used to open the file.

At the beginning of the main loop, the screen is cleared again and the menu is displayed. The user is asked to assign a command number to the variable Command$.

The value of Command$ is used to make a CASE statement selection, and an appropriate subroutine is called. If this number is not between 1 and 5, an error message is displayed and the loop is repeated until a valid command is entered. If command 5 is chosen, the program exits the main loop, the directory file is closed, and the program ends.

CREATE Subroutine

The first subroutine executes the Create command. This command creates a new directory file after closing the current file. Creating a new directory just establishes the new file, it does not place any information in the file. The Add command must be run after a new directory has been created to write information on the file.

```
SUB Create (#9)
    ! Create new directory file.
    CLEAR
    CLOSE #9
    CALL OpenFile ("New directory file name", "new", #9)
END SUB
```

After the screen is cleared, the old directory file is closed, and a new file is opened with the same file number. To open the new file, we call the same OpenFile subroutine that we introduced in Example Program 9-9.

ADD Subroutine

The next subroutine executes the Add command. There are two items or lines of information for each directory entry, the name of a person and the corresponding telephone number. Here is an outline of this subroutine.

Set directory file to end of file.
Top of loop.
  Request name and telephone number.
  Exit loop if name is a null string.
  Print namc and number on directory file.
Bottom of loop.
End subroutine.

We use this outline to write the following subroutine:

```
SUB Add (#9)
    ! Add data to the directory.
    CLEAR
    RESET #9: end
    PRINT "Press ENTER key after Name prompt to stop."
    PRINT
```

```
            LINE INPUT prompt "Name: ": Name$   ! Pressing just ENTER
            DO until Name$ = ""                 ! gives a null string.
            LINE INPUT prompt "Phone number: ": Phone$
            PRINT #9: Name$
            PRINT #9: Phone$
            PRINT
            LINE INPUT prompt "Name: ": Name$
        LOOP
    END SUB
```

Before writing any information on the directory, the file pointer is set to the end of the file so that new information will be added to existing information. A loop is established for entering new values into the variables Name$ and Phone$. The values of Name$ and Phone$ are written on the directory file with two separate PRINT # statements, ensuring that each value is written as a separate line.

The user is told to press the Enter key in response to the Name prompt to stop adding new information. This action produces a null string in Name$, and if the program finds that value, it exits the loop.

LIST Subroutine

The List subroutine is next and again we start by writing down an outline.

Set directory file to beginning of file.
Initialize a line counter.
Top of loop.
  Input name and telephone number from file.
  Exit loop if end of file is reached.
  Display name and number on the screen.
  If screen is full, pause and reset counter.
Bottom of loop.
Pause again to view the last screen.
End subroutine.

The directory file pointer is set to the beginning of the file for reading. Information is read from the file and displayed on the screen. A counter variable Count keeps track of the number of lines displayed on the screen. After the column headings and a blank line have been printed, the counter is set to 2 because two lines are displayed.

When 21 lines are displayed on the screen, the program pauses until the user presses any key. This technique prevents information from scrolling off the screen faster than it can be read. A similar pause is placed at the end of the module, where the user must press a key before the program will return to the command menu.

```
SUB List (#9, Page)
    ! List the directory file.
    CLEAR
    PRINT "Name"; tab(30); "Phone"
    PRINT
    LET Count = 2
    RESET #9: begin
    DO until end #9
       LINE INPUT #9: Name$, Phone$
       PRINT Name$; tab(30); Phone$
       LET Count = Count + 1
       IF Count >= Page then
          LET Count = 0
          PRINT "Press any key to continue."
          GET KEY Dummy
          PRINT
       END IF
    LOOP
    PRINT
    PRINT "Press any key to return to menu."
    GET KEY Dummy
END SUB
```

The first pause is created by the GET KEY statement. Program execution stops until any key is pressed. The code value of the pressed key is assigned to the variable Dummy, but is not used in the program. A second, similar pause is used at the end of the subroutine.

SEARCH Subroutine

The next subroutine executes the Search command. Here is an outline for this command.

Set directory file to beginning of file.
Request target name.
Top of loop.
  Input name and telephone number from file.
  Exit loop if end of file is reached.
  Compare name from file and target name.
  If equal, display number and stop the search.
Bottom of loop.
If name is not found, display an error message.
Pause to view the screen.
End subroutine.

The user is asked to specify a name and then the directory file is searched sequentially, from the beginning, until the desired name is found. If the name is found, the corresponding telephone number is displayed. If it is not found, the user is informed that the name is not in the directory. Sequential searching is a simple search technique, adequate for small files but too slow for large files. A large file might be one with a thousand records or more.

When making comparisons, True BASIC tests for an exact match between the entered name and the directory name. For example, the name ''Peter Toms'' does not match the name ''PETER TOMS''. To avoid this kind of mismatch, both names are converted to uppercase characters before a comparison is made.

```
SUB Search (#9)
    ! Search for a name.
    CLEAR
    LET Found$ = "false" ! set to "true" if name is found
    LINE INPUT prompt "What name? ": Target$
    RESET #9: begin
    DO until end #9 or Found$ = "true"
       LINE INPUT #9: Name$, Phone$
       IF ucase$(Name$) = ucase$(Target$) then
          PRINT "Phone number: "; Phone$
          LET Found$ = "true"
       END IF
    LOOP
    IF end #9 and Found$ = "false" then
       PRINT "This name is not in the directory."
    END IF
    PRINT
    PRINT "Press any key to return to menu."
    GET KEY Dummy
END SUB
```

This command module asks the user to specify a target name that is assigned to the variable Target$. A flag variable named Found$ is set to false. Each record in the directory file is read, one by one, and the value of Target$ is compared with the value of Name$. The search is continued until a match is found or the end of file is reached. Variable Found$ is set to true if a match is found.

If the end of file is reached and Found$ has a value of false, the user is told that the target name is not in the directory. Variable Found$ is is used here to suppress the ''not in directory'' message if the desired name happens to be the last name in the file. As before, a pause is placed at the end of the module so the screen can be read before the menu is displayed.

The complete program consists of the main program unit and the four external subroutines. This is a substantial program, but easy to understand if you examine it module by module. Additional subroutines might be written to delete a name from the directory (see Practice Program 10), or to search for a telephone number and display the associated name.

```
! Example Program 9-10.
! Telephone Directory Program.

CLEAR                  ! Clear the screen
LET Page = 21          ! Number of lines displayed
LET Ins = 20           ! Tab inset for command menu
CALL OpenFile ("Directory file name", "old", #1)
```

```
DO ! top of main loop
   CLEAR
   PRINT tab(Ins); "Command Menu"
   PRINT
   PRINT tab(Ins); "1.....create a new directory file"
   PRINT tab(Ins); "2.....add data to the directory"
   PRINT tab(Ins); "3.....list the directory file"
   PRINT tab(Ins); "4.....search for a name"
   PRINT tab(Ins); "5.....quit"
   PRINT
   PRINT tab(Ins); "Your selection";
   LINE INPUT Command$

   SELECT CASE Command$
   CASE "1"  ! Create new directory file
        CALL Create (#1)
   CASE "2"  ! Add data to the directory
        CALL Add (#1)
   CASE "3"  ! List the directory file
        CALL List (#1, Page)
   CASE "4"  ! Search for a name
        CALL Search (#1)
   CASE "5"  ! Quit the program
   CASE else
        PRINT tab(Ins); "Enter number between 1 and 5."
        PRINT tab(Ins); "Press any key to continue."
        GET KEY Dummy
   END SELECT
LOOP until Command$ = "5"  ! bottom of main loop
CLOSE #1
END

SUB Create (#9)
    ! Create new directory file
    CLEAR
    CLOSE #9
    CALL OpenFile ("New directory file name", "new", #9)
END SUB

SUB Add (#9)
    ! Add data to the directory.
    CLEAR
    RESET #9: end
    PRINT "Press ENTER key after Name prompt to stop."
    PRINT
    LINE INPUT prompt "Name: ": Name$    ! Pressing just ENTER
    DO until Name$ = ""                  ! gives a null string.
       LINE INPUT prompt "Phone number: ": Phone$
       PRINT #9: Name$
       PRINT #9: Phone$
       PRINT
       LINE INPUT prompt "Name: ": Name$
    LOOP
END SUB

SUB List (#9, Page)
    ! List the directory file
    CLEAR
    PRINT "Name"; tab(30); "Phone"
    PRINT
```

```
    LET Count = 2
    RESET #9: begin
    DO until end #9
       LINE INPUT #9: Name$, Phone$
       PRINT Name$; tab(30); Phone$
       LET Count = Count + 1
       IF Count >= Page then
          LET Count = 0
          PRINT "Press any key to continue."
          GET KEY Dummy
          PRINT
       END IF
    LOOP
    PRINT
    PRINT "Press any key to return to menu."
    GET KEY Dummy
END SUB

SUB Search (#9)
    ! Search for a name
    CLEAR
    LET Found$ = "false"  ! set to "true" if name is found
    LINE INPUT prompt "What name? ": Target$
    RESET #9: begin
    DO until end #9 or Found$ = "true"
       LINE INPUT #9: Name$, Phone$
       IF ucase$(Name$) = ucase$(Target$) then
          PRINT "Phone number: "; Phone$
          LET Found$ = "true"
       END IF
    LOOP
    IF end #9 and Found$ = "false" then
       PRINT "This name is not in the directory."
    END IF
    PRINT
    PRINT "Press any key to return to menu."
    GET KEY Dummy
END SUB

SUB OpenFile (Prompt$, Mode$, #9)
    ! Prompt for file name and open file.
    LET FileOpened$ = "false"
    DO
        WHEN error in
             PRINT Prompt$;
             LINE INPUT FileName$
             LET X = pos(FileName$, ":")
             IF X = 0 then
                INPUT prompt "On disk in which drive? ": Drive$
                LET FileName$ = Drive$[1:1] & ":" & FileName$
             END IF
             OPEN #9: name FileName$, create Mode$
             LET FileOpened$ = "true"
        USE
             PRINT "Error: "; extext$
             PRINT "Check file name and try again."
             PRINT
        END WHEN
    LOOP until FileOpened$ = "true"
END SUB
```

9.8 OTHER TYPES OF FILES

True BASIC supports two other types of files in addition to sequential text files. *Record files* store information in fixed-length records that can be accessed directly. Direct access means that you can move directly to any record in the file and write information on or read information from that record. Record files are often used to store information that is to be searched at random.

Byte files store information as a sequence of bytes with no concern about what data types these bytes represent. These files provide the most efficient method for storing information on a disk, but they are difficult to read and write and are not often used in simple application programs.

We will discuss record files in Chapter 11 and refer you to the language reference manual for further information about byte files.

IMPORTANT POINTS

Spaces or blank characters are not allowed in file names.

When a text file containing text is opened for writing, you can start to write only at the end of the file.

It is good practice to erase a temporary file before writing on it.

It is good practice to close a file after you are through using it, especially if you have written new information on it.

We recommend that you use the PRINT statement with only a single variable, expression, or constant when writing on a file.

You cannot start reading somewhere in the middle of a sequential text file, only at the beginning.

If you are reading string values from a text file, we recommend that you use the LINE INPUT statement.

If an item on a text file represents a number, it can be read into a numeric variable with the INPUT statement.

File numbers can be passed as parameters to subroutines, but not to functions.

SELF-TEST QUESTIONS

Unless specified otherwise, the word "file" in these questions means a sequential text file.

1. Is a True BASIC program file (for example, MYPROG.TRU) a sequential text file?
2. What delimiter is used to separate lines of text in a file?
3. Can you start to read a file (a) at the beginning of the file, or (b) in the middle of the file?

4. Can you start to write new information on an existing file (a) at the beginning of the file, (b) in the middle of the file, or (c) at the end of the file?
5. When you have opened a new file for writing, but have not yet written anything on it, where is the file pointer?
6. Which of these file names are allowed in MS-DOS?
   a) HW1.DAT
   b) NEW TEXT.DOC
   c) 3WAYS.TXT
   d) FINALLY
   e) RESERVATIONS.DAT
7. What is the default value of the ACCESS mode in an OPEN statement when a file is opened?
8. How many files can be open in a program at the same time?
9. If the first file opened in a program is assigned a file number of 1, does the next file opened have to be assigned a file number of 2?
10. Can the first file opened in a program be assigned a file number of (a) 9, (b) −9, (c) 990, or (d) 1,900?
11. Is it possible to write information on a file that has not been assigned a file number?
12. What is the default value of the CREATE action in an OPEN statement when a file is opened?
13. What ORGANIZATION type is assumed when a new file is opened and a line of characters is written to the file?
14. What statement is used to set the file pointer (a) to the end of file #3, or (b) to the beginning of file #3?
15. What is a disadvantage of having more than one variable in a PRINT statement used to write information on a file?
16. If a file has been opened as file #1, what statement must you execute before you can open another file as file #1?
17. Can you read a file that has been opened with an ACCESS mode of OUTPUT?
18. What is an advantage of the LINE INPUT #N statement over the INPUT #N statement when reading lines of text from a file?
19. If each line in file #1 represents a number, what statement or statements can you use to read a line and assign it to a variable named Num?
20. What is the value of the logical function END #1 if file #1 contains several lines of text and the file pointer is (a) at the beginning of the file, or (b) at the end of the file?
21. Can file numbers be passed as parameters (a) to external subroutines, or (b) to external functions?
22. If a file is opened in an external function, is that file open or closed when control returns to the calling unit?
23. If a file is specified as file #1 in the CALL statement of an external subroutine, does it have to be specified as file #1 in the heading statement of the subroutine?
24. What is the value of the logical function MORE #1 if the logical function END #1 has a value of true?
25. A file is opened for writing with the statement

```
OPEN #1: name "PROB07", create new
```

What file name will be used by MS-DOS to identify this file?

26. A file is opened for reading with the statement

```
OPEN #1: name FileName$
```

What value must be assigned to FileName$ if the desired file is named HOMEWORK and is located in the directory named LECTURE7 on the disk in drive B?

PRACTICE PROGRAMS

1. Write a text file consisting of lines of characters. A user specifies the file name and then enters text from the keyboard. Signify the end of text by entering a period as the first and only character in a line. Do not write this period on the file.

Test your program by writing the preceding lines to a file named FIRST.TXT.

2. Ask a user to specify the name of a text file. Read the file and display the text on the screen. Notify the user when the last line has been displayed.

Test your program using the file FIRST.TXT written in Practice Program 1.

3. A text file named GRADES.DAT contains student grades, stored as ASCII characters, one grade per line. Read the file and calculate the average grade, the minimum grade, and the maximum grade. Display these three values on the screen with appropriate labels.

4. A text file named NAMES.DAT contains customer names, stored one name per line in the format of first name, optional middle initial, last name. Examples are

John H. Williams
Judith Spencer

Enter a last name from the keyboard. Search through the file and display the names of all customers who have that last name. Your search should be insensitive to case; that is, both SMITH and smith should match Smith.

Test your program using the names WILLIAMS, smith, and SMITH.

5. Rewrite Practice Program 2 to display only 20 lines on the screen and then display the prompt "More?". A reply of Y (or YES or yes) displays 20 more lines. A reply of Q or N stops the program.

Test your program using the file PREFACE.TXT.

6. A file named PARTS.DAT is a text file, containing four lines of inventory information on each part:

part number
part name
quantity in stock
unit cost

A file named ORDER.DAT is a text file, containing three lines of ordering information on each part:

part number
minimum quantity before reordering
quantity to reorder

Read the information for each item from file PARTS.DAT and check the quantity in stock against the minimum quantity before reordering in file ORDER.DAT. If an order is indicated, display the following information on the screen, using one line for each item:

quantity to order
part name
total cost for this item

At the end, display the grand total cost for the entire order. This screen display could be used to generate an order for replacing inventory.

7. Write an external subroutine that copies information from one text file onto a second text file. The names of both files will be passed as parameters. If the first file does not exist, notify the user and allow the file name to be entered again. If the second file exists, it should be erased. Your program should handle strings that are up to 1024 characters long.

   Use this subroutine in a program for copying text files where the user specifies both file names. Test your program by copying the contents of file PREFACE.TXT into a file named COPY.TXT.

8. Rewrite Example Program 8-8, storing the array Room in a file named STATUS.DAT. Test the program by renting three motel rooms with two occupants per room.

9. Rewrite Example Program 8-12, reading the list of cities and table of distances from two files named CITIES.DAT and DISTANCE.DAT. File CITIES.DAT contains one city per line. File DISTANCE.DAT contains one distance per line. Test your program by finding the distance from Chicago to Miami.

10. Add a command to Example Program 9-10 that deletes a specified name and its associated telephone number. Use statements similar to those used in the Search command to find the name.

    Deleting items from a sequential file requires that you open another temporary file (possibly named TEMP.DAT) with OUTIN access. Assume that you have found the specified name, and it is the fourth name in the directory file. To delete this name, read the first three names and telephone numbers from the directory file, one by one, and write them on the temporary file. Next read the fourth name and number from the directory file, but do *not* write it on the temporary file. Then read all the remaining names and numbers, one by one, from the directory file and write them on the temporary file.

    The temporary file now contains all the information in the directory file except the specified name and telephone number. Erase the directory file and copy everything in the temporary file onto the directory file. Note that the directory file must also have OUTIN access. The temporary file can then be deleted using the program statement UNSAVE "TEMP.DAT".

    Test your command by deleting the names John Williams and Jane Carey from the directory file named PHONES.DAT, and then list the modified file.

10 Formatted Reports and Displays

10.1 INTRODUCTION

In many computer applications, the final product of a computer program is a printed report. The quality of this report is judged, in part, by its appearance. To produce an attractive and high-quality report, we must be able to control its format.

We develop further variations of the PRINT USING statement that provide us with better control of the format of information printed on paper or displayed on the screen. We show how to divide the screen into two or more independent windows so that more than one display can be observed simultaneously. We discuss methods for determining the current position of the cursor on the screen and for changing this position.

10.2 THE PRINT USING STATEMENT WITH NUMBERS

We have limited control over the format of printed reports and screen displays through use of commas and semicolons as variable separators in PRINT statements. The TAB function provides additional formatting control. It is difficult, however, to format a complicated report with just these capabilities.

The general form of the PRINT USING statement is

```
PRINT USING Format$: Item1, Item2,...
```

The expression *Format$* is either a string variable or a string constant containing special characters called format characters. You will remember that we used a simple version of this statement in Chapter 3. We list the format characters here and discuss most of them in subsequent paragraphs.

Numeric format characters are

#	any digit, print leading zeroes as spaces
%	any digit, print leading zeroes as zeroes
*	any digit, print leading zeroes as asterisks
+	print number with leading plus or minus sign
−	print number with leading space or minus sign
$	print number with leading dollar sign
^	print the exponent field of a number

String format characters are

#	any character
<	any character, left-justify string
>	any character, right-justify string

The format characters are used to control the appearance of the values of *Item1*, *Item2*, and so forth. As with the regular PRINT statement, these items can be constants, variables, or expressions. Note that the items in the PRINT USING statement are separated by commas. These commas are used only as separators; they do not cause the item values to be displayed in different print zones. Semicolons cannot be used as separators.

Commas and semicolons cannot be used to format the output of PRINT USING statements. An exception is the trailing semicolon that suppresses the normal carriage return and line feed after the statement is executed, keeping the cursor on the same line.

Displaying Simple Numbers

We will discuss first those special format characters used to control the display of numbers. The format character (#) represents any digit. Here again is the example program from Chapter 3.

```
! Example Program 10-1 (same as 3-16).
! Display numbers with the PRINT USING statement.

PRINT using "####": 125
PRINT using "####": 1285.9
PRINT using "####": 34562
PRINT
PRINT using "###.##": 12.5
PRINT using "###.##": -12.521
PRINT using "###.##": -133.33
END
```

This program produces the following display:

```
 125
1286
****

 12.50
-12.52
******
```

The format string in a PRINT USING statement may be a string variable instead of a string constant:

```
LET Format$ = "####"
PRINT using Format$: 125
```

The quantity to be printed may be a variable instead of a constant:

```
LET Number = 125
LET Format$ = "####"
PRINT using Format$: Number
```

Any characters included in the format string, other than format characters, will be displayed as entered. For example,

```
PRINT using "The total is ###,###."; 56752
```

displays the sentence

```
The total is 56,752.
```

The letters, spaces, and period are not format characters and are displayed as entered. The comma behaves a little differently—it is only displayed if there are four or more digits in the number.

Displaying Dollar Amounts

A common use of the PRINT USING statement is to display numbers representing dollars and cents with the decimal points properly aligned. For this purpose, we use the dollar sign ($) as a format character. A period is included in the format string to mark the column where the decimal point will be located. **Commas or other characters cannot be inserted between the dollar signs.**

If you wish to display an amount with a leading dollar sign, use a statement such as

```
PRINT using "$$$$$$.##": N
```

The dollar sign will ''float'', remaining always just to the left of the first digit. All the dollar signs, except the first one, are place holders for digits, so the largest number that can be printed using this format string is 99999.99. **This format string can only be used with numeric constants, variables or expressions.**

If you want the dollar sign to appear always in the same column, use a statement such as

```
PRINT using "$#####.##: N
```

Here is a program to display a column of dollar amounts, with a floating dollar sign in front of each number and the decimal points aligned.

```
! Example Program 10-2.
! Display a column of dollar amounts.

DO while more data
   READ Cost
   PRINT using "$$$$$$.##": Cost
LOOP

DATA 23.75, 1244.82, .237, 31112.5
END
```

The output of the program will look like this:

```
  $23.75
 1244.82
    $.24
$31112.50
```

Displaying Leading Signs

The regular PRINT statement places a blank space in front of a number if it is positive and a minus sign in front of a number if it is negative. To achieve the same format with the PRINT USING statement, place a minus sign (−) as a format character at the beginning of the format string. A plus sign (+) as a leading format character will display a plus sign if the number is positive and a minus sign if the number is negative. Multiple plus or minus signs in the format string cause a single ''floating'' plus or minus sign to be displayed.

```
! Example Program 10-3.
! Control display of numeric signs.

LET N = 12
LET X = -35
PRINT using "-###": N
PRINT using "-###": X
PRINT using "+++#": N
PRINT using "+++#": X
PRINT using "---#": N
PRINT using "---#": X
PRINT using "##": N
PRINT using "##": X
END
```

Here is the display

```
  12
- 35
 +12
 -35
  12
 -35
12
**
```

Note that the last PRINT USING statement displays error symbols (*) because the number −35 requires a format string of at least three characters.

If the PRINT USING statement has more variables than there are format character groups in the format string, then the format string is used over and over again until all the variable values have been printed. Any remaining characters in the format string are ignored after the last variable is displayed. The example

```
! Example Program 10-4.
! Repeated use of a format string.

LET One = 77.5
LET Two = 925
LET Three = 1.75
LET Form$ = "|##.##    ####|"
PRINT using Form$: One, Two, Three
END
```

produces the display

```
|77.50   925|| 1.75
```

Note that we use vertical bars (|) in this and several later examples to help you see the exact space occupied by the displayed values. A vertical bar is not a format character and thus is just displayed when it occurs in the format string.

Displaying Leading Zeroes

The usual format character (#) displays numbers with leading blank spaces. An alternate format character, the percent sign (%), will display numbers with leading zeroes. This format is sometimes used when displaying such items as part numbers or zip codes. The two format characters cannot be mixed in a single format character group.

For example, the statement

```
PRINT using "%%%%": 32
```

displays

```
0032
```

The statement

```
PRINT using "%#%#": 32
```

is not allowed.

Displaying Numbers with Exponents

The exponential notation for numbers is seldom used in business applications. However, the PRINT USING statement can display numbers in this form, and we show a few examples. The caret (^) is used as a format character to indicate the size of the exponent field—this field must be a least three characters long.

The example program

```
! Example Program 10-5.
! Display numbers in exponential form.

PRINT using "###^^^": 2.5e+7
PRINT using "#.##^^^": 2.5e7
PRINT using "#.##^^^^^": 2.5E7
PRINT using "##^^^": 25000000
END
```

produces the display

```
250e+5
2.50e+7
2.50e+007
25e+6
```

10.3 THE PRINT USING STATEMENT WITH STRINGS

String variables may also be formatted with PRINT USING statements. The same format character (#) is used to indicate the field in which the string value will be displayed. If the field is longer than the string value, the value will be centered in the field. If the field is shorter, a string of asterisks (*) will be printed.

If the leftmost format character (#) is replaced by another format character, the left angle bracket (<), then the string value will be left-justified in the field. A right angle bracket (>) in the same position will right-justify the string value. **Angle brackets cannot be used to justify numeric values.**

For example, the program

```
! Example Program 10-6.
! Display a string variable.

LET Title$ = "abc"
PRINT using "|#######|": Title$
PRINT using "|<######|": Title$
PRINT using "|>######|": Title$
PRINT using "|##|": Title$
END
```

produces the display

```
| abc |
|abc   |
|   abc|
|**|
```

Displaying Both Strings and Numbers

A format string can be used to control the display of a combination of strings and numbers. Here is an example that displays typical lines from a price list, showing the part number, description, and price.

```
! Example Program 10-7.
! Display both strings and numbers.

LET Format$ = "%%%%   <##############   $$$.##"
DO while more data
   READ PartNum, Item$, Price
   PRINT using Format$: PartNum, Item$, Price
LOOP

DATA 245, "Cleat, 4 inch", 12.50
DATA 1705, Bow Light, 34.50
DATA 12, Boat Cushion, 3.95
DATA 717, Shackle, 5.50
DATA 718, Pin, 2.25
END
```

This program displays the price list:

```
0245  Cleat, 4 inch   $12.50
1705  Bow Light       $34.50
0012  Boat Cushion     $3.95
0717  Shackle          $5.50
0718  Pin              $2.25
```

Printing on Files and on a Printer

Printing on files can be formatted with a modified PRINT USING statement. The statement

```
PRINT #1, using Format$: Title$
```

will print the value of the variable Title$ on file #1, using the format string contained in Format$. Remember that an attached printer can be thought of as a file and given a file number with the statement

```
OPEN #N: printer
```

Here is the previous program rewritten to print the price list on an attached printer. Be sure that a printer is connected to your computer and is turned on before running this program.

```
! Example Program 10-8.
! Print both strings and numbers on a printer.

OPEN #1: printer
LET Format$ = "%%%%   <#############   $$$.##"
DO while more data
   READ PartNum, Item$, Price
   PRINT #1, using Format$: PartNum, Item$, Price
LOOP

DATA 245, "Cleat, 4 inch", 12.50
DATA 1705, Bow Light, 34.50
DATA 12, Boat Cushion, 3.95
DATA 717, Shackle, 5.50
DATA 718, Pin, 2.25
END
```

10.4 EXAMPLE OF A PROPOSAL REPORT

Our example program prepares a proposal report for a school microcomputer laboratory. This report is shown in Figure 10-1 on page 180.

Information for the report is read from a sequential text file named PROPOSAL.DAT, whose contents are shown in the following list. We will explain the meaning of each individual data item as we discuss the program.

```
3
Computer Laboratory Proposal
for
Newtown High School
3
Hardware
20
ABC microcomputers, 2295
20
Model 15 monochrome monitor, 175.5
5
Model XX-50 printer, 520
5
Printer cable, 31.75
-1
Software
```

20
DOS 4.0 operating system, 60
20
BASIC interpreter, 40
20
Pascal compiler, 49.95
−1
Furniture
10
"Table, 3 ft. x 7 ft.", 180
20
Chair, 37.5
−1

```
                 Computer Laboratory Proposal
                              for
                      Newtown High School

============================================================
NO.            ITEM                        PRICE        COST
============================================================

Hardware:

20      ABC microcomputers               2295.00    45900.00
20      Model 15 monochrome monitor       175.50     3510.00
 5      Model XX-50 printer               520.00     2600.00
 5      Printer cable                      31.75      158.75

                                       Subtotal:   $52168.75

Software:

20      DOS 4.0 operating system           60.00     1200.00
20      BASIC interpreter                  40.00      800.00
20      Pascal compiler                    49.95      999.00

                                       Subtotal:    $2999.00

Furniture:

10      Table, 3 ft. x 7 ft.              180.00     1800.00
20      Chair                              37.50      750.00

                                       Subtotal:    $2550.00

                                          Total:   $57717.75
```

Figure 10-1 Proposal report produced by Example Program 10-9.

We look first at an outline of the program:

Display the report title.
Create format strings.
Display column headings.
For each category of items,
  Display quantity, item, unit price, cost;
  Display subtotal cost for the category;
  Display the grand total cost.

The program is written so that it can be modified easily to write the report on any output device. As written, it will display on the screen that is designated file #0. If you want to write the report on an attached printer or on a file, add the appropriate file opening statement to the program and assign a different value to the file number variable N.

The first section of the program opens the data file and displays the general title. The data file is designated as file #1 and is opened for reading only. We assume that this file is in directory CH10 on a disk in drive B. Note that this designation of the data file as #1 means that the output file number, N, must have a different number.

To display the title, we use the technique discussed earlier for centering lines of text, using the TAB function. The program is designed to handle a multiline title, the number of lines being specified by a variable TitleLines that is the first item read from the data file.

```
! Example Program 10-9.
! Program to produce a formatted report.

! Open the data file and display the title.
! You may need to change the disk
! drive letter (B:) in the file name.
OPEN #1: name "B:\CH10\PROPOSAL.DAT", access input
LET N = 0                    ! N is the output file number
LET Width = 60               ! width of the page in columns
SET #N: margin Width
INPUT #1: TitleLines         ! number of lines in title
FOR I = 1 to TitleLines
    INPUT #1: Line$
    PRINT #N: tab((Width - len(Line$))/2); Line$
NEXT I
PRINT #N
```

The variable TitleLines has a value of three, indicating that the next three items read from the data file are lines of the title. The report is designed to fit on a page that is 60 columns wide and that value is assigned to the variable Width. A TAB function in the PRINT statement centers the string Line$ in this page width. The SET statement makes sure that the screen is set to the same width.

The format strings for column headings and values are placed in the next section. By placing these strings together, it is easy to see how the values, either text or numbers, line up under the individual column headings.

The heading format string H$ and the value format string F$ are written in two parts that are then concatenated together. This procedure avoids a program statement that is too long to be displayed as a single line on the screen.

```
! Create format strings for headings and values.
LET H1$ = "###      ####                           "
LET F1$ = "##     <##############################"
LET H2$ = "      #####          ####  "
LET F2$ = "     ####.##     #####.##"
LET H$ = H1$ & H2$
LET F$ = F1$ & F2$
```

The next section displays column headings. We use the REPEAT$ function to display two horizontal lines that separate the column headings from the rest of the table.

```
! Display column headings.
PRINT #N: repeat$("=", Width)
PRINT #N, using H$: "NO.", "ITEM", "PRICE", "COST"
PRINT #N: repeat$("=", Width)
PRINT #N
```

The main section of the program displays the report table itself. We use the F$ format string to format each line. The table is divided into NumCat categories, where the variable NumCat is the next item read from the data file. In this example, there are three separate categories in the report. We calculate a cost subtotal within each category and a total cost for the complete project.

We use two summing variables, SubTotal and GrandTotal. SubTotal is used to calculate the total cost for a category, while GrandTotal is used to calculate the total cost for the project. Note that SubTotal must be reset to zero at the beginning of each category. The number -1 is read from the data file and is used as a dummy trailer in each category to indicate that there are no more data items for that category.

```
! Display the main table.
LET GrandTotal = 0
INPUT #1: NumCat
FOR I = 1 to NumCat
    INPUT #1: SubHeading$
    PRINT #N: SubHeading$; ":"
    PRINT #N
    LET SubTotal = 0      ! reset for each category
    INPUT #1: Number
    DO until Number < 0  ! stop at negative trailer
       INPUT #1: Item$, UnitPr
       LET Cost = Number * UnitPr
       LET SubTotal = SubTotal + Cost
       PRINT #N, using F$: Number, Item$, UnitPr, Cost
       INPUT #1: Number
    LOOP
    PRINT #N
    PRINT #N: tab(Width - 20); "Subtotal: ";
    PRINT #N, using "$$$$$$.##": SubTotal
    PRINT #N
    LET GrandTotal = GrandTotal + SubTotal
```

```
NEXT I
PRINT #N: tab(Width - 17); "Total: ";
PRINT #N, using "$$$$$$$.##": GrandTotal
END
```

Let's look at this section in more detail. First we set the variable GrandTotal to zero. The number of categories is read from the data file, and a FOR loop with this number is used to print all the categories. In this example, there are three categories of items.

For each category, we read and print a subheading and set the variable SubTotal to zero. A small loop reads the quantity and then the description and price of each item from the data file, calculates the cost for this quantity of the item, and prints a line of the report. The value of SubTotal is updated.

As we mentioned earlier, a quantity value of -1 signifies the end of a category of items. At this point, the value of SubTotal is printed with an appropriate label and is added to the grand total cost. The FOR loop then goes to the next category of items. After all categories have been printed (as determined by the value of NumCat), the value of GrandTotal is printed with an appropriate label.

Looking again at the data file, note that one of the item descriptions is enclosed in quotes. If this is not done, the comma after ''Table'' will be interpreted as a data separator and the wrong description will be printed. Moreover, the program will halt with an error message when a nonnumeric string is read for the item price.

Here is the complete program:

```
! Example Program 10-9.
! Program to produce a formatted report.


! Open the data file and display the title.
! You may need to change the disk
! drive letter (B:) in the file name.
OPEN #1: name "B:\CH10\PROPOSAL.DAT", access input
LET N = 0                     ! N is the output file number
LET Width = 60                ! width of the page in columns
SET #N: margin Width
INPUT #1: TitleLines          ! number of lines in title
FOR I = 1 to TitleLines
    INPUT #1: Line$
    PRINT #N: tab((Width - len(Line$))/2); Line$
NEXT I
PRINT #N


! Create format strings for headings and values.
LET H1$ = "###            ####              "
LET F1$ = "##     <#############################"
LET H2$ = "     #####      ####  "
LET F2$ = "    ####.##    #####.##"
LET H$ = H1$ & H2$
LET F$ = F1$ & F2$
```

```
! Display column headings.
PRINT #N: repeat$("=", Width)
PRINT #N, using H$: "NO.", "ITEM", "PRICE", "COST"
PRINT #N: repeat$("=", Width)
PRINT #N

! Display the main table.
LET GrandTotal = 0
INPUT #1: NumCat
FOR I = 1 to NumCat
    INPUT #1: SubHeading$
    PRINT #N: SubHeading$; ":"
    PRINT #N
    LET SubTotal = 0        ! reset for each category
    INPUT #1: Number
    DO until Number < 0     ! stop at negative trailer
       INPUT #1: Item$, UnitPr
       LET Cost = Number * UnitPr
       LET SubTotal = SubTotal + Cost
       PRINT #N, using F$: Number, Item$, UnitPr, Cost
       INPUT #1: Number
    LOOP
    PRINT #N
    PRINT #N: tab(Width - 20); "Subtotal:   ";
    PRINT #N, using "$$$$$$$.##": SubTotal
    PRINT #N
    LET GrandTotal = GrandTotal + SubTotal
NEXT I
PRINT #N: tab(Width - 17); "Total:   ";
PRINT #N, using "$$$$$$$.##": GrandTotal
END
```

10.5 CONTROLLING THE SCREEN DISPLAY

We have discussed ways to control the format of the display screen, using a format string in a PRINT USING statement. Another method of format control is to specify the position of the cursor, thus designating the position where a display will start.

Setting the Cursor Position

For the purposes of this section, the display screen consists of 80 columns and 24 rows. The statement

```
SET CURSOR Row, Column
```

moves the cursor to the location specified by the values of Row and Column. For example,

```
SET cursor 1,1
```

moves the cursor to the upper left corner of the screen.

The first time a SET CURSOR statement is executed in a program, the screen will be cleared and configured as a single display window, filling the entire area of the screen. When the program ends, the display will return to the normal split screen showing both program and command windows.

You may have as many SET CURSOR statements as you wish in a program. You may move the cursor up or down, right or left on the screen. You may not, however, move the cursor off the screen. This means that the column value must be between 1 and 80 (assuming a screen width of 80), and the row value between 1 and 25.

The SET CURSOR statement is used in an example program to draw a box around a menu on the screen. We use the familiar menu from our telephone directory program of Chapter 9.

Figure 10-2 shows how the screen display will appear.

A major part of this program is a subroutine that draws a box of width W columns and height H rows on the screen, centered at location column X and row Y. Here is an outline for the subroutine.

Assign special characters for box outline.
Assign box boundaries.
Check if box will fit on screen.
Draw the box.
Draw the top edge.
Draw both vertical edges.
Draw the bottom edge.

The special characters used to draw the outline of the box are assigned to variables in the section labeled "Box components." The boundaries of the box are calculated and assigned to variables Xminus, Xplus, Yminus, and Yplus. The next section of the subroutine checks to make sure that the box is not too big to fit on the screen. This is another example of good defensive programming.

The box is drawn by first drawing the top edge, then drawing the two vertical edges, and finally drawing the bottom edge. Note that special IBM graphics characters are used to draw the edges and the four corners of the box. See Appendix F for a complete list. If your printer will not reproduce these characters and you need a paper copy of

```
+------------------------------------+
|                                    |
|    Telephone Directory Commands    |
|                                    |
|     1. . . .create a new directory |
|     2. . . .add data to the directory |
|     3. . . .list the directory file |
|     4. . . .search for a name      |
|     5. . . .quit                   |
|                                    |
+------------------------------------+

         Your selection. . . . . . . . . . . . .
```

Figure 10-2 Screen display produced by Example Program 10-10.

your results, use a plus sign (+) for the corner characters, a minus sign (−) for the horizontal characters, and a vertical bar (|) for the vertical characters.

Returning to the main program, a SET CURSOR statement is used to place the cursor inside the box and the menu is displayed. A SET CURSOR statement must be used before each PRINT statement. Another SET CURSOR statement moves the cursor outside the box so that the command prompt can be displayed.

```
! Example Program 10-10.
! Use cursor control to display menu in box.

LET BoxOK$ = "true"
CALL Box (40, 8, 40, 12, BoxOK$)
IF BoxOK$ = "false" then
   PRINT "Press any key to stop."
   GET KEY Dummy
   STOP
END IF
SET cursor 9,26
PRINT "Telephone Directory Commands"
SET cursor 11,24
PRINT "1.....create a new directory file"
SET cursor 12,24
PRINT "2.....add data to the directory"
SET cursor 13,24
PRINT "3.....list the directory file"
SET cursor 14,24
PRINT "4.....search for a name"
SET cursor 15,24
PRINT "5.....quit"
SET cursor 18,28
PRINT "Your selection.........";
LINE INPUT prompt "": Command$
END

EXTERNAL SUB Box (W, H, X, Y, BoxOK$)
    ! Display box centered at column X, row Y.
    ! Box has width W and height H.

    ! Box components.
    LET ULCorner$ = chr$(218)
    LET URCorner$ = chr$(191)
    LET LLCorner$ = chr$(192)
    LET LRCorner$ = chr$(217)
    LET VertLine$ = chr$(179)
    LET HorLine$ = chr$(196)

    ! Box boundaries.
    LET Xminus = X - W/2
    LET Xplus = X + W/2
    LET Yminus = Y - H/2
    LET Yplus = Y + H/2

    ! Check parameter values.
    CLEAR
    ASK max cursor Height, Width
```

```
IF Xplus > Width or Xminus < 0 then
   PRINT "Screen is not wide enough for this box."
   LET BoxOK$ = "false"
   EXIT SUB
END IF
IF Yplus > Height or Yminus < 0 then
   PRINT "Screen is not high enough for this box."
   LET BoxOK$ = "false"
   EXIT SUB
END IF


    ! Display the box.
    SET cursor Yminus, Xminus
    PRINT ULCorner$;
    FOR I = (Xminus + 1) to (Xplus - 1)
        PRINT HorLine$;
    NEXT I
    PRINT URCorner$
    FOR Row = (Yminus + 1) to (Yplus - 1)
        SET cursor Row, Xminus
        PRINT VertLine$;
        SET cursor Row, Xplus
        PRINT VertLine$
    NEXT Row
    SET cursor Yplus, Xminus
    PRINT LLCorner$;
    FOR I = (Xminus + 1) to (Xplus - 1)
        PRINT HorLine$;
    NEXT I
    PRINT LRCorner$
END SUB
```

A CLEAR statement at the beginning of the subroutine clears the entire screen for use by the program. An ASK MAX CURSOR statement (discussed in the next section) determines the width and height of the screen. You will notice that the flag BoxOK$ is set to false if the subroutine is exited because the box is too big. If this flag is set, there is a pause in the main program so that the error message can be read and, when a key is pressed, the program stops.

Try running this program again after changing the "CALL Box" statement to specify a box that is wider than the normal screen width of eighty columns. The following statement specifies a box width of ninety columns.

```
CALL Box (90, 8, 40, 12, BoxOK$)
```

Another example demonstrates what happens when a program contains a large number of PRINT statements, causing the display to scroll up when the bottom of the screen is reached, and further PRINT statements are executed. The SET CURSOR statement then refers to the current screen, not the original screen. Try the following example program to see what we mean:

```
! Example Program 10-11.
! Demonstration of how the set cursor statement
! works when the screen scrolls.

! Mark two corners of the screen with asterisks.
SET cursor 1,1
PRINT "*"
SET cursor 24,80
PRINT "*"
! Pause to observe the display.
PRINT "Press any key to continue.";
GET KEY Dummy

! Scroll screen up 25 rows.
FOR I = 1 to 25
  PRINT
NEXT I

! Mark opposite corners with asterisks.
SET cursor 1,80
PRINT "*"
SET cursor 24,1
PRINT "*"
PRINT "Press any key to continue.";
GET KEY Dummy   ! pause again
END
```

Note that we pause at two points so the user can view the screen display. We then print an explanatory message and use the GET KEY statement with a dummy variable to sense if a key has been pressed. **If pauses are not inserted, the display will flash by so quickly that it cannot be seen.** The lower asterisk is displayed at row 24, not 25, so that there is room on the screen for the explanatory message.

Finding the Cursor Position

The statement

```
ASK CURSOR Row, Column
```

determines the current position of the cursor, assigning the current cursor row value to the variable Row and the column value to the variable Column. The statement

```
ASK MAX CURSOR Height, Width
```

determines the size of the screen measured in rows and columns. The variable Height will be assigned the maximum number of rows that are allowed (usually 25 for IBM PC-compatibles), and Width will be assigned the maximum number of columns (usually 80). We used this statement in Example Program 10-10.

We can also turn the cursor on and off by using the statement

```
SET CURSOR Condition$
```

where the string variable Condition$ may have only the values of "off" or "on" (in uppercase or lowercase letters). A companion statement

```
ASK CURSOR Value$
```

will assign the value of ON or OFF to the variable Value$, indicating whether the cursor is on or off.

Other variable names may be used in any of the cursor statements. The only restriction is that the variables must be of the correct type, string or numeric, for each case.

10.6 SCREEN WINDOWS

When writing True BASIC programs, we use a screen divided horizontally into two windows, a program window and a command window. In the previous section, the SET CURSOR statement changed the display to a single window. The CLEAR statement also clears the screen and displays a single window with the cursor located in the upper left corner.

Application programs are often easier to use if the screen can be divided into two or more separate and independent windows. You already know how convenient it is in True BASIC to have both the program window and command window open at the same time. Several modern screen editors allow two files to be displayed on the screen at one time, each file in its own window. Information can be read from one file while the other file is being edited.

True BASIC allows us to write programs that divide the screen into several independent windows and to move as we wish from one window to another. Each window is denoted by a window number. These window numbers are similar to file numbers, and in fact, both window numbers and file numbers are also called channel numbers. **The same channel number cannot be used as both a file number and a window number in a program.**

Creating Windows

The default window is designated as window #0 and includes the entire screen. Another window can be opened with the statement

```
OPEN #N: screen Left, Right, Bottom, Top
```

where N is the window number. The numeric expressions *Left, Right, Bottom* and *Top* define the position where the window will appear on the screen. For these expressions, True BASIC uses screen coordinates of 0 to 1 in both the horizontal and vertical directions. The coordinates of the lower left corner of the screen are (0,0), while those of the upper right corner are (1,1). Thus the values of *Left, Right, Bottom* and *Top* must be between 0 and 1.

Figure 10-3 is a picture of window #0, showing the coordinates of each corner. (See page 190.)

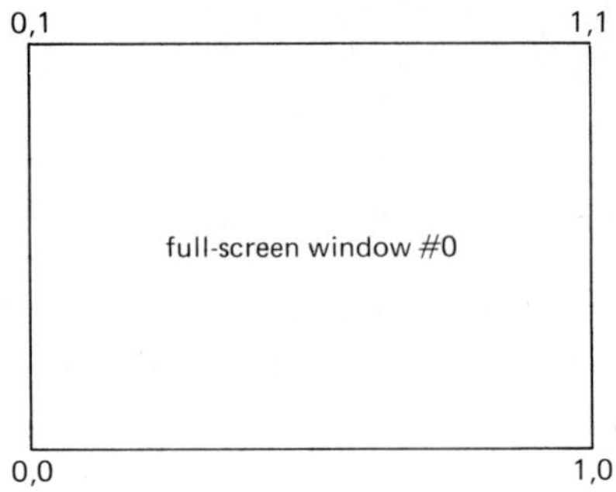

Figure 10-3 A full-screen window.

For example, the statement

```
OPEN #1: screen 0, 0.5, 0, 1
```

designates the left half of the display screen as window #1. When this window is opened, it becomes the current window. All further display operations take place in the current window. If another window is opened, it then becomes the current window. The statement

```
OPEN #2: screen 0.5, 1, 0, 1
```

opens a second window on the right half of the screen. Overlapping windows should be avoided because, on some computers, information written on one window can erase information on another overlapping or underlying window. These two windows are shown in Figure 10-4.

The statement

```
CLOSE #N
```

is used to close window #N when it is no longer being used. When any window is closed, window #0, the default window, is automatically reopened.

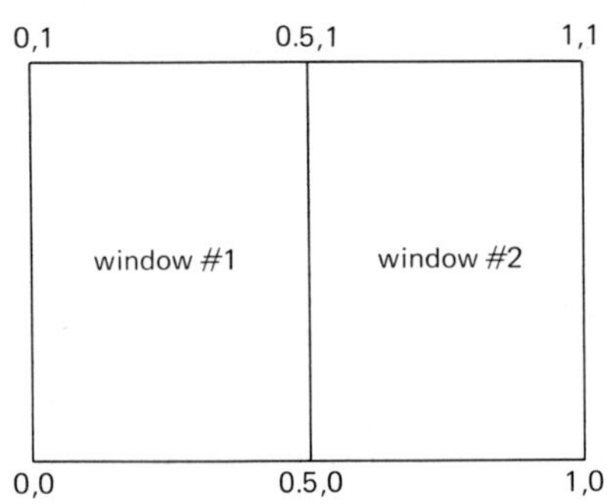

Figure 10-4 Two half-screen windows.

Moving Between Windows

We can move from one window to another by using the statement

```
WINDOW #N
```

which switches to window #N as the active window. True BASIC remembers the current cursor location, color, window coordinates, and so forth and automatically restores these values when we switch back to a window.

We can control the cursor location in a window by using the SET CURSOR statement that we introduced in the last section. **Note that the row and column values specifying cursor location are relative to the current window, not the entire screen.** We use the ASK MAX CURSOR statement to determine the maximum row and column values for the current window. An error message is displayed if we try to move the cursor outside the window.

Here is an example program that divides the screen into two windows. The left window is used to display a table of the months. The right window asks the user to enter a number and then displays the name of the corresponding month. At the same time, an arrow is moved to mark that particular month in the left window table.

```
! Example Program 10-12.
! Demonstrate use of two screen windows.

! Display table of months in first window.
DIM Month$(12)
OPEN #1: screen 0, 0.5, 0, 1
PRINT tab(7); "MONTHS"
PRINT
FOR I = 1 to 12   ! read month names into an array
    READ Month$(I)
    PRINT tab(7); Month$(I)
NEXT I

! Draw dividing line between windows.
FOR I = 1 to 24
    SET cursor I, 39
    PRINT chr$(179)   ! vertical line
NEXT I

! Run program in second window.
OPEN #2: screen 0.5, 1, 0, 1
PRINT "Type 0 to stop."
CALL GetMonth (Num)     ! get a month number
DO until Num = 0
   PRINT "You have selected "; Month$(Num)
   PRINT
   ! Mark month in first window.
   WINDOW #1
   ! Erase the old arrows and print new arrow.
   ! Month names are displayed in rows 3 thru 15
   FOR I = 3 to 15
       SET cursor I, 3     ! arrow starts at column 3
       PRINT "   "         ! erase old arrow
   NEXT I
   ! Mark the specified month.
   SET cursor Num + 2, 3
   PRINT "-->"             ! mark month with arrow
   ! Return to second window.
   WINDOW #2
   CALL GetMonth (Num)   ! get next month number
LOOP

DATA January, February, March, April
DATA May, June, July, August
DATA September, October, November, December
END
```

```
EXTERNAL SUB GetMonth (Number)
DO
  INPUT prompt "Number of month? ": Number
  IF Number > 12 or Number < 0 then
    PRINT "Enter number between 0 and 12."
    PRINT
  END IF
LOOP until Number >= 0 and Number <= 12
END SUB
```

Window #1 is opened first and a table of the months is displayed. Then window #2 is opened and the subroutine GetMonth is called that asks the user to enter a number. Number 0 stops the program. Any number less than 0 or greater than 12 is considered an error, and the user is asked to enter the number again. When a valid number has been entered, the name of the corresponding month is displayed in window #2. Display is switched to window #1, any old arrows are erased, and a new arrow is printed next to the current month. Display is switched back to window #2, and the name of another month is requested.

IMPORTANT POINTS

Commas and semicolons (except trailing semicolons) cannot be used to format the output of PRINT USING statements.

A format string containing dollar signs and periods cannot be used with string variables.

Commas cannot be inserted between the dollar signs in a format string.

Angle brackets in a format string cannot be used to justify numeric values.

When changing windows or clearing the screen, you may need to insert pauses so the display will not be erased before you are able to read it.

The same channel number cannot be used for both a file number and a window number in a program.

Character numbers between 128 and 255 produce special characters on IBM PC-compatible computers. See Appendix F.

Row and column values specifying the cursor location are relative to the current window, not the entire screen.

SELF-TEST QUESTIONS

1. Which of the following characters can be used as format characters in a format string?
   - a) #
   - b) %
   - c) $
   - d) ?
   - e) <
   - f) ;
   - g) *
   - h) +
   - i) =
   - j) −
2. Can semicolons be used to separate items in a PRINT USING statement?
3. Is a trailing semicolon allowed in a PRINT USING statement? If so, what does it do?
4. What is displayed when the number 12345 is printed with a format string of "####"?
5. (a) Is "$$###" a valid format string? If not, why not? (b) Is "%%###" a valid format string? If not, why not?
6. What is displayed when the number 12.5 is printed (a) with a format string of "−##.##", and (b) with a format string of "+##.##"?
7. Is the string "$$,$$$.##" a valid format string? If not, why not?
8. Can the format string ">###" be used to print a numeric variable Num containing the value 256?
9. Can the number −999 be printed with a format string of "###"?
10. (a) If the string "THE" is printed using a format string of "#####", will it be left-justified or right-justified in the five-character field? (b) How will the string "THE END" be displayed using the same format string?
11. Can a single format string be used to print both a numeric variable value and a string value? Explain.
12. What statement is used to assign an attached printer to a file number of 9?
13. Can the PRINT USING statement be used to write numeric variable values on a disk file?
14. (a) What is the purpose of the CLEAR statement? (b) What is the location of the cursor after this statement is executed?
15. What file number is used to designate the display unit?
16. What is the purpose of a "trailer" value in a DATA statement?
17. In the statement

```
SET cursor A, B
```

what is the meaning (a) of variable A, and (b) of variable B?

18. What statement (a) moves the cursor to the center of your screen, and (b) turns off the cursor?
19. If the statement

```
ASK max cursor A, B
```

is executed, what is the value (a) of A, and (b) of B?

20. What happens when the statement

```
GET KEY Dummy
```

276

is executed?

21. If a window is opened as window #1, can you also open a file (a) as file #2, or (b) as file #1?

22. (a) What coordinate system is used to specify the size of a window? (b) Is this system different from the coordinate system used to specify the position of the cursor?

23. What statement is used (a) to open window #3, (b) to move the cursor to window #3, and (c) to close window #3?

24. Can you use the SET CURSOR statement to move the cursor from window #1 to window #2?

PRACTICE PROGRAMS

1. Read accounts payable information, the name of the payee and the amount owed, from a sequential text file named ACCOUNTS.DAT. Print or display a check for each payee in the format shown, separating one check from another with three blank lines. See Example Program 10-10 and the accompanying discussion about special characters to create the outline of the check. Enter the desired date and the number of the first check from the keyboard. Number the following checks sequentially. Identifiers in angle brackets will be replaced by actual values.

```
ACME SALES CORPORATION                         <check date>
     Detroit, Michigan


Pay to: <payee>                                    <amount>


No: <check number>                 ______________________
                                                     Treas.
```

Test your program using the file ACCOUNTS.DAT.

2. Read names and addresses from a sequential text file named MAILING.DAT. The following information is available for each person:

name
street address
city
state
zip code

Each item of information (field) is stored on a separate line in the file. Print or display mailing labels in the format of two labels across the page, as shown:

John H. Smith	Mary Z. Wheeler
25 Oak Drive	1350 Main Street
Richmond, VA 23219	Willowdale, VA 23230

Each label has a maximum width of 36 columns. If any line in a label exceeds 36 characters, your program must have an algorithm for reducing its length. The two-character state abbreviation and the five character zip code cannot be shortened.

Test your program using the file MAILING.DAT.

3. Modify the Box subroutine of Example Program 10-10 to draw a double box as shown:

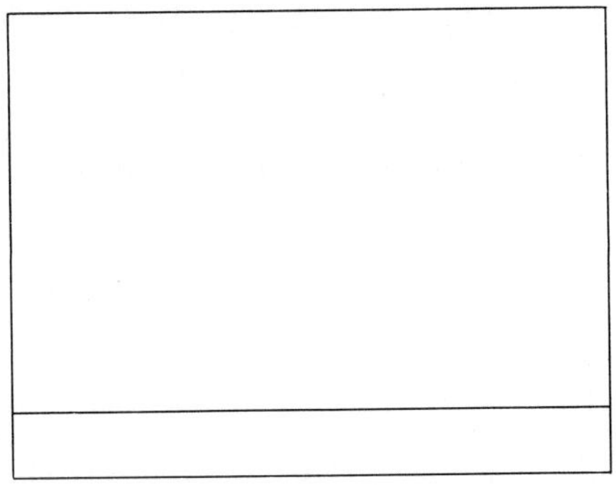

The height of the upper part of the box is H1 and of the lower part is H2. If you can display or print IBM graphics characters, use character 195 to form the left end of the dividing line and character 180 to form the right end. See Appendix F for more information.

Rewrite the program to place the menu in the upper part of the box and the command prompt in the lower part. Test your program by showing how the menu of Example Program 10-10 will look with the new box.

4. It is often useful to be able to display and compare two text files at the same time. Divide the screen horizontally into two equal windows. Ask the user for the names of two text files, file A and file B. Display the first 10 lines of file A in the top window and the first 10 lines of file B in the bottom window.

If a user presses the Alt-1 key (hold down the Alt key and press the 1 key), 8 more lines of file A will be displayed in the top window. If a user presses the Alt-2 key, 8 more lines of file B will be displayed in the bottom window. If a user presses any other key, the program will stop.

Note that when using the GET KEY statement, the Alt-1 key returns a numeric code of 376 and the Alt-2 key returns a numeric code of 377. See Appendix I for more information.

Test your program using the file UPPER.TXT for file A and LOWER.TXT for file B. Show the screen displaying the first 10 lines of file A and the lines of file B after it has scrolled up 16 lines.

11 Applications and Record Files

11.1 INTRODUCTION

We introduce two algorithms that are used frequently in business applications: a sorting algorithm arranges the contents of files into ascending or descending order, a binary search algorithm quickly finds a specified item in a sorted file.

To search a file record by record, we must be able to read any particular record. We introduce the concept of a record file that allows us to access any record directly.

Another useful application is the conversion of data files from one format to another. We discuss an example of this technique.

11.2 A SIMPLE SORTING TECHNIQUE

The need to sort lists into numeric or alphabetic order occurs frequently in computer programs. Sorting time can be a significant part of a program's execution time, and so considerable research effort has been devoted to developing fast and efficient sorting algorithms. Unfortunately, many of these fast sorting methods are complicated and difficult to understand.

As a simple example of sorting, we will use the *bubble sort* algorithm. This is not a fast method of sorting, but it is easy to understand. Our program will sort a list of names that has been placed in a string array.

Comparing Two Strings

We need to understand how the computer determines if one string is larger than another string. Let's compare two string variables named A$ and B$. We want to know if the logical expression (A$ > B$) is true or false.

Comparison of two strings is done character by character and is based on the ASCII values of the characters. The computer compares the ASCII value of the first character of A$ with that of the first character of B$. If the character in A$ has the greater value, then the expression (A$ > B$) is true. Remember that an uppercase letter and the corresponding lowercase letter are different characters and have different ASCII values.

"C" is greater than "B", and "a" is greater than "A".

If the character in A$ has the lesser value, then the expression (A$ > B$) is false. If the first characters in A$ and B$ are identical, then a comparison is made between the ASCII values of the second character in each string.

This process continues until (1) the value of a character in one string is greater or less than the value of the corresponding character in the other string, or (2) the end of one string is reached while the other string still contains more characters, or (3) the ends of both strings are reached because they are equal in length and have the same sequence of characters.

If the ASCII value of a character in string A$ is greater or less than the ASCII value of the corresponding character in string B$, then the last comparison determines whether the expression is true or false.

"ABC" is greater than "ABB".

If A$ is longer than B$ and the two strings have an identical sequence of characters up to the end of string B$, then string A$ is considered the greater and the expression is true.

"QED" is greater than "QE".

If both strings, A$ and B$, are of equal length and have the same sequence of characters, then the two strings are equal and the expression (A$ > B$) is false.

"xyz" is equal to "xyz".

The Bubble Sort Algorithm

Now let's examine the bubble sort algorithm and see how it works. We go through our list of names, from one end of the list to the other end, comparing names in pairs. The first pair consists of the first name and the second name, the second pair consists of the second name and the third name, and so forth. We call this process scanning the list.

If a pair is in the wrong alphabetic order, we swap or interchange the two names. If a pair is in the correct alphabetic order, we move on to the next pair.

This process repeats until we can scan the list without having to swap any names. Then we know that the list is in sorted order.

Swapping Two Values

You have to use a third temporary variable when swapping two names. To swap the values of A$ and B$, put the value of A$ into the variable Temp$, assign the value of B$ to A$, and then assign the value of Temp$ to B$. The program statements might look like this:

```
LET Temp$ = A$      ! put value of A$ in Temp$
LET A$ = B$         ! put value of B$ in A$
LET B$ = Temp$      ! put value of Temp$ in B$
```

Using a Logical Flag

We have used string variables as logical flags in several previous examples. **In this case, a logical flag tells the program when the list has been scanned without any interchanges.** Each time we start to scan the list, we set the flag to true (assign the flag variable a value of "true"). If we make an interchange during this scan of the list, the flag is changed to false. We then examine the flag at the end of each scan, and if it is true, we know that no interchanges were made during the last scan through the list and that the list is in sorted order.

11.3 SORTING A LIST OF NAMES

Our program consists of three tasks:

Reading names from a file.
Sorting the array in memory.
Writing the array back out to the file.

This program assumes that we have enough memory so that the entire file can be placed in a memory array. It is much easier and quicker to sort a list in memory, than it is to sort a list in a disk file. The program contains a subroutine for the actual sorting.

Here is an outline of the sorting subroutine.

Begin loop.
  Set the sorted flag to true.
  For each pair of strings:
    Compare the two string values;
    Swap the two values if not in proper order;
    Set the sorted flag to false.
Loop until the sorted flag is true.

The sorting subroutine uses an array A$ containing N string values. A flag variable named Sorted$ is used to determine when to stop scanning the array.

```
! Example Subprogram 11-1.
! Subroutine for bubble sort algorithm.
! Sort array in ascending alphabetic order.
! Parameters:  A$()   array of strings
!              N      no. of strings in array

EXTERNAL SUB Sort (A$(), N)
    DO
       LET Sorted$ = "true"
       FOR I = 1 to (N - 1)
           IF A$(I) > A$(I + 1) then
              LET Temp$ = A$(I)
              LET A$(I) = A$(I + 1)
              LET A$(I + 1) = Temp$
              LET Sorted$ = "false"
           END IF
       NEXT I
    LOOP until Sorted$ = "true"
END SUB
```

The flag Sorted$ is set to true at the beginning of the scan loop. Pairs of names denoted by A$(I) and A$(I+1) are compared, and are swapped if not in sorted order. If swapping occurs, the flag is set to false. The scan loop continues until the flag remains true.

Note that the FOR loop only goes up to I = N−1 because one index in the comparison is I+1 and the last name in the list is A$(N). If the index I were assigned a value of N, the program would try to compare the string elements A$(N) and A$(N+1) and would stop with an error because no name has been assigned to A$(N+1).

This subroutine will sort a list of strings in ascending alphabetic order. To sort in descending order, reverse the logical sense of the comparison, making it

```
IF A$(I) < A$(I + 1) then
```

The program assumes that the names are stored in a text file, one name per line. The array that will hold the names is dimensioned by the user.

Here is the complete program:

```
! Example Program 11-2.
! Sort a text file containing names.

DIM List$ (1)
PRINT "Maximum number of names that you plan to sort";
INPUT Capacity
MAT List$ = nul$(Capacity)
LINE INPUT prompt "File name? ": File$
LET X = pos(File$, ":")
IF X = 0 then
   INPUT prompt "On disk in which drive? ": Drive$
   LET File$ = Drive$[1:1] & ":" & File$
END IF
OPEN #1: name File$, organization text
LET Count = 0
RESET #1: begin

DO while more #1
   LET Count = Count + 1
   LINE INPUT #1: List$(Count)
LOOP
CALL Sort (List$, Count)
ERASE #1
FOR I = 1 to Count
    PRINT #1: List$(I)
NEXT I
CLOSE #1
PRINT "File "; File$; " has been sorted."
END

SUB Sort (A$(), N)
    ! Bubble sort a string array
    ! in ascending alphabetic order.
    DO
       LET Sorted$ = "true"
       FOR I = 1 to (N - 1)
           IF A$(I) > A$(I + 1) then
              LET Temp$ = A$(I)
              LET A$(I) = A$(I + 1)
              LET A$(I + 1) = Temp$
              LET Sorted$ = "false"
           END IF
       NEXT I
    LOOP until Sorted$ = "true"
END SUB
```

The user is asked to enter the file name and the file is opened as a text file. As a precaution, we set the pointer to the beginning before starting to read from the file. A small loop reads the names into an array named List$, counting the number of names that are read. The subroutine Sort is called and the array is sorted.

True BASIC will not write over existing text in a file, so the original contents of the file are erased (which sets the file pointer to the beginning) and the sorted list of names is written to the file from the array List$. Finally, the file is closed and the user is told that the file has been sorted.

Another, and perhaps safer, option is to write the sorted array on a different file. We avoid the risk of having the computer stop unexpectedly after the original file has been erased and before the sorted file has been completely written.

To test the sorting program, we need a short text file containing several names. The following program will create such a file, named TEST.DAT.

```
! Example Program 11-3.
! Create a test file.

! You may need to change the disk
! drive letter (B:) in the file name.
OPEN #1: name "B:\CH11\TEST.DAT", create newold
ERASE #1  ! if file already exists
DO while more data
   READ Name$
   PRINT #1: Name$
LOOP
CLOSE #1

DATA John, Mary, Elizabeth, William, Spencer
DATA Jules, Johnson, Bruce, Aaron, Ruth
END
```

Our program, as written, will not sort a file containing more than the maximum number of names specified by the user. As the size of the array is made larger, we will soon reach a practical limit because small computers cannot hold very large arrays in memory. More sophisticated sorting algorithms have been developed that allow large disk files to be sorted quickly and efficiently.

11.4 SEARCHING TECHNIQUES

When we developed the database program in Chapter 9, we included a command to search the file for a specified string. We now discuss searching techniques in more detail, examining two common methods for searching a file or list.

Searching a Nonsorted List

If a list or file has been created by adding items to it from time to time, it will usually not be in sorted order. The sorting method we used in Chapter 9 to search such a text file is called a *sequential search*. As you remember, we asked the user to specify a target name. Starting at the beginning of the file, we read each name from the file, in sequence, and compared it to the target name. If the two names were equal, we reported success. If the target name was not equal to any name in the file, we reported failure.

A sequential search can take a long time with a large list or file. **However, if the names in a list are not sorted, but arranged in random order, a sequential search is probably the best and simplest method to use.**

Searching a Sorted List

When the items in a list or file are in sorted order, we can use another, faster searching method called a *binary search*. This method works by repeatedly dividing or halving the list, resulting in a shorter list to search.

Assume that the list is sorted in ascending order, with the highest-valued item at the bottom, and a target name has been specified. We compare the target name with name at the middle of the list. If the target name is greater than the middle name, we can confine further searching to the bottom half of the list. If the target name is less than the middle name, we search only the top half of the list. One comparison has effectively cut the length of the list in half, and the process is repeated until the desired name is found or the search fails.

We will use the binary search method to search a sorted file of names. This method requires that we be able to access any name in the file. We cannot use a text file because that file structure will not allow us to read directly an individual name in the middle of the file. We can only start reading at the beginning and read through to the end of the file. Thus we interrupt our discussion of searching to introduce a new kind of file structure, the *record file*.

11.5 USING RECORD FILES

A *record* in a record file is defined as a fixed amount of space on the disk, containing a single data item. The data item may be a numeric expression or a string expression. The contents of a record are stored in an internal format, not in the ASCII character format used in text files. This means that the stored information cannot be viewed directly on the screen, but can only be read by a True BASIC program. Reading and writing information on record files is faster than on text files.

The fixed size of each record allows the computer to know exactly where each record begins and ends. This knowledge is not available with a sequential text file where every line may be of a different length. **Thus any record in a record file can be accessed directly for either reading or writing.** True BASIC allows you to write new information on an existing record without fear of overflowing that record and causing damage to an adjoining record. If the information item that you are writing is larger than the record size, a run-time error message is displayed and the program stops.

Opening a Record File

The record size must be specified before a record file can be used. You can do this in the OPEN statement by including the RECSIZE phrase.

```
OPEN #1: name Fname$, create new, recsize 128
```

The record size has been set to 128 bytes in this example.

You can also add the phrase ORGANIZATION RECORD to the OPEN statement, specifying that the file will be created as a record file. This type of organization will be assumed, however, as soon as the record size is specified, and thus the ORGANIZATION RECORD phrase is not really necessary.

A program knows that it is reading from a record file because (1) the OPEN statement contains an ORGANIZATION RECORD phrase, (2) the OPEN statement contains a RECSIZE phrase, or (3) the first item read is in record file format, not text file format. The latter method is commonly used to determine whether an existing file is a record file.

You need a record size of eight bytes for a record that will hold a numeric value. A record that will hold a string value must have a size equal to or greater than the number of characters in the string. If a file is opened without the RECSIZE phrase, you can specify the record size with a separate SET statement:

```
SET #1: recsize 128
```

You should use one of these two methods of specifying the record size before you write information on a record file. The only way to change the record size of an existing record file is to erase the file, using the ERASE #N statement, and then set a new record size.

Setting the File Pointer

There are several SET statements for moving the file pointer in a record file. One of the most useful is the statement

```
SET #N: record R
```

which sets the file pointer to the beginning of record R. For example, the statement

```
SET #1: record 5
```

moves the file pointer to the start of record 5 in file #1. You can also use the statement

```
ASK #N: record X
```

to find out the present location of the file pointer, where the variable X returns the record number.

Other SET statements are

```
SET #N: pointer begin     ! set pointer to beginning of file
SET #N: pointer end       ! set pointer to end of file
SET #N: pointer next      ! set pointer to next record
SET #N: pointer same      ! set pointer to previous record
```

The abbreviated forms of these statements in True BASIC are

```
RESET #N: begin
RESET #N: end
RESET #N: next
RESET #N: same
```

Record numbering starts with record 1. You cannot move the pointer before the beginning of the file or beyond the end of the file.

Writing on a Record File

Writing on a record file is done with the WRITE statement. The format is

```
WRITE #N: Expr1, Expr2,...
```

The expression items can be constants, expressions or variables, either string or numeric. Each item is written on a separate record. The first item is written on the record at the current pointer position, and the pointer then advances to the next record. If you try to write past the end of the file, the file is extended by creating a new record.

As with text files, it is common practice to write only a single variable with each WRITE statement. This variable is often a string variable, possibly containing several items of information in substrings. Each substring is called a *field* and a record may contain one or more fields. If you try to write an item (usually a string) that is longer than the record length, you will get a run-time error.

As an alternative to placing each item in a substring, each item can be written to a different file record, and these several file records then constitute a logical record. We usually prefer the first method, using a substring for each field.

Reading from a Record File

Reading from a record file is done with the READ statement. The format is

```
READ #N: Var1, Var2,...
```

The variables can be either numeric or string. An item written on the file as a string value must be read as a string value and assigned to a string variable. An item written as a numeric value must be assigned to a numeric variable. Unlike text files, you cannot read a string of numeric characters and assign them to a numeric variable.

The first item is read from the record at the current pointer position, and the pointer then advances to the next record. If you try to read past the end of the file, you will get an error message.

Here is a simple demonstration program using a record file for both reading and writing. The file is opened with a record size of 30 bytes or characters. Five expense ledger titles are read from a DATA statement and written on the file, one title in each record. Then the user is asked to specify a record number and the title in that record is displayed.

```
! Example Program 11-4.
! Demonstration of a record file.

! You may need to change the disk
! drive letter (B:) in the file name.
OPEN #1: name "B:\CH11\NAME.REC", create newold
ERASE #1  ! if the file already exists
SET #1: recsize 30

! Add information to the file.
RESET #1: begin
FOR I = 1 to 5
    READ Title$
    WRITE #1: Title$
NEXT I

! Specify a record number.
PRINT "Enter zero to stop."
INPUT prompt "Display what record? ": RecNum
DO until RecNum = 0
   SET #1: record RecNum
   READ #1: Title$
   PRINT "Title: "; Title$
   PRINT
   INPUT prompt "Display what record? ": RecNum
LOOP

DATA Labor, Equipment, Supplies, Travel, Utilities
END
```

There are times when you would like to know how many records are being used in a record file. This information is available from the FILESIZE statement whose syntax is

```
ASK #N: filesize Size
```

When this statement is executed, the variable Size will contain a value representing the number of records in file #N.

Dividing a Record into Fields

If a record file is used to store general information, each record usually consists of a single string. Remember that a string can be over 32,000 characters long. The record is often subdivided into several fields, each field containing a different item of information.

One way to create fields is to divide the record string into fixed-length substrings. Each substring field must be long enough to hold the longest item that will be stored in that field. If the item string is shorter than this maximum length, it must be padded with blanks to increase its length to the fixed value.

We introduce fixed-length fields in Chapter 14. This method requires some effort to add and remove the padding blanks, and the space they occupy on the disk does not hold useful information. Fixed-length fields work best when most items to be stored in a field are of about the same length.

Another and simpler way to create fields is to use variable-length substrings for each field. It is then necessary to place a special character as a separator between adjacent fields. The separator character must be one that is never used in a field value.

The record string consists of a concatenation of variable-length field strings and separators. It is also of variable length, but must be no longer than the fixed length of the record. For example, a typical name-and-address record, using a backslash (\) character as the separator, might look like this:

```
John Butler\13 South St.\Worcester\MA\03120
```

Here is another example program with two items of information placed in each record. The variable Entry$ contains both a name field and a telephone number field, separated by a backslash (\), and is written on the file record.

The file is subsequently read and a value is read from a record and assigned to a string variable. Then the value assigned to the variable is separated into the two field values, name and telephone number, using substrings.

```
! Example Program 11-5.
! Another demonstration of a record file
! with two items of information in each record.

! You may need to change the disk
! drive letter (B:) in the file name.
OPEN #1: name "B:\CH11\PHONES.REC", create newold
ERASE #1            ! if the file already exists
SET #1: recsize 60
CALL Add (#1)       ! add information to the file
CALL Sort (#1)      ! sort the file by name

! Specify a record number.
PRINT "Enter zero to stop."
INPUT prompt "What record? ": RecNum
DO until RecNum = 0
   SET #1: record RecNum
   READ #1: Item$
   LET X = pos (Item$, "\")
   LET Name$ = Item$[1:X-1]
   LET Phone$ = Item$[X+1:len(Item$)]
   PRINT "Name: "; Name$; tab(40); "Phone: "; Phone$
   PRINT
   INPUT prompt "What record? ": RecNum
LOOP
END  ! main program

EXTERNAL SUB Add (#9)
    ! Add information to the file.
    RESET #9: begin
    DO while more data
       READ Name$, Phone$
       LET Entry$ = Name$ & "\" & Phone$
       WRITE #9: Entry$
    LOOP
    DATA Jane Ulan, 293-9788, Bill Miller, 924-0103
    DATA Susan Moody, 977-1882, Joe Stove, 977-1586
    DATA Robert Heilman, 293-9017
END SUB
```

```
EXTERNAL SUB Sort (#9)
    ! Sort a record file.
    ASK #9: filesize N
    DO
       LET Sorted$ = "true"
       FOR I = 1 to (N - 1)
           RESET #9: record I
           READ #9: First$, Second$
           IF First$ > Second$ then
              RESET #9: record I
              WRITE #9: Second$, First$
              LET Sorted$ = "false"
           END IF
       NEXT I
    LOOP until Sorted$ = "true"
END SUB
```

The subroutine Add is called first to add names and telephone numbers to the file. These items are read from DATA statements in the subroutine. The subroutine Sort is called next to sort the file in ascending order. We still use the bubble sort algorithm, but sort the file directly rather than copying the file to an array and sorting the array. Note particularly how two record values are interchanged; they are read from the file in one order (First$, then Second$) and written back to the file in opposite order (Second$, then First$).

The file is sorted in ascending alphabetic order by full name. This order is not the one we would choose if we were printing an alphabetized list, because ''Bill Miller'' comes before ''Robert Heilman''. It is the proper order, however, for searching when the target name (the name to find) is entered as a full name.

After the file is written and sorted, the user is asked to specify a record number. The string value in this record is assigned to the variable Item$. The POS function is used to find the location of the backslash, and string Item$ is then separated into two substrings, one consisting of the characters before the backslash and the other consisting of the characters after the backslash. These substrings are assigned to the variables Name$ and Phone$, which are displayed.

11.6 THE BINARY SEARCH METHOD

Returning to the problem of searching a sorted list, we develop a program using the binary search method. The program asks a user to enter a name to be found, called the target name. We assume the list of names is an indexed list (an array) and is sorted in ascending order from top to bottom.

Searching an Array

We define a top end point, a bottom end point and a midpoint. When we start, the top end point is the index of the first name in the list. This index is usually one. The bottom end point is the index of the last name in the list. The midpoint is approximately half way between the top and bottom end points.

We use the midpoint (rounded to an integer value) as an index and designate the name with that index the midpoint name. We compare the target name to the midpoint name. If the target name equals the midpoint name, we have completed our search. If the target name is less than the midpoint name, we know that our search can be confined to the top half of the list. We leave the top end point unchanged, but designate a new bottom end point equal to the midpoint minus one. In effect, the length of list to be searched has been cut in half, as shown in Figure 11-1.

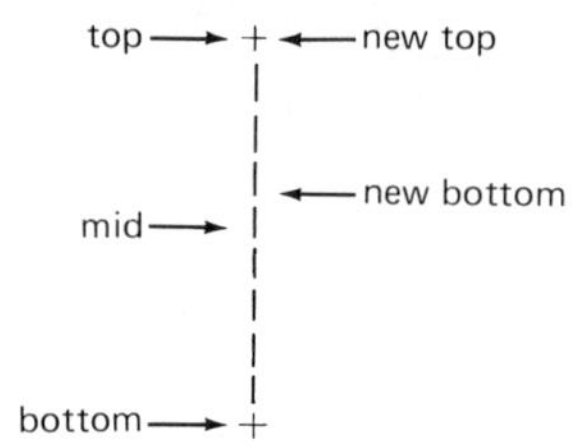

Figure 11-1 Target name is in top half of list.

Conversely, if the target name is greater than the midpoint name, we know that our search can be confined to the bottom half of the list. We leave the bottom end point unchanged and designate a new top end point equal to the midpoint plus one. Figure 11-2 shows the result.

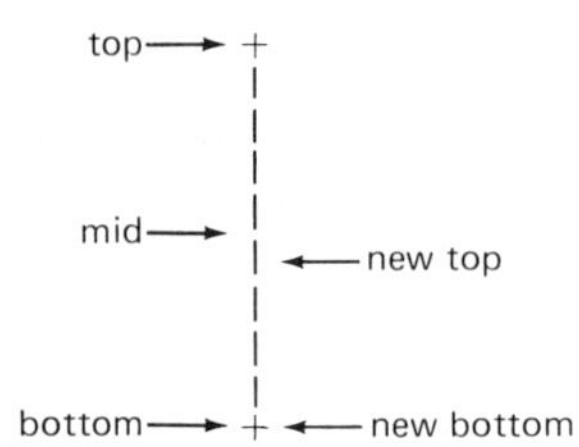

Figure 11-2 Target name is in bottom half of list.

Here is the list of names we used in a previous section (Example Program 11-3), sorted in ascending order from top to bottom:

1 Aaron
2 Bruce
3 Elizabeth
4 John
5 Johnson
6 Jules
7 Mary
8 Ruth

9 Spencer
10 William

An outline of the search process looks like this:

Target name is Ruth.
Top end point is 1.
Bottom end point is 10.
Calculate midpoint, its rounded value is 6.
Midpoint name for index of 6 is Jules.
Note that Ruth is greater than Jules.
Set new top end point at 7.
Bottom end point remains at 10.

Here is the reduced list to be searched:

7	Mary	top end point
8	Ruth	
9	Spencer	
10	Williams	bottom end point

The search process continues:

Calculate new midpoint of 9.
Midpoint name for index of 9 is Spencer.
Note that Ruth is less than Spencer.
Top end point remains at 7.
Set new bottom end point at 8.
Calculate new midpoint of 8.

We observe that the midpoint name for an index of 8 is our target name, Ruth.

Searching a Record File

As an example of a searching program, we will look for a specified name in a sorted record file. This file contains the same list of names as the sorted text file produced by Example Program 11-2. You remember that this program produced a sequential text file, a type of file structure that cannot be searched effectively with the binary search algorithm. We must first convert the text file to a record file and then search the latter file.

The first example program converts the sorted text file named TEST.SRT to a sorted record file named TEST.REC. We will use a record length of ten bytes or characters.

```
! Example Program 11-6.
! Convert sequential file TEST.SRT
! to record file TEST.REC.

! You may need to change the disk
! drive letter (B:) in the file names.
OPEN #1: name "B:\CH11\TEST.SRT", organization text
OPEN #2: name "B:\CH11\TEST.REC", create newold
ERASE #2  ! if the file already exists
SET #2: recsize 10
RESET #1: begin
DO while more #1
   LINE INPUT #1: Item$
   WRITE #2: Item$
LOOP
CLOSE #1
CLOSE #2
END
```

The next example program searches a sorted record file for a given name. If the name is found, its record number is displayed. The user is told if the name cannot be found. This version of the program allows the user to enter several names, one at a time. Entering the letter "Q" tells the program to stop.

The main program is straightforward, asking for the file name and the target name. The results of the search are displayed. Two parameters, the file name and the target name, are passed to the function named Search. Note that the file must be opened in the function because file numbers cannot be passed to functions.

In the function Search, the local variable Top is the number of the record at the top end of the search range, initially record 1. The number of records in the file is determined by the ASK FILESIZE statement and is assigned to variable N. Variable Bottom is the number of the record at the bottom end of the search range, initially record N.

Variable Mid is the number of the record in the middle of the search range. This record is read and its value compared to the target string value. If they are equal, function Search is assigned the value of Mid (the number of the desired record), and control returns to the main program. If they are not equal, either the top or bottom end of the search range is changed, a new value of Mid is calculated, and the comparison process repeated.

A search is considered unsuccessful when the top and bottom end points cross, and this result is denoted by assigning a value of zero to the function Search. Remember that the technique of binary searching depends on having a file in sorted order. If the file is not in sorted order, the program will usually fail to find the requested record.

```
! Example Program 11-7.
! Search a sorted record file for a given name.

DECLARE FUNCTION Search
LINE INPUT prompt "File name? ": File$
```

```
LET X = pos(File$, ":")
IF X = 0 then
  INPUT prompt "On disk in which drive? ": Drive$
  LET File$ = Drive$[1:1] & ":" & File$
END IF
PRINT "Enter the letter Q to stop the program."
PRINT
LINE INPUT prompt "Name to find? ": Name$
DO until ucase$(Name$[1:1]) = "Q"
   LET Result = Search(File$, Name$)
   IF Result = 0 then
      PRINT Name$; " cannot be found."
   ELSE
      PRINT Name$; " is in record"; Result
   END IF
   PRINT
   LINE INPUT prompt "Name to find? ": Name$
LOOP
END

EXTERNAL FUNCTION Search (FileName$, Look$)
    ! Search a record file using
    ! the binary search algorithm.
    ! Look$ contains the target name.
    OPEN #9: name FileName$, organization record
    LET Top = 1
    ASK #9: filesize N
    LET Bottom = N
    LET Found$ = "false"
    LET Look$ = ucase$(Look$)
    DO
       LET Mid = round((Top + Bottom)/2)
       SET #9: record Mid
       READ #9: Rec$
       IF Look$ = ucase$(Rec$) then
          LET Found$ = "true"
       ELSEIF Look$ > ucase$(Rec$) then
          LET Top = Mid + 1
       ELSE
          LET Bottom = Mid - 1
       END IF
    LOOP until Bottom < Top or Found$ = "true"
    IF Found$ = "true" then
       LET Search = Mid
    ELSE
       LET Search = 0
    END IF
    CLOSE #9
END FUNCTION
```

Note that all strings are converted to uppercase before comparisons are made. If the function returns a value of zero, a search failure message is displayed. Otherwise, the record number and the value of the desired record are displayed.

11.7 STRING AND FILE CONVERSIONS

A common requirement in BASIC programs is the ability to convert dates or times from one format to another. True BASIC has system variables, Date$ and Time$, that contain the current date and time. These values may not be in the desired format and will have to be converted before being displayed.

The system variable Date$ has the current date value stored in YYYYMMDD format. For example, the value might be

```
19830307
```

and we would like to change it to the more readable format

```
March 7, 1983
```

Table Look-up

In the next example, we introduce the idea of using a table of values from which a certain value can be selected. Let's say that we have the names of the months, stored in order and one per line, in a text file named MONTHS.DAT. We can read the file sequentially and assign each name to an array element.

This technique gives us a table in memory containing the names of all the months. If we want to find the name of the third month, we look at the third element in the array and note that it contains the value ''March''. The technique would normally be used with a much larger table, the only limit on size is having enough memory to hold the array.

Our program is designed to change the format of the current date, stored in the system variable Date$, into a format with the name of the month spelled out. A subroutine opens the file containing the month names and these names are assigned to an array. A function is used to convert the date to the new format.

```
! Example Program 11-8.
! Display the current date in expanded format.
! Table of month names is read from a file.

DECLARE FUNCTION LongDate$
DIM Month$(12)
CALL MonthTable (Month$)
PRINT "The current date is "; LongDate$(Month$)
END

EXTERNAL SUB MonthTable (M$())
    ! Read file and create table of month names.
    OPEN #1: name "B:\CH11\MONTHS.DAT", access input
    FOR I = 1 to 12
        INPUT #1: M$(I)
    NEXT I
END SUB
```

```
EXTERNAL FUNCTION LongDate$(M$())
    ! Convert current date to an expanded format.
    LET Year$ = Date$[1:4]
    LET Num = val(Date$[5:6])
    LET Day$ = Date$[7:8]
    IF Day$[1:1] = "0" then LET Day$ = Day$[2:2]
    LET LongDate$ = M$(Num) & " " & Day$ & ", " & Year$
END FUNCTION
```

The current date in Date$ is broken up into substrings for the year, month, and day. If the day substring has a leading zero, it is stripped off. The month number Num is used as an index for the month name array M$. A new string is created by concatenating the month name, the day and the year, and is assigned to the function LongDate$.

Conversion of File Formats

Many professionals who know BASIC do not write large programs. They use their computers for running application programs such as electronic spreadsheets and database managers. They sometimes find that the file produced by one application cannot be read by another application.

One solution to that problem is to write your own True BASIC program to convert the format of a file. If the file is a text file containing only ASCII characters, such a conversion is easy to accomplish.

Our example demonstrates the conversion of a file of information, commonly called a data file. This file consists of names (data items) separated from each other by blank spaces. The names themselves do not contain any spaces. Thus the only role of spaces is to serve as data item delimiters or separators. The data items are contained in text lines that end with the usual carriage return and line feed characters.

This data file will be read by an application program that requires that every data item be enclosed in quotes and that the items be separated from each other by commas. Spaces are not allowed. Carriage return and line feed characters are expected at the end of each line.

Here is a line from the original data file:

```
JOHN WILLIAM MARY PETER SUSAN JENNIFER
```

Here is how the line must look for the application program:

```
"JOHN","WILLIAM","MARY","PETER","SUSAN","JENNIFER"
```

As you can imagine, it would be a time-consuming job to convert such a data file by hand. We will write a True BASIC program to make the conversion.

Both an input file and an output file are opened. A line of text is read from the input file, its format is changed, and it is written on the output file. The process continues until the end of the input file is reached.

The conversion is accomplished by scanning a line of text, using the POS function to find the location of the first space. The characters to the left of the space are enclosed in quotes. Note the odd-looking string """" that represents a double quotation mark as a string constant. The characters to the right of the space are the remainder of the old line of text, and this line is analyzed again as the program searches for the next space. A new line of text is gradually constructed and, when finished, is written on the output file. The process continues until the entire input file has been read.

Here is the conversion program:

```
! Example Program 11-9.
! Convert the format of a text data file.
! Input file strings are separated by spaces.
! Output strings are in quotes and separated by commas.

PRINT "Include disk drive letter in each file name."
LINE INPUT prompt "Input file: ": InName$
OPEN #1: name InName$
LINE INPUT prompt "Output file: ": OutName$
OPEN #2: name OutName$, create new

DO while more #1                    ! read a line
   LINE INPUT #1: Old$
   LET New$ = ""
   DO                               ! scan old line
      LET X = pos(Old$, " ")        ! look for a space
      IF X = 0 then
         LET New$ = New$ & """" & Old$ & """"
      ELSE
         LET Temp$ = Old$[1:X-1]
         LET Old$ = Old$[X+1:Maxnum]
         LET New$ = New$ & """" & Temp$ & """,""
      END IF
   LOOP until X = 0
   PRINT #2: New$                   ! write modified line
LOOP
CLOSE #1
CLOSE #2
END
```

Try running this program using as input the file NAMES.DAT in directory CH11 on the example program disk.

IMPORTANT POINTS

When strings are compared in logical expressions, they are compared character by character, using the ASCII values of the characters.

A third temporary variable is needed when interchanging the values of two variables.

A logical flag can be used to indicate whether or not a certain task has been accomplished.

A sequential search is an acceptable searching technique for a list in unsorted order.

The binary search technique works only for a list in sorted order.

A record file contains fixed-length records. Each record may contain one or more fields.

Any record in a record file can be accessed directly and information can be either read from or written in the record.

SELF-TEST QUESTIONS

1. What is the name of the sorting algorithm used in the example programs in this chapter?
2. Which string in each of the following pairs of strings is larger?
   a) ZY or XY
   b) JOHN or John
   c) qe35 or QE37
   d) ABC or CBA
   e) simplification or simplifications
3. Write a three-statement program fragment that will swap the values of variables Num1 and Num2.
4. Does a list need to be in sorted order (a) for a sequential search, and (b) for a binary search?
5. When making a binary search of a list sorted in ascending order, if the target name is greater than the midpoint name, what is the new index value (a) of the top end point, and (b) of the bottom end point?
6. Will your answers in the previous question be different if the list is sorted in descending order? If yes, what are the index values of the new end points?
7. What statement moves the file pointer to record 7 of a record file denoted as file #2?
8. If record 10 of a record file contains information, can you overwrite the old information with new information?
9. What happens if you write a string containing 45 characters on a record file whose record size is 44?
10. What statement establishes the record length of a record file?
11. What statement moves the file pointer (a) to the beginning of the next record, and (b) to the beginning of the same record?
12. Given the statement

    ```
    READ #1: Name1$, Name2$
    ```

    the value of what record is assigned to Name1$ if Name2$ is assigned the value of record 5?
13. What statement tells you the number of records in a record file?
14. What appears on the screen if you use the TYPE command of MS-DOS to display the contents of a record file?
15. What format is used to display the current date stored in the system variable Date$?
16. If you are copying all the information from record file #1 to record file #2, what test can you use to stop the program when everything has been copied?

PRACTICE PROGRAMS

1. The bubble sort algorithm in Example Program 11-2 scans through the entire list, each time comparing each contiguous pair of elements in the list. You will note that the first scan positions the largest element at the right end of the list. This means that the second scan needs to cover only the first N − 2 pairs of elements, not N − 1 pairs.

   Rewrite Example Program 11-2 to take advantage of this fact. Your FOR statement might be

   ```
   FOR I = 1 TO ScanLimit
   ```

   where ScanLimit starts at N − 1 and is decreased by one after each scan.

   Test your program by reading the file of names, TEST.DAT, created in Example Program 11-3, and writing the sorted list of names to a new file named TEST1.DAT.

2. Rewrite the sorting algorithm of Example Program 11-2 so that it will sort an array in either ascending or descending order. You will need to pass a third parameter to the subroutine, a string variable containing the letter "A" for ascending sort or the letter "D" for descending sort.

   Test your program by reading the file of names, TEST.DAT, created in Example Program 11-3, and writing the sorted list of names to a new file named TEST2.DAT.

3. True BASIC has two system time variables. The string variable Time$ contains the current 24-hour clock time in HH:MM:SS format. The numeric variable Time contains a value representing the current time expressed in seconds since midnight.

   Assuming that your system has a built-in clock, modify Example Program 11-2 to measure the elapsed time taken by the sorting algorithm in that program. Be sure to include only the time used for sorting, not the time taken to read the file.

   Test your program using the file RANDOM.DAT, which contains 80 ten-character strings of random characters.

4. In our example programs we read unsorted data from DATA statements or a record file into an array and then sort the array. Assume that you have the ten unsorted names of Example Program 11-2 stored in a record file, similar to the file TEST.REC produced by Example Program 11-6.

   Modify the bubble sort subroutine to sort this record file directly instead of sorting an array containing information read from the file. The only parameter needed by the subroutine is the file number. Use the timing procedure of Practice Program 3 to compare the time required to sort a record file and the time required to sort an array.

   Test your program using the record file TEST4.REC, writing the sorted list to a file named TEST4.NEW.

5. It is difficult to compare different sorting methods when using short lists because the time differences may be very small. It is also difficult to think of a large number of different names, say, 100 names, to create a longer test list.

   Write a program to create a text file with the number of lines specified by the user. Each line is a ten-character string, consisting of a random group of letters selected using the RND function discussed in Chapter 5. Create a test file named LONG.DAT containing 200 strings.

   Use this file to measure the performance of the sorting routine in Example Program 11-2 (with timing statements added) and one other sorting routine (We recommend the routine in Practice Problem 1.). Measure sorting times only and do not write output files.

6. Assume that you want to sort a file containing two or more items per logical record, such as the database file we used in Chapter 9. There are at least two ways to store this information in an array.

   One method, as illustrated in Example Program 11-5, is to combine the two items, name and telephone number, in a single string with a backslash separator. The strings are then stored in a one-dimensional array and sorted using the subroutine we have already developed.

   Another method is to store the information in a two-dimensional array, with names stored in column 1 and telephone numbers stored in column 2, as shown:

John H. Smith	217-202-3132
Mary White	617-627-0030
Clarence Goode	804-213-3137

   Develop a sorting subroutine to sort a two-dimensional string array with two columns, where sorting orders the elements in the first column in ascending order. Pass as parameters the array and the number of rows.

   Write a test program to show how your subroutine works, using the file PHONES.DAT in directory CH11 on the example program disk. This file contains the same information as the file with the same name in directory CH09, but has the first and last names in reverse order.

7. Extend the concepts of Practice Program 6 to write a more general sorting subroutine. This subroutine will sort an array containing a variable number of columns, where sorting orders the elements in a specified column. Pass as parameters the array, the number of rows, the number of columns, the column number designated for sorting, and the letter ''A'' or ''D'' for an ascending or descending sort.

   Demonstrate how your subroutine works by sorting a price list array with 4 columns containing part number, item name, quantity and unit price. Sort the price list in ascending order by unit price (column 4). Remember that all values in the array are string values, so you will have to be careful when comparing prices. Use the file PARTS.DAT in directory CH11.

8. Using the file PHONES.REC produced by Example Program 11-5, write a program that allows a user to specify the name of a telephone subscriber. A binary file search is used to find the name and the corresponding telephone number is then displayed. The program should make all comparisons with names converted to a single case.

   Test your program with the names Susan Moody, James Jones, and Bill Miller.

9. If several string items are to be concatenated together and written on a file as a single string, you must use a method that allows you to separate the individual items when the file is read. One method is to use a separator character, such as a backslash, that will not be used within any of the items. Another method is to convert variable-length strings to fixed-length strings before concatenation.

   Write a subroutine that converts a variable-length string to a fixed-length string by adding blanks to the end of the string. Pass the string variable name and the new fixed length as parameters. Be sure to check that the current string length is not longer than the new fixed length.

   Test your subroutine in a program, using a string value of ''Oars'' and a length of 20, also a string value of ''Inflatable row boats'' and the same length.

10. A record file has records with fixed-length strings, each string containing three items of information. The fixed-length string is 30 characters long and is divided as follows:

Item description	20 characters
Reorder point	4 characters
Reorder quantity	6 characters

The first item is padded with trailing blanks. The other two items are padded with leading zeroes. The file is ordered in ascending order, sorted alphabetically by item description.

Write a program containing a binary search subprogram (function or subroutine) to search for a specified record by item description. Ignore uppercase and lowercase differences when searching. Display the record items with appropriate labels after stripping off trailing blanks and leading zeroes.

Test your program using the record file REORDER.REC and the item names ''Oars'', ''Paddle'', and ''Turnbuckle''.

11. A text file contains information stored as one string per line. A logical record consists of six lines containing the following information:

last name
first name
department
current salary
date when last hired
date of last pay increase

Create a new text file with a different format. Each line of the new file will contain the six strings of a logical record, each string enclosed in quote marks and separated from one another by commas.

Test your program using the input file PAYROLL.DAT and the output file NEWPAY.DAT.

12. A word processor named XyWrite is used to write an article containing True BASIC programs. It is easy to isolate a program from the surrounding text and write it on a separate file, but the program still contains special formatting characters that keep it from executing.

Ask the user to specify the name of an input file containing True BASIC program statements, and the name of an output file. Read and examine each line of the input file. Delete any block of characters that starts with the double left angle bracket (ASCII value 174) and ends with the double right angle bracket (ASCII value 175). The characters within these double angle brackets are formatting instructions to the word processor. Write the corrected line to the output file.

Test your program using the input file XYWRITE.TXT and an output file named ASCII.TXT.

12 Computer Graphics

12.1 INTRODUCTION

True BASIC provides extensive capabilities for creating graphics images on the display screen. We define a high-resolution graphics mode and show how window coordinates can be established. We then examine the graphics primitives: statements for plotting points, lines, areas, and text.

Several advanced graphics statements allow us to draw simple figures such as rectangles and circles, to save and retrieve graphics figures, and to change their color or intensity. The external picture unit provides a graphics subprogram capability similar to the external subroutine. Picture units may be transformed using either user-designed or built-in transformation routines.

A final section shows how to use the graphics capabilities of True BASIC in two application programs. One example program draws the front elevation of a simple house. The other program demonstrates how interactive graphics can be used to draw diagrams on the screen.

12.2 SETTING THE GRAPHICS ENVIRONMENT

The display unit screen is normally used to display characters, most often in a format of 24 or 25 lines containing up to 80 characters per line. Each character is composed of a number of illuminated dots or *pixels* on the screen.

This same screen can also be used to display other images by selecting and illuminating a pattern of pixels. Maximum flexibility can be achieved when each pixel is controlled by one or more bits of computer memory. This mode of display is called *bit-mapped* computer graphics.

To use the graphics capability of your computer, you must have a display unit, with its associated control card, that will support graphics. On the IBM PC, the color display unit supports graphics. The monochromatic display unit will support graphics only if a special control card, such as the Hercules graphics card, has been installed. Many IBM PC compatibles (such as the AT&T 6300 and the Compaq portable) support graphics on their standard monochromatic display unit.

Computer graphics is a complicated subject, dependent on both the type of computer and the specific display unit being used. Our discussion of computer graphics in True BASIC will not be comprehensive, but rather will focus on a particular mode of graphics display on IBM PC-compatible computers. If you need information on other graphics displays, especially multiple-color displays, consult the language reference manual.

Text Mode

The statement that establishes the type of graphics is

```
SET MODE Type$
```

where Type$ must contain one of a list of predefined values. If you are using a black-and-white or monochromatic display unit (where white is usually displayed as green or amber, depending on the unit), the default value of Type$ is probably either ''80'' or ''bw80''. Both these modes have the following attributes:

Screen can display 80 columns of text.
All 256 characters are available.
Text characters are white.
Background is black.
Graphics is not supported.
Blinking cursor is displayed.

In our discussion, we will call this mode the *text mode,* displaying the *text screen.* It is the normal mode of operation of the display unit.

Graphics Mode

A different mode must be used to display graphics on the screen. Most color display units support several modes of graphics display. A low-resolution mode (meaning that the illuminated pixels are larger and thus fewer in number) permits multiple colors to be displayed on the screen. A high-resolution mode allows only one foreground color and a black background to be displayed.

The mode that supports the highest-resolution graphics (on the IBM PC and on most compatibles) is called "hires". Your program must contain a statement similar to

```
SET mode "hires"
```

to initiate this mode of display.

Hires mode has the following attributes:

Screen can display 80 columns of text.

Only the basic ASCII characters, code values 0 through 127, are available.

Text and graphics may be in any one color, this color is white on a black and white console.

Background color is black.

Graphics is supported with a resolution of 640 by 200 pixels.

Cursor is not displayed.

In our discussion, we will call this mode the *graphics mode,* displaying the *graphics screen*. The hires mode is the only graphics mode that we will discuss and use.

When the computer executes the mode statement for hires graphics, the current screen clears and a screen capable of supporting graphics, with no cursor, is displayed. After the program ends, **you must press the Enter key to return to the previous text mode** and the familiar split screen with command and program windows.

Here is a simple program that demonstrates the graphics screen:

```
! Example Program 12-1.
! Accessing the hires graphics mode.

SET mode "hires"
LINE INPUT prompt "Enter a sentence: ": Phrase$
PRINT Phrase$
PRINT "Press ENTER to leave graphics mode."
END
```

Another version of this program asks for the mode when the program starts, using the ASK MODE statement, and then returns to that specific mode after the graphics screen has been displayed. A PAUSE statement is used to halt the computer for three seconds so the graphics screen display can be observed.

```
! Example Program 12-2.
! Accessing the hires graphics mode.

ASK mode Type$
SET mode "hires"
LINE INPUT prompt "Enter a sentence: ": Phrase$
PRINT Phrase$
PAUSE 3
SET mode Type$
END
```

You will notice that the text characters on the graphics screen have less detail than, and are not as clear as, corresponding characters on the text screen.

The Graphics Window

Having established the graphics mode, the next step is to establish a *graphics window* on the screen. This window may include the entire screen or only part of the screen (see Chapter 10). Most of our example programs use full-screen windows. To refer to a point in the window, a system of *window coordinates* must be defined.

The vertical or Y coordinate is used to locate the vertical position of a point between the bottom and top of the window. A minimum value of Y (Ymin) is assigned to the bottom of the window and a maximum value of Y (Ymax) to the top. The vertical position of any point in the window can then be described by specifying a Y value between Ymin and Ymax. In the same manner, a horizontal or X coordinate can be defined by assigning values for Xmin and Xmax. The position of any point can now be specified by giving its X and Y coordinate values, usually in the format (X value, Y value).

The SET WINDOW statement is used to establish a coordinate system. The general form of the statement is

```
SET WINDOW Xmin, Xmax, Ymin, Ymax
```

Figure 12-1 shows how the screen and window appear.

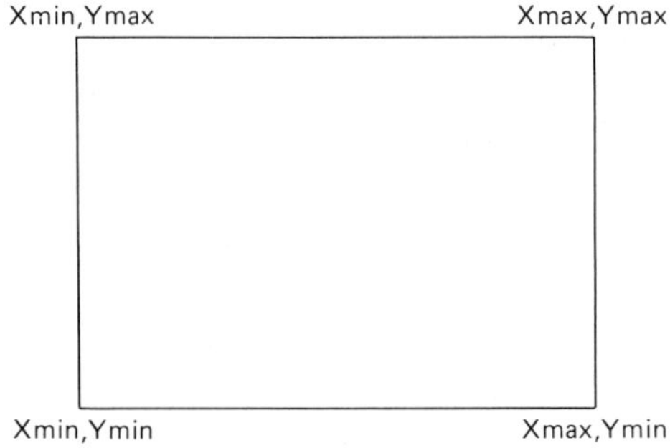

Figure 12-1 Graphics window and coordinate system.

If a graphics window has already been established, you can determine its boundaries with the statement

```
ASK WINDOW Xmin, Xmax, Ymin, Ymax
```

As an example, suppose that you want the horizontal coordinate to go from 0 to 100 and the vertical coordinate to go from −10 to +10. The proper statement is

```
SET window 0, 100, -10, 10
```

Note that the lower left corner of the window is the point (0, −10), while the upper right corner is the point (100, 10). The result is shown in Figure 12-2.

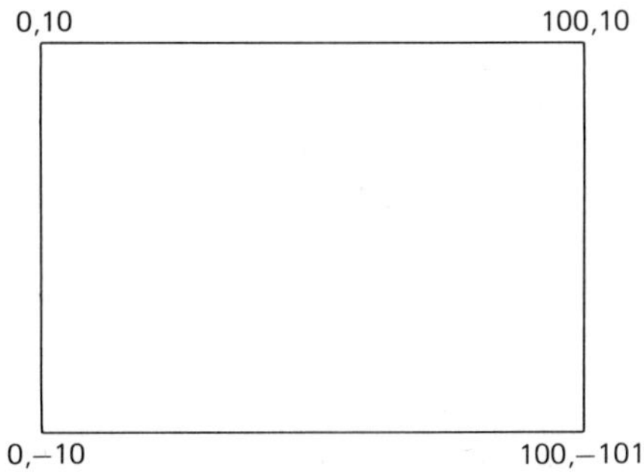

Figure 12-2 A specific graphics coordinate system.

When using the graphics screen, you do not need to be concerned about the screen resolution or number of pixels. True BASIC makes an automatic translation from window coordinates to pixel position on the screen.

If you do not include a SET WINDOW statement in your program, the default window coordinates are 0, 1, 0, 1. Note that the graphics screen coordinate system is different from the row-and-column coordinate system used in the text screen.

Selecting an Aspect Ratio

Almost any appropriate coordinate system can be chosen for the graphics window if you are plotting a graph. However, if you are drawing a geometric figure, you must consider the *aspect ratio* of your particular screen.

The aspect ratio is the ratio of the horizontal dimension of the screen to the vertical dimension. Most display screens are not square, but rectangular, with the wide dimension horizontal. Thus if a unit length is to be the same in both horizontal and vertical directions, the number of unit lengths in the horizontal or X direction must be greater than the number in the vertical or Y direction.

On the particular computers we used when writing this book, satisfactory screen aspect ratios are between 1.2 and 1.5. The IBM PC monochromatic screen and the Compaq Portable screen have an aspect ratio of about 1.4, while the AT&T PC6300 monochromatic screen has a ratio of about 1.28.

To produce squares that look square and circles that are round on an AT&T display unit, we usually use the statement

```
SET window 0, 128, 0, 100
```

or

```
SET window -64, 64, -50, 50
```

to establish the screen coordinate system. The first statement puts the origin at the lower left corner of the screen, while the second statement centers the origin on the screen.

On an IBM monochromatic display unit, these statements are

```
SET window 0, 140, 0, 100
```

or

```
SET window -70, 70, -50, 50
```

Later in this chapter, we will show you how to adjust your coordinate system to produce figures that are geometrically correct.

It is important to note that the aspect ratio of your printer may be different from the aspect ratio of your screen. This means that a square that looks correct on the screen will appear rectangular when printed on paper. The only solution is to use different versions of the program with different aspect ratios for displaying and printing.

12.3 FUNDAMENTALS OF DRAWING

Drawing Points

The True BASIC statement to draw or plot a point at the position X,Y on the graphics screen is

```
PLOT POINTS: X,Y
```

In many applications, you want to plot several points and then the statement becomes

```
PLOT POINTS: X1,Y1; X2,Y2;...
```

The position identifiers X1, X2, Y1, and Y2 can be numeric variables, constants or expressions. Each position pair, X and Y, is the coordinate of a point to be plotted. The pairs are separated by semicolons. As usual in most graphics statements, these positions are expressed in terms of the window coordinate system.

You can, of course, use the PLOT POINTS statement in a loop to plot a sequence of points. Here is an example:

```
! Example Program 12-3.
! Plot a sequence of points.

SET mode "hires"
SET window 0,10,0,100
FOR X = 0 to 10 step 0.1
    LET Y = X*X
    PLOT POINTS: X, Y
NEXT X
PRINT "Press ENTER key to clear screen."
END
```

This program plots the equation $Y = X^2$, a parabolic curve. After you run the program and the curve is displayed, press the Enter key to return to the normal text screen. We tried this program first without the ''step 0.1'' phrase, but like it better the way it is now written, with the points plotted closer together. You might want to try plotting it both ways yourself.

Drawing Lines

The statement

```
PLOT LINES: X1,Y1; X2,Y2
```

is used to draw a line between points (X1, Y1) and (X2, Y2). You can connect several points together with lines by using the statement

```
PLOT LINES: X1,Y1; X2,Y2; X3,Y3;...
```

If the coordinates of the first point are the same as those of the last point, you will produce a closed figure; that is, the line will close on itself.

Here is our previous example, rewritten to display a line plot rather than a point plot:

```
! Example Program 12-4.
! Plot a line between points.

SET mode "hires"
SET window 0,10,0,100
FOR X = 0 to 10
    LET Y = X*X
    PLOT LINES: X, Y;
NEXT X
PRINT "Press ENTER key to clear screen."
END
```

Note the trailing semicolon in the PLOT LINES statement, which causes a line to be drawn from one point to the next point. In this case, we use a step of one so that the curve is drawn more quickly.

This program produces the graph shown in Figure 12-3.

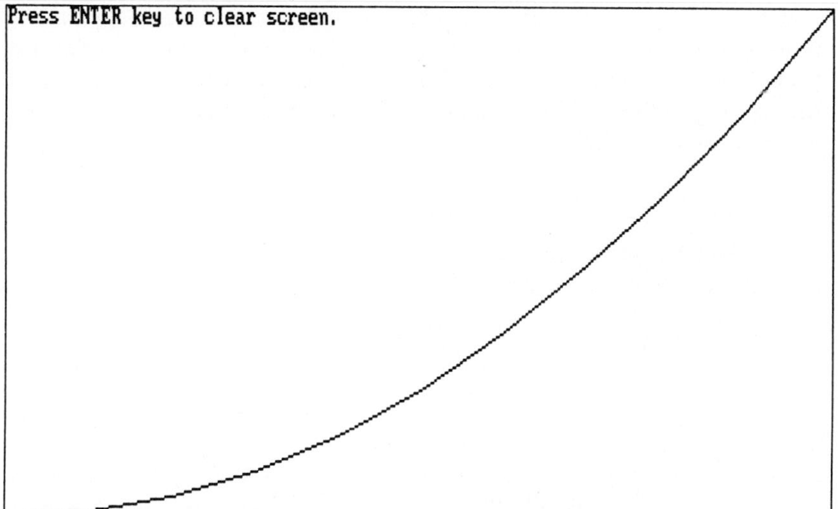

Figure 12-3 Graph produced by Example Program 12-4.

Drawing Areas

Having learned to draw lines, you can now connect lines together to produce a figure, still using the PLOT LINES statement. This technique produces an outline figure. The PLOT AREA statement can be used to fill in the area enclosed by the outline. Here is an example program that uses both statements. The program first draws an outline of a square and then, after a short pause, fills in the square.

```
! Example Program 12-5.
! Display outline and filled figures.

SET mode "hires"
LET Ratio = 1.4
SET window 0,(100*Ratio),0,100

! Display an outline square.
PLOT LINES: 10,10; 10,50; 50,50; 50,10; 10,10
PAUSE 2

! Display a filled square.
PLOT AREA: 10,10; 10,50; 50,50; 50,10; 10,10
PRINT "Press ENTER key to clear screen."
END
```

Note that we choose a coordinate system to match a screen aspect ratio of 1.40. By assigning the aspect ratio to a variable named Ratio, it is easy to change this variable if we run the program on computers with different display unit aspect ratios.

Using Colors

We have not yet talked about the possibility of displaying figures in color. Of course, if you have only a black-and-white display unit, your ''hires'' figures will be in white (which may actually be green or amber, depending on your display unit) on a black background. If you have a color display, you can choose one of several colors for your figures, depending on the computer and display unit that you are using. The statement to establish a new color is

```
SET COLOR Name$
```

where Name$ contains the name of the desired color. In general, True BASIC will support at least the following colors:

red	cyan
magenta	brown
yellow	white
green	black
blue	background

Note that the color "background" means the figure will be displayed in the same color as the background (which is always black in hires mode), thus effectively erasing an existing figure. Here is an example:

```
! Example Program 12-6.
! Show method for erasing a figure.

SET mode "hires"
LET Ratio = 1.4
SET window 0,(100*Ratio),0,100

! Display an outline square.
PLOT LINES: 10,10; 10,50; 50,50; 50,10; 10,10
PAUSE 2

! Now erase the figure.
SET color background
PLOT LINES: 10,10; 10,50; 50,50; 50,10; 10,10
PRINT "Press ENTER key to clear screen."
END
```

Displaying Text

It is often desirable to display text in a graphics window. Text capability is needed for such purposes as labeling figures or displaying instructions for a user.

The familiar PRINT statement can be used, but it may not place the text just where you want it. A more useful statement is

```
PLOT TEXT, AT X,Y: Label$
```

where Label$ is a string variable containing the desired text. This text will be located in the window so that the lower left corner of the first character is at coordinate position (X, Y). The next program plots a bar graph, also called a *histogram,* of data values.

```
! Example Program 12-7.
! Display a bar graph with labels.

SET mode "hires"
SET window 0,120,0,100
FOR X = 20 to 100 step 20
    READ Y
    PLOT AREA: X-5,0; X-5,Y; X+5,Y; X+5,0
    LET Label$ = str$(Y)
    PLOT TEXT, at X-3,Y+5: Label$
NEXT X

DATA 52.3, 21.7, 72.8, 30.1, 66.7
END
```

Note that the label must be a string value and thus the numeric variable Y must be converted to a string. Each individual label starts with a different character having a different lower left point. This fact causes each label to be located in a slightly different position with respect to its histogram bar. The graph produced by this program is shown in Figure 12-4.

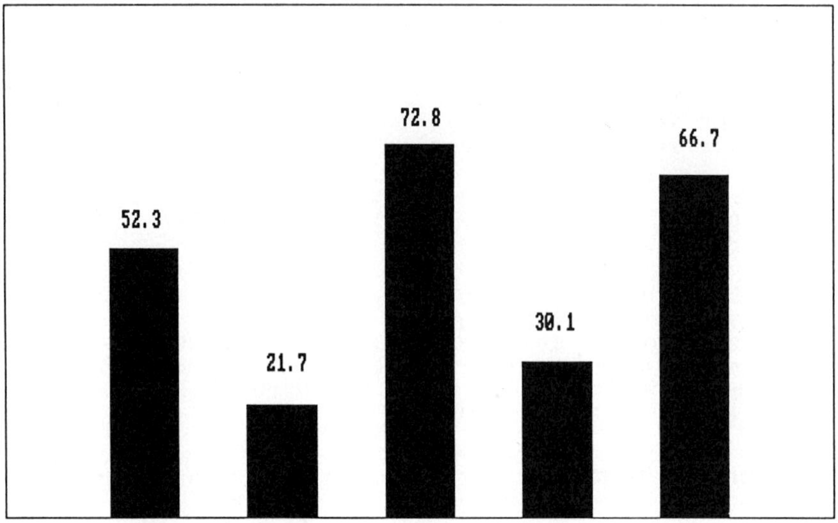

Figure 12-4 Histogram produced by Example Program 12-7

Determining the Aspect Ratio

We now present a program that you can use to determine the aspect ratio of your own screen. Run the program and measure carefully the width and height of the square displayed on the screen. If these two dimensions are not the same, try again when prompted and enter a new aspect ratio. If the square as displayed is too wide, increase the aspect ratio; if too narrow, decrease the ratio.

Both Ymin and Xmin are set to zero. Ymax is set to 100 and Xmax is set to 100 times the aspect ratio. When a new aspect ratio is entered, the value of Xmax is recalculated and the test square is displayed again in the modified coordinate system.

```
! Example Program 12-8.
! Determine the aspect ratio of your screen.

! Display instructions.
CLEAR
PRINT "Program to Determine Screen Aspect Ratio"
PRINT
PRINT "Carefully measure the width and height of"
PRINT "the displayed square.  If it is too wide,"
PRINT "increase the aspect ratio; if too narrow,"
PRINT "decrease the aspect ratio."
PRINT
PRINT "Press any key to display the square.";
GET KEY Dummy
```

```
! Set mode and initial aspect ratio.
ASK mode Type$
SET mode "hires"
LET Ratio = 1.4
DO
   CLEAR
   LET Xmax = 100*Ratio
   SET window 0,Xmax,0,100
   ! Display a filled square.
   PLOT AREA: 30,20; 30,80; 90,80; 90,20; 30,20
   LET Label$ = "Aspect ratio is " & str$(Ratio)
   PLOT TEXT, at 40,90: Label$
   ! Check for another display.
   LINE INPUT prompt "Try again? ":Reply$
   LET Reply$ = ucase$(Reply$[1:1])
   ! Ask for new aspect ratio and display square again.
   IF Reply$ <> "N" then
      INPUT prompt "Aspect ratio? ": Ratio
   END IF
LOOP until Reply$ = "N"
SET mode Type$
END
```

12.4 DRAWING SIMPLE SHAPES

The PLOT statements described in the previous section can be used to draw any figure consisting of straight lines. Another set of statements, the BOX statements, allows simple figures to be drawn more easily and more quickly. The additional drawing speed makes BOX statements a good choice for animation programs where drawings must change rapidly.

Drawing with BOX Statements

Rectangles can be drawn and erased using the following statements:

```
BOX LINES Xmin, Xmax, Ymin, Ymax
BOX AREA Xmin, Xmax, Ymin, Ymax
BOX CLEAR Xmin, Xmax, Ymin, Ymax
```

The BOX LINES statement draws a rectangle that extends horizontally from Xmin to Xmax and vertically from Ymin to Ymax. This is a line drawing, similar to that produced by the PLOT LINES statement. The BOX AREA statement draws a solid rectangle in the selected color, with dimensions again determined by the values of Xmin, Xmax, Ymin, and Ymax. The BOX CLEAR statement erases a rectangle drawn previously by either the BOX LINES or BOX AREA statement. See Example Program 12-9 on page 230.

```
! Example Program 12-9.
! Use of BOX statements to draw rectangles.

SET mode "hires"
LET Ratio = 1.4
SET window 0,(100*Ratio),0,100
! Draw a rectangle.
BOX LINES 10,60,10,60
PAUSE 2
! Erase the rectangle.
BOX CLEAR 10,60,10,60
PAUSE 2
! Draw a solid rectangle.
BOX AREA 70,120,40,90
PAUSE 2
! Erase again.
BOX CLEAR 70,120,40,90
PRINT "Press ENTER key to clear screen."
END
```

PAUSE statements have been inserted to separate the different BOX statements. Note particularly the speed with which the BOX AREA statement fills a rectangle, compared to the speed of the PLOT AREA statement. We have included a PRINT statement in the program to remind the user to press the Enter key to return to the text screen.

Another BOX statement draws an ellipse or circle within a rectangular area. Remember that a circle is just the special case of an ellipse drawn within a square. This statement has two forms:

```
BOX ELLIPSE Xmin, Xmax, Ymin, Ymax
```

or

```
BOX CIRCLE Xmin, Xmax, Ymin, Ymax
```

Here is an example:

```
! Example Program 12-10.
! Use of a BOX statement to draw a circle.

SET mode "hires"
LET Ratio = 1.4
SET window 0,(100*Ratio),0,100
! Draw a square.
BOX LINES 10,60,10,60
PAUSE 2
! Erase the square.
BOX CLEAR 10,60,10,60
PAUSE 2
! Draw a circle.
BOX CIRCLE 10,60,10,60
END
```

If you prefer, you can use the statement BOX ELLIPSE instead of BOX CIRCLE—

the results will be identical. Note that in this and subsequent example programs, we no longer remind the user to press the Enter key to leave graphics mode.

Coloring an Area

The FLOOD statement lets a user "fill in" any outline figure with solid color. The coordinates in the FLOOD statement can be any point within the outline figure. Here is the same program again, but the ellipse is now drawn within a rectangle, not a square, and is filled in with the default color (usually green or amber on a monochromatic display unit).

```
! Example Program 12-11.
! Use of a BOX statement to draw an ellipse.

SET mode "hires"
LET Ratio = 1.4
SET window 0,(100*Ratio),0,100
! Draw a rectangle.
BOX LINES 10,120,30,80
PAUSE 2
! Erase the rectangle.
BOX CLEAR 10,120,30,80
PAUSE 2
! Draw an ellipse.
BOX ELLIPSE 10,120,30,80
PAUSE 2
! Flood the ellipse with color.
FLOOD 50,50
END
```

Note that the coordinates of the FLOOD statement must refer to a point inside the ellipse. Try running this program with different FLOOD statement coordinates and see what happens.

Saving Graphics Figures

Two additional BOX statements are used to save and redisplay a portion of the graphics screen. This process is much faster than erasing and redrawing the figure. The statements are

```
BOX KEEP Xmin, Xmax, Ymin, Ymax IN Var$
BOX SHOW Var$ AT Xmin, Ymin
```

The BOX KEEP statement saves a portion of the graphics screen (actually a portion of the computer's display memory) in the string variable Var$. The BOX SHOW statement allows the contents of Var$ to be displayed at any selected point on the graphics screen, with the lower left corner of the saved figure placed at Xmin, Ymin.

Here is an example that first draws a circle, then saves the circle figure and erases the screen, and finally displays the saved figure again at four new locations.

```
! Example Program 12-12.
! Save and redisplay a graphics image.

SET mode "hires"
LET Ratio = 1.4
SET window 0,(100*Ratio),0,100
! Draw and flood a circle.
BOX CIRCLE 60,70,45,55
FLOOD 65,50
PAUSE 2
! Save and erase this figure.
BOX KEEP 60,70,45,55 in Figure$
BOX CLEAR 60,70,45,55
PAUSE 2
! Display the figure in four new locations.
BOX SHOW Figure$ at 10,10
BOX SHOW Figure$ at 10,80
BOX show Figure$ at 110,80
BOX SHOW Figure$ at 110,10
END
```

Selecting Different Colors

We assume that your computer has either a black-and-white display unit capable of displaying graphics or a color display unit. In the former case, different colors will probably appear as different intensities on the screen. The range of color numbers for IBM PC-compatible computers goes from 0 through 15. Some color display units have a limited color capability and display the same color for two different color numbers. For most computers, number 0 represents the color black, the same color as the background in hires mode. Thus a figure drawn in color 0 will not be visible.

Here is a program that allows you to investigate the colors or intensities available on your computer. For each color or intensity number, a filled box is drawn and the color number is displayed. There is a short pause between each display.

```
! Example Program 12-13.
! Examine different colors or intensities.

SET mode "hires"
LET Ratio = 1.4
SET window 0,(100*Ratio),0,100
! Display individual colors by number.
FOR Color = 0 to 15
    SET color Color
    BOX AREA 30,70,30,70
    LET Msg$ = "Color number is " & str$(Color)
    PLOT TEXT, at 30,10: Msg$
    PAUSE 2
NEXT Color
END
```

Another version of the program displays the same figures, but identifies each figure by color name rather than by color number. It uses the eight color names that are generally available on all color display units.

```
! Example Program 12-14.
! Examine different color names.

SET mode "hires"
LET Ratio = 1.4
SET window 0,(100*Ratio),0,100
! Display individual colors by name.
DO while more data
   READ Color$
   SET color Color$
   BOX AREA 30,70,30,70
   LET Msg$ = "Color is " & Color$ & "     "
   PLOT TEXT, at 37,10: Msg$
   PAUSE 2
LOOP
DATA blue, green, cyan, red
DATA magenta, brown, white, yellow
END
```

Note the trailing blanks in the statement that assigns the color name string to Msg$. These blanks ensure that the old name is completely erased. If you leave out the blanks, part of an old color name may appear at the end of a new color name.

12.5 PICTURE SUBPROGRAMS

A graphics program unit is called a *picture*. It is the graphics equivalent of a True BASIC subroutine. While both internal and external pictures are allowed, we will discuss only external pictures.

External Picture Units

An external picture unit must start with the statement

```
EXTERNAL PICTURE Name (Parameters)
```

where *Name* is the picture name and *Parameters* is a list of variable names. The picture name must follow the same rules that apply to variable names (see Chapter 3). In True BASIC, the word EXTERNAL may be omitted, but the picture unit must be placed after the main program END statement. The parameters are local variable names, separated from one another by commas. Information is passed to these parameters by reference, just as in subroutines. In fact, the use of temporary variables, passing of file or channel numbers and so forth, all behave with pictures as they do with subroutines.

The last statement in a picture unit must be END PICTURE and other exit points are identified by the EXIT PICTURE phrase. A picture unit is invoked from another program unit by the statement

```
DRAW Name (Parameters)
```

where the *Parameters* may be variables, constants or expressions.

Here is an example program that uses a picture unit to draw a circle at a specified location. The user is asked to enter the radius of a circle to be drawn on the screen. If the radius is zero, the program stops. The user is then asked to enter the center coordinates of the circle and an external picture is called to draw the figure.

```
! Example Program 12-15.
! Use picture unit to draw a circle.

ASK mode Type$
DO
   CLEAR
   PRINT "Enter zero to stop the program."
   INPUT prompt "Radius of circle? ": Radius
   IF Radius > 0 then
      INPUT prompt "Center coordinates (X,Y)? ": X, Y
      SET mode "hires"
      LET Ratio = 1.4
      SET window -50*Ratio, 50*Ratio, -50, 50
      DRAW Circle (Radius, X, Y)
      PAUSE 3
      ! Set original mode.
      SET mode Type$
   ELSEIF Radius < 0 then
      PRINT
      PRINT "You cannot have a negative radius."
      PAUSE 2
   END IF
LOOP until Radius = 0
END

PICTURE Circle (R, X, Y)
    ! Draw a circle of radius R at point X, Y.
    BOX CIRCLE X-R, X+R, Y-R, Y+R
END PICTURE
```

The initial screen mode is saved in a variable named Type$. A user is asked to specify the radius and center coordinates of the circle, and the display mode is changed from text to graphics. An external picture named Circle draws the figure, with the radius and center coordinates passed as parameters. Upon returning to the main program unit, the screen is restored to its original text mode so that text prompts with a cursor can be displayed.

Transforming a Graphics Figure

One advantage of using picture units for computer graphics is that the figures specified in the picture unit can be transformed when the picture is drawn. Transforming a picture means changing its appearance by some geometric process, such as rotation or shifting. The transformation statement is

```
DRAW Pic WITH Trans
```

where Pic is the name of a picture unit and Trans is the name of a transformation. If you wish to apply more than one transformation, use the statement

```
DRAW Pic WITH Trans1*Trans2*...
```

where Trans1, Trans2, and so forth are the same or different transformations.

True BASIC has five standard or built-in transformations. They are:

SHIFT (A, B) Move the figure A units in the X direction and B units in the Y direction. Every point plotted at (X, Y) is moved to (X + A, Y + B).

SCALE (A) Change the size of the figure by A. Every point plotted at (X, Y) is moved to (X * A, Y * A).

SCALE (A, B) Change the size of the figure by A in the X direction and by B in the Y direction. Every point plotted at (X, Y) is moved to (X * A, Y * B).

ROTATE (A) Rotate the figure A radians or degrees counterclockwise about the origin of the window coordinate system. **Note that the figure is not rotated about its own center.** Radians are used unless your program contains an OPTION ANGLES DEGREES statement.

SHEAR (A) Tilt all vertical lines in the figure to the right (clockwise) by A radians or degrees. Every point plotted at (X, Y) is moved to (X + (Y * TAN(A)), Y). Radians are used unless your program specifies the use of degrees.

If you are going to transform a picture unit, it must contain PLOT statements, not BOX statements, because figures drawn with the latter cannot be transformed. In addition to the built-in transformations just listed, you can develop and apply your own custom transformations. We will not discuss the process here, but it is covered in many advanced books on computer graphics. See the language reference manual for further information.

Here is an example program using a picture unit with transformations. It first draws a simple square and then redraws the same figure with several different transformations applied. Remember to press the Enter key after the figures are displayed to return to the True BASIC divided screen.

```
! Example Program 12-16.
! Using transformations with a picture.

SET mode "hires"
LET Ratio = 1.4   ! Change to 1.6 for HP LaserJet
SET window -(50*Ratio),(50*Ratio),-50,50
OPTION ANGLE degrees

DRAW Square(10,-35,25)
PLOT TEXT, at -60,5: "Original square"
```

```
DRAW Square(10,35,25) with shear(10)
PLOT TEXT, at 5,5: "Sheared 10 degrees clockwise"

DRAW Square(10,0,0) with rotate(45)*shift(35,-25)
PLOT TEXT, at 5,-45: "Rotated 45 degrees"

DRAW Square(10,-25,-25) with scale(1.5,1)
PLOT TEXT, at -60,-45: "Lengthened 50 percent"
END

PICTURE Square (Size, X, Y)
    ! Draw a square centered at the point X, Y.
    LET P = Size/2
    PLOT LINES: -P+X,P+Y; P+X,P+Y;
    PLOT LINES: P+X,-P+Y; -P+X,-P+Y; -P+X,P+Y
END PICTURE
```

We specify a window coordinate system that is centered on the screen. To rotate a square, we draw it so its center coincides with the center of coordinates. When we rotate the square, it rotates about its own center and after rotation, we move it to the desired position.

Figure 12-5 shows the drawing produced by this program.

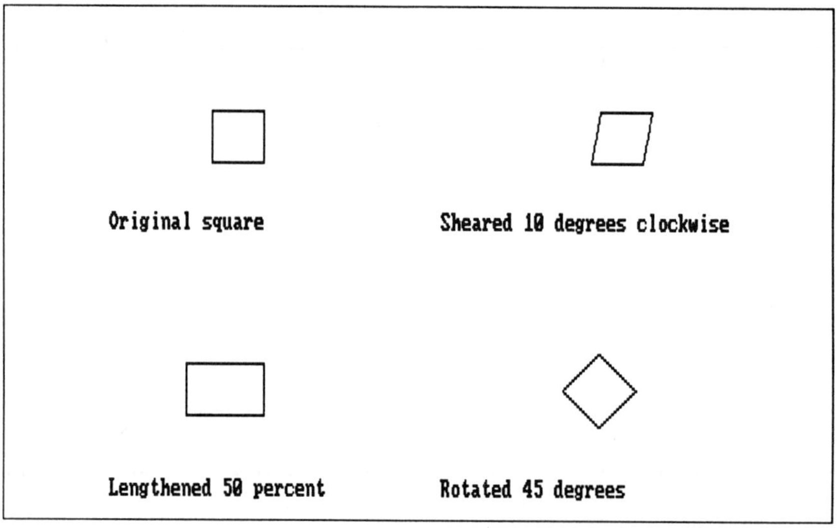

Figure 12-5 Screen display produced by Example Program 12-16.

Picture Libraries

Library files of pictures can be created in the same manner as library files of functions or subroutines. A file named GRAPHLIB.TRU is distributed with True BASIC and contains picture units for drawing polygons, arcs of circles, window axes, line graphs, and bar graphs.

To use any of the pictures in this library, add the statement

```
LIBRARY "GRAPHLIB"
```

to the beginning of your program. You can find out how to use these library pictures by examining the GRAPHLIB.TRU file.

12.6 EXAMPLES OF COMPUTER GRAPHICS APPLICATIONS

In this final section of Chapter 12, we present two example programs that illustrate computer graphics applications.

Computer-Aided Design

The process of using computer graphics to assist architects and engineers to create drawings is called *computer-aided design (CAD)*. Most CAD systems produce drawings that are much more complicated and detailed than our example, the front view or elevation of a simple house.

The house we design is 30 feet wide and the peak of the roof is 27 feet off the ground. It has an exterior chimney on the left side that is 3 feet wide. The front door is 3.5 feet by 7 feet. Most of the windows are 2.5 feet by 4 feet, but one small attic window is only 1.5 feet by 1.5 feet. There is a 4 foot wide step at the front door. Two horizontal lines on the chimney show where its depth is reduced at 5 feet off the ground. Our design is shown in Figure 12-6.

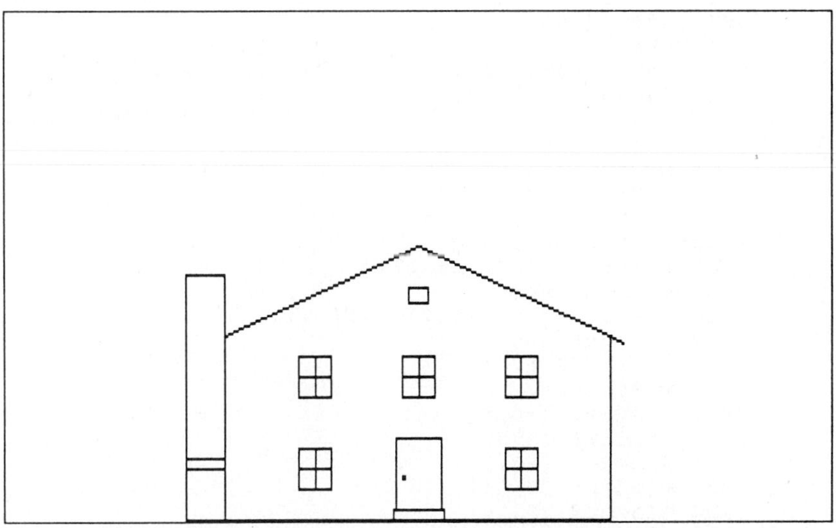

Figure 12-6 Front view of house produced by Example Program 12-17.

We choose a coordinate system so that the screen width represents 70 feet and the screen height represents 50 feet. This gives an aspect ratio of 1.4, the correct ratio for an IBM PC computer. You can easily change the aspect ratio to match your particular computer.

Here is the outline of our program:

Draw front outline of house.
Draw chimney.
Draw roof overhang.
Draw front step.
Use picture to draw front door.
Use pictures to draw windows.

CAD systems for architects usually have libraries or collections of detail drawings for such items as doors and windows. An architect may be able to choose from several dozen door and window designs and place these items where needed on the drawing. In our program, we have one external picture that draws a 3.5 foot by 7 foot door. We pass the coordinates of the center of the door when we call the picture unit.

We use two different types of windows and thus have two external picture units for windows. The first draws a standard 2.5 foot by 4 foot window. The second draws a small 1.5 foot by 1.5 foot window. We specify the center of a window when we call a picture unit. In an actual CAD program, the door and window drawings would show a lot more detail than in our example.

```
! Example Program 12-17.
! Draw the front view of a house.

SET mode "hires"
LET Ratio = 1.4
SET window -(25*Ratio), (25*Ratio), 0, 50
! Draw house outline.
PLOT LINES: -15,0; -15,18; 0,27; 15,18; 15,0; -15,0
! Draw chimney.
PLOT LINES: -18,0; -18,24; -15,24; -15,0; -18,0
PLOT LINES: -18,5; -15,5
PLOT LINES: -18,6; -15,6
! Draw roof overhang.
PLOT LINES: 15,18; 16,17.4
! Draw front step.
PLOT LINES: -2,0; -2,1; 2,1; 2,0
! Draw front door.
DRAW Door1 (0,4.5)
! Draw windows.
DRAW Window1 (-8,5)
DRAW Window1 (8,5)
DRAW Window1 (-8,14)
DRAW Window1 (0,14)
DRAW Window1 (8,14)
DRAW Window2 (0,22)
END

EXTERNAL PICTURE Door1 (X,Y)
    ! Draw 3.5 foot by 7 foot door, centered at X, Y.
    LET Xmin = X - 1.75
```

```
        LET Xmax = X + 1.75
        LET Ymin = Y - 3.5
        LET Ymax = Y + 3.5
        BOX LINES Xmin, Xmax, Ymin, Ymax
        ! Draw door knob.
        DRAW Circle (0.1, X - 1.2, Y - 0.4)
    END PICTURE

    EXTERNAL PICTURE Window1 (X,Y)
        ! Draw a 2.5 foot by 4 foot window, centered at X, Y.
        LET Xmin = X - 1.25
        LET Xmax = X + 1.25
        LET Ymin = Y - 2
        LET Ymax = Y + 2
        BOX LINES Xmin, Xmax, Ymin, Ymax
        ! Draw individual window panes.
        PLOT LINES: X, Y - 2; X, Y + 2
        PLOT LINES: X - 1.25, Y; X + 1.25, Y
    END PICTURE

    EXTERNAL PICTURE Window2 (X,Y)
        ! Draw a 1.5 foot by 1.5 foot window, centered at X, Y.
        LET Xmin = X - .75
        LET Xmax = X + .75
        LET Ymin = Y - .75
        LET Ymax = Y + .75
        BOX LINES Xmin, Xmax, Ymin, Ymax
    END PICTURE

    EXTERNAL PICTURE Circle (R, X, Y)
        ! Draw a circle of radius R, centered at X, Y.
        BOX CIRCLE X - R, X + R, Y - R, Y + R
    END PICTURE
```

The main program draws the house outline, chimney, roof overhang, and front step. It calls external pictures to draw the front door and the six windows.

Interactive Computer Graphics

All our previous example programs have drawn screen figures based on coordinate values in graphics statements. If we wanted to draw another figure, we would have to change these values, or even the statements themselves. An interactive graphics program allows us to draw a figure by moving an indicator on the screen, and thus a large number of different figures can be drawn using the same program.

The indicator we will use is called a set of *cross-hairs* and we move it with the cursor arrow keys. As you might expect, the left arrow key moves the cross-hairs left, the up arrow key moves the cross-hairs up, and so forth. The movement is fairly slow, but if the arrow key is held down, the cross-hairs will move continuously in the specified direction. If the control key (Ctrl) is held down when the arrow key is pressed, the cross-hairs move to the edge of the screen in the specified direction.

The statement that produces the cross-hairs is

```
GET POINT: X,Y
```

This statement is the graphics input statement. When it is executed, cross-hairs are displayed at the center of the active window or at the last point specified on the graphics screen. The cross-hairs can be moved as described, and when they are at the desired point, the Enter key is pressed. This action assigns the coordinates of that point to the variables X and Y.

The pixel is now illuminated at the point that was chosen and appears as a small bright spot on the screen. As many points as desired can be chosen and the coordinates of each point will be assigned to the GET POINT statement variables.

For example, to draw a line between two points, use the program fragment

```
GET POINT: X1, Y1
GET POINT: X2, Y2
PLOT LINES: X1,Y1; X2,Y2
```

The first GET POINT statement assigns the coordinate values of the first point to X1 and Y1, while the second statement assigns values to X2 and Y2. The PLOT LINES statement then draws a line between the two designated points.

Our example program creates a split screen, with the upper window a graphics window and the lower window a command window. A border is drawn around the graphics window. The prompt ''Command?'' appears in the command window. No cursor is visible because the entire screen is placed in hires graphics mode.

The available commands are

h . . . . . help, display the available commands
l . . . . . draw a single line between two points
b . . . . . draw a rectangular box
t . . . . . write a single line of text
−l . . . . . erase a line
−b . . . . . erase a box
−t . . . . . erase text and its enclosing box
q . . . . . quit the program

The Help (h) and Quit (q) commands are self-explanatory. The Line (l) command draws a line after you mark two points. Move the cross-hairs to the first point and press the Enter key; then repeat for the second point. A line appears immediately, joining the two points.

The Box (b) command draws a box after you mark the locations of its lower left and its upper right corners. Follow the same procedure of moving the cross-hairs and pressing the Enter key as you did with the Line command. The Text (t) command first asks you to enter a line of text in the command window. It writes that text in the graphics window after you move the cross-hairs to the position where the first character (specifically, its lower left corner) will be placed, and press the Enter key.

The Minus Line (−l) command erases a line after you mark both ends with the cross-hairs. The Minus Box (−b) command erases a box in the same way, but in this case you must mark the lower left and the upper right corners of the box. The Minus Text (−t) command erases a line of text **only if the line is enclosed in a box.** Place the cross-hairs anywhere inside the box and press the Enter key—both the text and the box will disappear.

Here is the complete program:

```
! Example Program 12-18.
! Draws lines, boxes and text on the screen,
! and allows these figures to be erased.

! Open windows and establish coordinates.
SET mode "hires"
OPEN #1: screen 0, 1, 0, .08
SET window 1, 80, 1, 2
OPEN #2: screen 0, 1, .08, 1
SET window 1, 80, 1, 22
BOX LINES 1, 80, 2, 22
! Coordinates of center, window #2
LET X = 40
LET Y = 12

DO  ! main command loop
   WINDOW #1
   LINE INPUT prompt "Command? ": Action$
   ! Prefix with minus sign to erase.
   IF Action$[1:1] = "-" then
      LET Action$ = ucase$(Action$[2:2])
   ELSE
      LET Action$ = lcase$(Action$[1:1])
   END IF
   SELECT CASE Action$

   CASE "l"  ! single line between points
        WINDOW #2
        DRAW Line (X, Y)

   CASE "L"  ! erase a line
        WINDOW #2
        ASK color Hue$
        SET color background
        DRAW Line (X, Y)
        SET color Hue$

   CASE "b"  ! rectangular box
        WINDOW #2
        DRAW Box (X, Y)

   CASE "B"  ! erase a box
        WINDOW #2
        ASK color Hue$
        SET color background
        DRAW Box (X, Y)
        SET color Hue$
```

```
   CASE "t"  ! line of text
        LINE INPUT prompt "Text? ": Text$
        WINDOW #2
        DRAW Text (X, Y, Text$)

   CASE "T"  ! erase text and enclosing box
        WINDOW #2
        ASK color Hue$
        GET POINT: X, Y ! point inside box
        FLOOD X, Y
        SET color background
        FLOOD X, Y
        SET color Hue$

   CASE "h", "H"  ! list the menu
        PRINT "Commands are Line, Box, Text, Help or Quit."
        PRINT "Precede command with minus sign to erase."

   CASE "q", "Q"  ! go to END SELECT

   CASE else
        PRINT "Commands are Line, Box, Text, Help or Quit."

   END SELECT
LOOP until Action$ = "q"
WINDOW #1
PRINT "Press ENTER to erase the screen."
END

PICTURE Set (X, Y)
    ! Set cross-hairs at position X, Y.
    ASK color Hue$
    PLOT POINTS: X, Y
    SET color background
    PLOT POINTS: X, Y
    SET color Hue$
END PICTURE

SUB Coords (X1, Y1, X2, Y2)
    ! Get coordinates of two points.
    GET POINT: X1, Y1
    PLOT POINTS: X1, Y1
    GET POINT: X2, Y2
    PLOT POINTS: X2, Y2
END SUB

PICTURE Line (X, Y)
    ! Draw line between two points.
    DRAW Set (X, Y)
    CALL Coords (X1, Y1, X2, Y2)
    PLOT LINES: X1,Y1; X2,Y2
    LET X = X2 + 1
    LET Y = Y2 + 1
END PICTURE

PICTURE Box (X, Y)
    ! Draw a rectangular box.
```

```
        DRAW Set (X, Y)
        CALL Coords (X1, Y1, X2, Y2)
        BOX LINES X1, X2, Y1, Y2
        LET X = X1 - 1
        LET Y = Y1 - 1
    END PICTURE

    PICTURE Text (X, Y, Text$)
        ! Display a line of text.
        DRAW Set (X, Y)
        GET POINT: X1, Y1
        PLOT TEXT, at X1, Y1: Text$
        LET X = X1 - 1
        LET Y = Y1 - 1
    END PICTURE
```

After opening the graphics and command windows, and prompting for a command, the program uses a SELECT CASE statement to execute the command. Most of the work is done in a series of five subprograms.

The Set picture unit establishes the location in the graphics window where the cross-hairs will appear. The first PLOT POINTS statement establishes a location and colors that location with the existing color. The second PLOT POINTS statement uses background color to make the location invisible. This location then becomes the point where the cross-hairs will appear when the next GET POINT statement is executed.

The Coords subroutine unit plots two points, one at location (X1, Y1) and the other at location (X2, Y2). These two points are used by other subprograms for drawing figures.

The Line picture unit first calls the Set picture unit to establish a location for displaying the cross-hairs. It calls the Coords subroutine to plot the two end points of a line and draws the line with a PLOT LINES statement. It then assigns new values to X and Y, establishing a new coordinate set near one end of the line for the next location of the cross-hairs.

The Box picture unit behaves similarly, establishing a cross-hairs location and plotting two points. It uses the BOX LINES statement to draw a rectangular box. It assigns new values to X and Y so that the next location of the cross-hairs will be near the lower left corner of the box.

The Text picture unit uses the GET POINT statement to locate a point and the PLOT TEXT statement to write a line of text in the graphics window. The next location of the cross-hairs will be near the first character in the text line.

The commands to erase a line or box are quite simple. The color is changed to background and the line or box is drawn again, effectively erasing it. It is important, of course, that the cross-hairs be used to mark the two ends of the line and the two proper corners of the box.

The command to erase text works a little differently. Before text can be erased, it must be enclosed in a box. The cross-hairs are then placed anywhere inside the box and the Enter key is pressed. The first FLOOD statement fills the entire box with a solid color, overwriting the text, and then the second FLOOD statement erases the box of solid color.

Many additional commands could be added to this example program to make it a more useful drawing tool. We suggest one or two extensions in the practice programs.

IMPORTANT POINTS

A cursor is not displayed when you are in the graphics mode.

When in graphics mode, press the Enter key to return to text mode.

If you are drawing a geometric figure, you should specify a window coordinate system that matches the aspect ratio of your display unit screen.

Drawing the same figure with color "background" will effectively erase an existing figure.

Transformations take place about the center of the coordinate system, not necessarily the center of the figure.

SELF-TEST QUESTIONS

1. (a) What is a pixel? (b) How many pixels are available on the graphics screen defined in this chapter?
2. If your console is set in "bw80" mode, (a) is graphics supported, and (b) are all 256 characters available for display?
3. If your console is set in "hires" mode, (a) is graphics supported, and (b) are all 256 characters available for display?
4. After you have displayed a graphics figure on the screen, what must you do to return to the normal text screen?
5. (a) Is the cursor displayed in graphics mode? (b) Can text be displayed in graphics mode?
6. What statement causes a program to halt execution for one minute?
7. What statement is used to establish window coordinates?
8. When we refer to the point (5, 10), (a) what is the Y coordinate value, and (b) is it measured horizontally or vertically?
9. (a) Why is it important to know the aspect ratio of your display screen? (b) What is the aspect ratio of your screen?
10. If your display screen has an aspect ratio of 1.5 and the vertical coordinate scale goes from 0 to 80, the horizontal coordinate scale should go from 0 to what value?
11. What are the default coordinates if your entire screen is designated a graphics window?
12. What statement plots a point at location X = 3, Y = 5?
13. What statement draws a line from location (3, 5) to location (10, 10)?
14. Write a statement to draw a square with one corner at location (0, 0) and another corner at location (20, 20).
15. Write a statement to erase the square drawn in Question 14.

16. (a) What statement displays the word "READY?" at location (20, 20) on the graphics screen? (b) What part of which letter is located at point (20, 20)?
17. When drawing a circle with the BOX ELLIPSE statement, how is the location of the circle specified?
18. (a) What statement saves a BOX figure? (b) Where is the saved figure stored?
19. What color is usually represented by the color number zero?
20. How is an external picture unit called by the calling program unit?
21. (a) What transformation statement rotates a figure 30 degrees clockwise? (b) The rotation is about what point? (c) What other statement is required in a program when an angle is specified in degrees?
22. What statement allows a program to use the GRAPHLIB.TRU library file?
23. How do you determine where the cross-hairs will be displayed when a GET POINT statement is executed?

PRACTICE PROGRAMS

Use the hires graphics mode. Unless otherwise specified, use a window with a vertical coordinate scale from 0 to 100 and a horizontal coordinate scale from 0 to (100 * A), where A is the aspect ratio of your screen.

1. Display a figure consisting of three square boxes, of side length 10, 20, and 30 units, all centered at the center of the screen.
2. Display a figure consisting of three concentric circles, of radii 10, 20, and 30 units, all centered at the center of the screen.
3. Write a picture unit that draws a circle of radius R with its center at location (X, Y). Pass as parameters the circle radius and the coordinates of the center of the circle. Display an error message if the circle overlaps any of the window boundaries.

   Test your picture unit in a program, using a radius of 30 units and center coordinates of X = 40 units, Y = 40 units. Also test with a radius of 50 units and the same center coordinates.
4. Display a bar graph showing the following information on student enrollment:

Year	Students
1970	13,000
1975	15,000
1980	16,000
1985	16,500

   Use the standard horizontal coordinate scale and a vertical coordinate scale from 0 to 20,000. Each bar should be 10 units wide. Place a label above each bar indicating the year.
5. Enhance the bar graph in Practice Program 4 by drawing a vertical axis with labels for enrollments of 0, 5,000, 10,000, 15,000, and 20,000.

6. The rise and subsequent fall in sales of a new computer company can be modeled by the equation

$$\text{Sales(T)} = \text{S} + \text{B}\,exp(\text{CT}) - \text{D}\,exp(\text{ET})$$

where T is the time in years and *exp* is the exponential function, one of the standard functions of True BASIC. The coefficient S is the sales rate (units per year) at the beginning of the time period. The coefficients B, C, D, and E are adjustable in order to model different predicted performances. Assume the following coefficient values:

S = 50,000
B = 50
C = 1.10
D = 5
E = 1.37

Use a horizontal coordinate range of -1 to 11, allowing 10 years to be plotted. Use a vertical coordinate range of $-10{,}000$ to 100,000, allowing sales of up to 100,000 units per year to be plotted. Define the sales growth function Sales(T) in your program. Assume the beginning year is 1977 and draw a horizontal axis for a ten-year period with each year labeled. Plot sales over this ten-year period or until sales fall to zero. Be sure to use a small enough step in your plotting routine to produce a smooth curve.

7. Write a picture unit to draw axes close to the left edge and bottom edge of the screen. Use a horizontal coordinate range of -1 to 10 and a vertical coordinate range of -10 to 100. Place the intersection of the two axes at the origin of your coordinate system. The X axis runs from 0 to 10; the Y axis from 0 to 100.

The horizontal axis has ticks (small lines perpendicular to the axis) spaced DeltaX units apart, while the vertical axis has ticks spaced DeltaY units apart. Pass DeltaX and DeltaY as parameters to the picture unit.

Test this picture unit in a program that displays the curve of Example Program 12-4. Use values of DeltaX = 1 and DeltaY = 10.

8. Example Program 12-18 is an interactive graphics program. Add two new commands to this program; one to draw a circle in the graphics window, using the Circle (c) command, and one to erase a circle, using the Minus Circle ($-$c) command. Position the circle by using the cross-hairs first to position its center and then to position a point on its circumference. Hint: The best way to erase a circle might be to flood it with a solid color and then flood it again with the background color.

13 Programming with Matrices

13.1 INTRODUCTION

The word *matrix* is another name for an array, usually an array of numbers. We introduced arrays in Chapter 8 and showed how to use them in solving problems. You will remember that we often used FOR-NEXT loops, either single loops or double nested loops, to assign values to array elements or to display these elements. All manipulation of arrays ultimately required manipulation of the individual elements.

In this chapter, we introduce MAT statements that simplify matrix or array operations. We also discuss simple matrix arithmetic, particularly the addition and subtraction of matrices.

13.2 MAT STATEMENTS

A set of special statements in True BASIC, called *MAT statements,* allows us to manipulate matrices as entities, according to the rules of matrix arithmetic. Manipulating matrices in matrix arithmetic is in many ways similar to manipulating numbers in ordinary arithmetic. MAT statements allow us to manipulate arrays of strings as well as arrays of numbers.

If you are not a mathematician, you may wonder why you should be concerned about matrix arithmetic and the MAT statements. One reason is that MAT statements allow you to do certain things with matrices or arrays, such as changing their size in the middle of a program, that cannot be accomplished in any other way. Another reason is that they allow you to write simpler programs, because a single MAT statement can often replace half-a-dozen ordinary statements.

13.3 READING AND WRITING MATRICES

A matrix is an array, and as you know, every array must be dimensioned in a DIM statement before it can be used or referenced in any other program statement. The DIM statement specifies the number of dimensions and the size of each dimension. This size can be specified by a single number or in terms of a lower bound and an upper bound. We will normally work with matrices having a lower bound of one and thus will specify the size with a single number. For example,

```
DIM Vector(100)
DIM Transform(3,3)
```

MAT statements can also be used with arrays having any legal lower bound and upper bound, such as

```
DIM Spread(0:100,0:50)
```

The MAT INPUT Statement

The fundamental statement to read matrix values from the keyboard or from a text file is the MAT INPUT statement. This statement reads in values and assigns them to the matrix elements. It assigns the first value to the first element of the first row and continues assigning values in that row, from left to right, until all elements in the row have been assigned values. It then starts assigning values to the elements in the second row and continues in this manner until values have been assigned to all matrix elements. This method of accessing elements and assigning values is often called *odometer order,* meaning that the last index (in this case, the second or column index) varies the fastest.

Here is an example program to read a matrix:

```
! Example Program 13-1.
! Read matrix from the keyboard.

DIM Ratio(5,4)
MAT INPUT Ratio
END
```

The MAT INPUT statement is similar to the regular INPUT statement. A question mark is displayed as a prompt to the user to enter element values. The first number entered is assigned to element Ratio(1,1), the second to element Ratio(1,2), and so forth. Several numbers, separated by commas, can be entered on the same line.

In this example, 20 numbers must be entered to fill the array. If you press the Enter key before all numbers have been entered, you will receive the message "Too few input items. Please add more." and another question mark prompt.

Compare the simplicity of Example Program 13-1 with the following example using nested FOR-NEXT loops.

```
! Example Program 13-2.
! Read matrix using nested loops.

DIM Ratio(5,4)
FOR I = 1 to 5
    FOR J = 1 to 4
        INPUT Ratio(I,J)
    NEXT J
NEXT I
END
```

Both programs accomplish the same task, but Example Program 13-1 is considerably shorter and probably easier to understand.

The MAT PRINT Statement

Having entered information into an array, we can use the MAT PRINT statement to display this information on the screen. The MAT PRINT statement displays the element values by rows, in odometer order.

```
! Example Program 13-3.
! Read matrix from keyboard
! and display on screen.

DIM Ratio(5,4)
MAT INPUT Ratio
MAT PRINT Ratio
END
```

Element values are displayed one to a print zone, just as if a comma had been placed between the elements in an ordinary PRINT statement. Each time the computer finishes displaying a complete row, the cursor moves to the beginning of the next row. If 20 single-digit numbers are entered in response to the MAT INPUT statement, here is what the output might look like

```
 9             4             5             7
-2             6             7             4
 1            -9             3             2
 9             8             7             6
 2             7             3             9
```

We choose our example carefully so that each row will fit on the page. If you have a matrix with more elements per row, you can either reduce the size of the print zone using the SET ZONEWIDTH statement or place a trailing semicolon after the MAT PRINT statement. We modify our program by adding a trailing semicolon

```
! Example Program 13-4.
! Use of trailing semicolon after MAT PRINT.

DIM Ratio(5,4)
MAT INPUT Ratio
MAT PRINT Ratio;
END
```

and produce the following result

```
 9  4  5  7
-2  6  7  4
 1 -9  3  2
 9  8  7  6
 2  7  3  9
```

Redimensioning Matrices

A powerful attribute of the MAT INPUT statement is its ability to redimension an array. The number of dimensions cannot be changed, but the size of each dimension can be modified. For example, the statement

```
MAT INPUT Ratio(10,10)
```

changes the size of the Ratio array from 5 by 4 (see Example Program 13-1) to 10 by 10. Remember that redimensioning only changes the value of the upper bound, not the lower bound. The following statements are all legal ways of changing the size of the array in our last example:

```
MAT INPUT Ratio(2,2)
MAT INPUT Ratio(1 to 3, 1 to 6)
MAT INPUT Ratio(J, 1 to K)
```

In the first example, Ratio is redimensioned to an array with two rows and two columns. In the second example, Ratio is redimensioned to an array with three rows, numbered 1 through 3, and six columns, numbered 1 through 6.

The third case is particularly interesting because it redimensions the array on the basis of variable values. These values can be assigned from within the program. In this example, Ratio is redimensioned to an array with J rows, numbered from 1 to J, and K columns numbered from 1 to K. The values stored in J and K will be used to redimension the matrix when the MAT INPUT statement is executed.

The MAT INPUT statement has a special form of redimensioning for numeric arrays of one dimension. If a MAT INPUT statement is written as

```
MAT INPUT NumList(?)
```

the array NumList is redimensioned to hold as many numbers as are typed in. **This special form of redimensioning applies only to one dimensional arrays of numbers.**

For example,

```
! Example Program 13-5.
! Use of variable array dimensioning.

DIM NumList(1)
MAT INPUT NumList(?)
PRINT "No. of items in list is"; ubound(NumList)
MAT PRINT NumList;
END
```

The size of NumList is set initially to one, knowing that it will be redimensioned later. This program allows a user to type in a sequence of numbers, separated by commas, and the size of the array is adjusted to conform to the number of items entered. The process of entering items terminates when the Enter key is pressed. The size of the array is then displayed on the screen and the array itself is printed.

If you enter the following sequence of numbers in response to the question mark prompt,

```
? 1,2,3,4,5,6,7,8,9
```

the program will display the following results:

```
No. of items in list is 9
 1  2  3  4  5  6  7  8  9
```

13.4 MORE ON READING AND WRITING MATRICES

Other MAT INPUT Statements

The general form of the MAT INPUT statement is

```
MAT INPUT Array1, Array2,...
```

In most cases, a program is easier to use and understand if the MAT INPUT statement is used to enter only a single array, and that will be our usual practice.

A prompt can be added to the MAT INPUT statement, using the format

```
MAT INPUT prompt Expr$: Array1, Array2,...
```

where *Expr$* is any string expression, variable, or constant. This statement displays the prompt and expects the user to enter a sequence of numbers, separated by commas.

If an array has string elements, the MAT LINE INPUT statement is allowed and preferred. Characters are entered into each string element until a carriage return is encountered. The general form is

```
MAT LINE INPUT Array1$, Array2$,...
```

or

```
MAT LINE INPUT prompt Expr$: Array1$, Array2$,...
```

The MAT LINE INPUT PROMPT statement is not very useful because **it displays the prompt string only for the first item entered.** A single question mark is displayed for each subsequent item. For this reason, we usually display a line of general input instructions rather than a prompt and then use the plain MAT LINE INPUT statement.

Our next example program enters names into an array. We again set the initial size of the array Name$ to one. The MAT LINE INPUT statement will accept lines containing commas, such as "John J. Williams, Jr." Note that this statement is used both to redimension the array and to accept input.

```
! Example Program 13-6.
! Enter names into an array.

DIM Name$(1)
INPUT PROMPT "Number of names to enter? ": Number
PRINT "Enter one name at each ? prompt."
MAT LINE INPUT Name$(Number)
PRINT Number; "names have been entered."
END
```

The disadvantage of this program is that the user must specify at the beginning how many names will be entered. If you want to enter an unknown number of names into an array, one solution is to dimension the array large enough to hold the maximum number of names and use a special entry to indicate when the last name has been entered. In this case, you must use a loop instead of a MAT statement.

Here is an example:

```
! Example Program 13-7.
! Use part of a large array to store names.

DIM Name$(100)
PRINT "No more than 100 names may be entered."
PRINT "To stop, press ENTER key after prompt."
LET Count = 1
LET Finished$ = "false"
DO
   LINE INPUT prompt "Name? ": Name$(Count)
   IF Name$(Count) = "" then
      LET Finished$ = "true"
   ELSE
      LET Count = Count + 1
   END IF
LOOP until Count > 100 or Finished$ = "true"
PRINT (Count - 1); "names have been entered."
END
```

Note that the counter Count is initialized to one and incremented only if a valid name is entered. If you enter a null value for Name$ to stop the entry process, the flag Finished$ is set to true. After exiting the loop, Count will be one larger than the number of names entered and must be decremented by one to represent the number of names.

Special redimensioning using the question mark (see the previous section) is not allowed with the MAT LINE INPUT statement. The Enter key is used in this statement to mark the end of each string and thus cannot also be used to identify the last string.

The MAT READ Statement

The MAT READ statement is used to read array element values from one or more DATA statements. The general format is

MAT READ *Array1, Array2,...*

As before, we prefer to read only a single array. The program must contain one or more DATA statements with numeric or string values separated from one another by commas.

If there are more values in the DATA statements than are required by the MAT READ statement, the extra values will be ignored. If there is an insufficient number of values, the error message ''Reading past end of data'' will be displayed.

Here is an example where only the first four data values are used:

```
! Example Program 13-8.
! Read element values from data statements.

DIM Table(1,1)
MAT READ Table(2,2)
MAT PRINT Table

DATA 1,2,3,4,5
END
```

When this program is executed, the following table will be displayed:

```
1                2
3                4
```

Note that the MAT READ statement can be used in the same way as the MAT INPUT statement to redimension an array.

Other MAT PRINT Statements

The general form of the MAT PRINT statement is

MAT PRINT *Array1, Array2,...*

This statement first displays *Array1*, then displays *Array2*, and so forth. To simplify formatting problems, we recommend that you use the MAT PRINT statement to display only a single array.

Commas not only separate the array names, but they also specify that the elements in a row be displayed in different print zones. Another form of the MAT PRINT statement, namely,

```
MAT PRINT Array1; Array2;...
```

will separate the elements in a row by only one or two spaces. It is even possible to use both separators in the same statement, such as

```
MAT PRINT Array1; Array2, Array3;
```

In this case, the elements in the rows of *Array1* will be separated by 1 or 2 spaces, those in the rows of *Array2* by 16 spaces (or the current print zone width), and those in the rows of *Array3* by 1 or 2 spaces. We repeat, however, that in most cases we prefer to display only a single array with each MAT PRINT statement.

A format string, used to control the format of array rows, can be included in the MAT PRINT USING statement. The syntax is

```
MAT PRINT using Format$: Array1, Array2,...
```

where *Format$* is a string constant or variable containing format specifications for displaying the elements in each row.

Here is an example program that displays a two-column array consisting of part numbers and unit prices.

```
! Example Program 13-9.
! Display an array of part numbers and prices.

DIM Inventory(6,2)
LET F1$ = "########            #####"
PRINT using F1$: "PART NO.", "PRICE"
PRINT
MAT READ Inventory
LET F2$ = "######              $$$.##"
MAT PRINT using F2$: Inventory

DATA 163151,12.85,177762,33.40,183926,18.75
DATA 205055,7.55,234965,81.60,309835,2.25
END
```

The output will look like this:

```
PART NO.     PRICE

163151      $12.85
177762      $33.40
183926      $18.75
205055       $7.55
234965      $81.60
309835       $2.25
```

13.5 STORING MATRICES ON FILES

The MAT PRINT # Statement

The general statement to write a matrix to a text file is

```
MAT PRINT #N: Array1, Array2,...
```

This statement writes matrix elements on file number N in the same format that they would be displayed on the screen. **The statement has limited usefulness because a file written with this statement cannot be read by a subsequent MAT INPUT statement.** You remember that we suggested you write text data files with one item per line and the MAT PRINT statement violates this principle. **Thus we will not use this statement in our examples.**

The MAT INPUT # Statement

Matrix element values can be read from a text file instead of from the keyboard, provided that they were written to the file in an appropriate format. We will assume one element value per line. The general statements are

```
MAT INPUT #N: Array1, Array2,...
MAT LINE INPUT #N: Array1$, Array2$,...
```

As mentioned earlier, it is usually preferable to read only a single array with either of these statements. The number N is the file or channel number, assigned to a file by the OPEN statement.

Here are two examples that use arrays and text files. Example Program 13-10 writes a list of names on a file, recording the number of names as the first element in the file. Example Program 13-11 reads these names from a file and places them in a one-dimensional array.

The first program uses subroutines to open the file and to enter names into an array. The latter task cannot be accomplished easily with a MAT statement because the number of names to be entered is not known. Thus the array holding the names cannot be redimensioned.

As an alternative to redimensioning, the array is dimensioned to a large size and only part of the array is used to hold names. The number of names is passed back to the calling program unit and written on the file as the first item. A FOR loop is used in the main program to write the names themselves on the file. MAT statements are not used in this program.

```
! Example Program 13-10.
! Enter list of names and write them on a file.
! Record number of names as first item in file.
```

```
DIM Name$(100)
CALL OpenWriteFile (#1)
LET Number = 0
CALL EnterNames (Number, Name$)
! Store number of names on the file
PRINT #1: Number
! Store the names themselves on the file.
FOR I = 1 to Number
    PRINT #1: Name$(I)
NEXT I
PRINT Number; "names written on file."
END  ! main program

EXTERNAL SUB OpenWriteFile (#99)
    ! Open an empty text file for writing.
    INPUT prompt "Name of file? ": FileName$
    LET X = pos(FileName$, ":")
    IF X = 0 then
       INPUT prompt "On which drive? ": Drive$
       LET FileName$ = Drive$[1:1] & ":" & FileName$
    END IF
    OPEN #99: name FileName$, create newold
    ERASE #99
END SUB

EXTERNAL SUB EnterNames (Count, List$())
    ! Enter names into an array.
    PRINT "No more than 100 names may be entered."
    PRINT "To stop, press ENTER key after prompt."
    LET Count = 1
    LET Finished$ = "false"
    DO
       ! Form the prompt string.
       PRINT "Name("; str$(Count); ")? ";
       LINE INPUT prompt "": List$(Count)
       IF List$(Count) = "" then
          LET Finished$ = "true"
       ELSE
          LET Count = Count + 1
       END IF
    LOOP until Count > 100 or Finished$ = "true"
    ! Adjust counter for number of entered names.
    LET Count = Count - 1
END SUB
```

Subroutine OpenWriteFile asks for a file name. If the name contains a colon, we assume that the disk drive has been specified. If not, the user is asked to enter the disk drive prefix.

Subroutine EnterNames prompts the user to enter a name. The index value of the name is displayed in the PRINT statement prompt. Note the use of a null string prompt in the LINE INPUT statement to suppress the normal question mark prompt of that statement. As before (see Example Program 13-7), the counter Count must be adjusted.

In the second example program, we can determine both the number of names and the names themselves by reading the file. This knowledge allows us to use a MAT statement and redimension the array into which the names are read. To display the names on separate lines, we set the print zone width to 80 columns and use the MAT PRINT statement.

```
! Example Program 13-11.
! Read names from file and store in array.
! Then display the list of names.

DIM Name$(1)
CALL OpenReadFile(#1)
INPUT #1: Size
MAT LINE INPUT #1: Name$(Size)
SET zonewidth 80
MAT PRINT Name$
END

EXTERNAL SUB OpenReadFile (#99)
    ! Open a text file for reading.
    INPUT prompt "Name of file? ": FileName$
    LET X = pos(FileName$, ":")
    IF X = 0 then
       INPUT prompt "On which drive? ": Drive$
       LET FileName$ = Drive$[1:1] & ":" & FileName$
    END IF
    OPEN #99: name FileName$
END SUB
```

The MAT WRITE # and MAT READ # Statements

MAT statements are also available to write information on and read information from record files. The statement

```
MAT WRITE #N: Array1, Array2,...
```

writes arrays on a record file, one array element per record. The MAT WRITE statement is usually used with only a single array. The array is written by rows, in odometer order, with element(1,1) being written on the first record, element(1,2) on the second record, and so forth.

The general statement for reading information from a record file is

```
MAT READ #N: Array1, Array2,...
```

Here is a simple program to read an array of numbers from DATA statements and write the array on a record file. The record size is set to 8 because the array elements are numbers and each number occupies 8 bytes on a record file.

```
! Example Program 13-12.
! Write an array on a record file.
```

```
DIM Array(3,3)
INPUT prompt "Name of file? ": FileName$
LET X = pos(FileName$, ":")
IF X = 0 then
   INPUT prompt "On disk in which drive? ": Drive$
   LET FileName$ = Drive$[1:1] & ":" & FileName$
END IF
OPEN #1: name FileName$, create newold
ERASE #1
SET #1: recsize 8
MAT READ Array
MAT WRITE #1: Array
CLOSE #1

DATA 2,5,3,7,5,8,7,9,1
END
```

A companion program reads the record file and displays the array.

```
! Example Program 13-13.
! Read an array from a record file.

DIM Array(3,3)
INPUT prompt "Name of file? ": FileName$
LET X = pos(FileName$, ":")
IF X = 0 then
   INPUT prompt "On disk in which drive? ": Drive$
   LET FileName$ = Drive$[1:1] & ":" & FileName$
END IF
OPEN #1: name FileName$
MAT READ #1: Array
MAT PRINT Array;
END
```

Note in this case that it is not necessary to specify a record size because the file has already been created. The trailing semicolon in the MAT PRINT statement displays the array in a compact tabular format, as shown:

```
2  5  3
7  5  8
7  9  1
```

Three points on using MAT statements are worth repeating:

1. **We recommend using a single array with each of these statements.** The resulting program is simpler and easier to understand.
2. In some cases, MAT statements will produce the best and simplest program; in other cases, a loop is required. You should use whichever structure is most appropriate.
3. A powerful feature of the MAT statements is their ability to redimension arrays, using a constant, variable, or expression to change the upper-bound value of any dimension.

13.6 MATRIX ARITHMETIC

A set of mathematical rules exists that allows us to manipulate matrices in much the same way that we manipulate numbers. We can assign a value to a matrix, which means assigning a value to every element of the matrix. We can use the common arithmetic operations with matrices, such as addition, subtraction, multiplication, and division, but with some restrictions and differences from number arithmetic.

Matrix arithmetic is useful in solving certain specialized business problems. We will discuss some of the simpler operations of matrix arithmetic and their implementation in True BASIC. If you are interested in learning more, we suggest that you read a book containing information on matrix arithmetic, such as *College Algebra*, second edition, by Fleming and Varberg, Prentice-Hall, Inc., 1984.

Matrix Assignments

The element values of one matrix can be assigned to the corresponding elements of another matrix. For example, if both A and B are matrices with two rows and columns, the statement

```
MAT A = B
```

assigns the value of B(1, 1) to A(1, 1), the value of B(1, 2) to A(1, 2), and so forth. Here is an example program:

```
! Example Program 13-14.
! Matrix assignment.

DIM A(2,2), B(2,2)
MAT INPUT B
MAT A = B
MAT PRINT A;
END
```

If you enter these values for B,

```
? 7,1,-2,8
```

the program will display these values for A:

```
 7  1
-2  8
```

You must watch out for one special feature of the matrix assignment statement. **The matrix assignment statement can redimension a matrix.** Remember that redimensioning can change only the size of a dimension (which it does by changing the upper bound), not the number of dimensions. The best way to demonstrate this feature is to write the previous example with a different matrix B.

```
! Example Program 13-15.
! Matrix assignment with redimensioning.

DIM A(2,2), B(2,3)
MAT INPUT B
MAT A = B
MAT PRINT A;
END
```

Note that matrix B is now dimensioned as a 2-by-3 matrix. When you run the program, you will have to enter six numbers to assign values to all the elements in B, as shown:

```
? 7,1,5,-2,8,3
```

Now the matrix assignment statement (MAT A = B) redimensions matrix A so that it is also a 2-by-3 matrix. The program then displays matrix A:

```
 7  1  5
-2  8  3
```

Matrix redimensioning is both a blessing and a curse. The ability to redimension a matrix with the MAT INPUT or MAT READ statements is a powerful and useful feature of True BASIC. Automatic redimensioning in a matrix assignment statement, however, can lead to unexpected results. When assigning the values of one matrix to another, we usually make sure that both matrices are of the same size so that redimensioning does not occur.

You can also use the matrix assignment statement to assign the same value to every element in an array. The value can be a constant or the value of a variable or an expression. Here is an example program

```
! Example Program 13-16.
! Assign a value to each array element.

DIM Table$(3,3)
MAT Table$ = ("xxxx")
MAT PRINT Table$
END
```

that produces the following display:

```
xxxx            xxxx            xxxx
xxxx            xxxx            xxxx
xxxx            xxxx            xxxx
```

Note that the parentheses around "xxxx" are not required in this case, but they are required if the expression on the right side of the assignment statement is anything other than a constant or a simple variable.

Matrix Addition and Subtraction

Adding two matrices means adding the values of the corresponding elements of the two matrices. If B and C are both 2-by-2 matrices, you create the sum matrix A with the statement

```
MAT A = B + C
```

where A(1, 1) = B(1, 1) + C(1, 1), A(1, 2) = B(1, 2) + C(1, 2), and so forth. Matrices B and C must have the same number of dimensions and be of the same size. If needed, matrix A will be redimensioned to the size of B and C, but as in the case of assignment, we recommend avoiding such redimensioning. Here is an example:

```
! Example Program 13-17.
! Matrix addition.

DIM A(2,2), B(2,2), C(2,2)
MAT READ B
MAT INPUT C
MAT A = B + C
MAT PRINT A;

DATA 3,3,3,3
END
```

If you enter the values

```
? 1,2,3,5
```

the program will display

```
4  5
6  8
```

Subtraction is similar to addition and here is a program that does both addition and subtraction:

```
! Example Program 13-18.
! Matrix addition and subtraction.

DIM A(2,2), B(2,2), C(2,2), D(2,2)
MAT READ B, C, D
MAT A = B + C
MAT A = A - D
MAT PRINT A;

DATA 1,2,3,5
DATA 2,1,1,2
DATA 3,7,1,4
END
```

This program displays the array

```
0 -4
3  3
```

Note that a single expression such as MAT A = B + C − D is not allowed. Only two matrices are permitted on the right side of the MAT expression and thus two MAT statements are needed to accomplish the addition and subtraction.

Matrix Multiplication and Division

Multiplication of two matrices is allowed only under certain conditions. Division of one matrix by another is not defined, but there is an equivalent process of multiplying one matrix by the inverse of another matrix. These operations really cannot be understood without some background in matrix arithmetic, and we will not discuss them here.

You should know, however, that True BASIC does have statements for multiplying two matrices and for inverting a matrix. If you need to use either of these operations, consult the previously recommended book on matrix arithmetic and the True BASIC reference manual.

Multiplying a matrix by a single constant, variable, or expression means multiplying each element of the matrix by the same value. The syntax is

```
MAT A = N * B
```

where N is a constant, variable, or expression and B is a matrix. Note that N must come before B—the statement MAT A = B * N is not allowed. If N is an expression, it must be enclosed in parentheses.

Here is an example where a list of prices is read from data statements and each price is increased by 20 percent (multiplied by 1.2).

```
! Example Program 13-19.
! Multiply an array by a constant.

DIM Price(4)
LET Increase = 20   ! percent increase
MAT READ Price
MAT Price = (1 + Increase/100) * Price
MAT PRINT Price

DATA 12.45, 13.95, 8.40, 2.95
END
```

The results displayed by this example program are

```
14.94              16.74              10.08              3.54
```

IMPORTANT POINTS

Accessing array elements in odometer order means accessing the elements so that the last index varies the fastest. In a two-dimensional array, this means accessing the elements by row, from left to right.

The MAT INPUT and MAT READ statements assign values to array elements in odometer order.

Any MAT INPUT or MAT READ statement can be used to redimension an array.

The MAT PRINT and MAT WRITE statements read values from array elements in odometer order.

The statement MAT INPUT Array(?) is a special form of redimensioning allowed only with one-dimensional arrays of numeric values.

The MAT LINE INPUT PROMPT statement displays its prompt only before the first value is entered, not before subsequent values.

The MAT PRINT # statement has only limited usefulness because a text file written with this statement cannot be read by a MAT INPUT # statement.

We recommend using only a single array variable with the MAT INPUT, MAT READ, MAT PRINT, and MAT WRITE statements.

The matrix assignment statement can be used to redimension an array.

SELF-TEST QUESTIONS

1. What is the difference, if any, between a matrix and an array?

2. In what order does the MAT INPUT statement assign values to array elements?

3. What are the differences, if any, between the displays produced by the statement

```
MAT PRINT Array;
```

and the statement

```
MAT PRINT Array
```

4. If an array Index is dimensioned by DIM Index(3,3), which of the following statements is allowed:

a) MAT INPUT Index(2,2)
b) MAT INPUT Index(5,5)
c) MAT INPUT Index(2,5)
d) MAT INPUT Index(1:3,2:5)
e) MAT INPUT Index(1:2,1 to 3)
f) MAT INPUT Index(7,0 to 7)

5. What is meant by the term ''odometer order''?

6. (a) Is the statement MAT INPUT Line$(?) a valid statement? (b) Is MAT INPUT Line(?) a valid statement?
7. Given an array dimensioned by DIM Name$(100), does the statement

```
MAT LINE INPUT prompt "Name? ": Name$
```

display the prompt before each name is entered?
8. In what format does the statement

```
MAT PRINT #1: Name$
```

store the elements of Name$ on file #1?
9. In what format does the statement

```
MAT LINE INPUT #1: Name$
```

expect to find the individual name values stored in file #1?
10. The statement

```
MAT WRITE #1: Array
```

is used to write an array on what type of file?
11. Are the following statements valid and legal?
    a) MAT A = B + C
    b) MAT A = B + C + D
    c) MAT A = B − C + D
12. In the statement MAT X = Y + Z, must (a) array Y be the same size as array X, and (b) array Y be the same size as array Z?
13. If A and B are arrays and N is a simple variable, are the following statements allowed?
    a) MAT A = B * N
    b) MAT A = N * B
14. What record size is required for a record file designed to store values of numeric variables?

PRACTICE PROGRAMS

Use MAT statements wherever possible in these programs.

1. A record file named CLIENTS.REC, with a record length of 40 bytes, contains name strings. These names are stored in the reverse format (last name, first name), with a comma serving as the field separator. Assume no other commas in the string.

   Open the file and determine the number of records. Transfer all names from the file to a redimensioned array. Write a modified array with the names in normal format (first name preceding last name). Display the names in the modified array on the screen.

2. A text file named EXPENSES.DAT contains expense categories (strings) and expense values (numbers), stored one item per line. The first line in the file contains a value representing the number of different expense categories. A sample file might contain:

```
3
Labor
32248.50
Feed
6742.82
Fertilizer
13840.00
```

Transfer all items from the file to a redimensioned array with two columns, one for expense categories and the other for expense values. Display an expense report in the following format:

```
              Farm Expenses

Labor                        $32248.50
Feed                          $6742.82
Fertilizer                   $13840.00
```

3. A record file named PRICES.REC contains a long list of prices, one per record. Due to inflation, all prices must be increased by 11.4 percent. Modify the file so that it contains the new prices.
4. Modify the PRICES.REC file discussed in Practice Program 3, decreasing all prices by 4.3 percent and adding a handling charge of $2.00 to each price.
5. Sales by division for the current year are shown in the following table:

SALES BY QUARTERS (MILLION $)

Division	1st	2nd	3rd	4th
1	3.6	3.7	3.8	3.6
2	1.7	1.5	1.9	2.0
3	5.1	4.8	4.9	5.2
4	1.0	1.0	0.9	1.1
5	8.5	8.5	8.5	8.4
6	5.2	5.4	5.6	5.8

Assuming that each division is required to produce a 9 percent increase in sales next year, calculate and display a revised table of estimated quarterly sales, using the same display format.

Calculate and display the row and column totals for this revised table, with appropriate labels.

14 An Indexed Database Program

We conclude our presentation of True BASIC with another database program that brings together many of the concepts and techniques discussed throughout the previous chapters. We will examine some points that are different from the example database program in Chapter 9, but there are certain areas of similarity.

AN INVENTORY DATA FILE

This example program accesses a file of inventory information. The inventory file is a record file, with all information on each inventory part stored in a record as a fixed-length string of 84 characters. Each item of information in the record is called a *field* and we have eight fields in our record. These fields are fixed length substrings of the record string.

We will use the part number as the primary identifier of a particular part. Because the inventory file is a large file, we also have an index file that tells us what record contains the information on a particular part. In this application, the part number field is called the *key field* .

Here is a outline of the inventory file record, showing the name and length of each field:

Field Name	Length (characters)
Part Number	6
Description	20
Quantity	8
Unit Price	8
Bin Number	4
Reorder Amount	8
Vendor Name	20
Vendor Phone	10
	84

USING AN INDEX FILE

To understand the concept and use of an index file, remember that one of the fastest ways to search a file or array is a binary search, but this search only works if the file or array is in sorted order. We could sort our inventory file on any field, say, part number, but each time we added a new part, we would have to sort the file again. This is a slow process because the file is long and the record size is large.

As an alternative, we can create another file, called an *index file,* that has small records containing only the part number and the record number. This file can be sorted more quickly than the inventory file. When we search the index file for a part number, we find the inventory file record number for that particular part. The index file gets its name because it is similar to an index in a book—it tells us which record in a file contains the desired information.

Here is how the information in the index file might look, displayed in an expanded form:

Part Number	Record Number
123161	15
202571	7
209115	113
399417	1
576102	23

As you see, we can easily determine the record number for any given part number. The part numbers are in sorted order, but not the record numbers. These record numbers are sometimes called *pointers* because they point to or indicate the record where information is stored for a particular part number.

Because the index file is a smaller file than the inventory file, it is often possible to read the index file into an array in memory and carry out the binary search in memory rather than on disk. This procedure yields a much faster search.

Another advantage of this type of organization is that we can have more than one index file. In addition to a file that is sorted by part number, we can have another file containing description and record number, and sorted by description. We can search this second index file for a particular description and find the corresponding record number in the inventory file.

PROGRAM OUTLINE

We design our program as a menu-driven program. We have a main program unit and several subprogram units. We include only three commands (plus a stop command) in our menu, and each command is executed from a separate subroutine. Other commands can be added and will be discussed in the practice programs at the end of the chapter.

Here is an outline of the main program unit:

Name inventory and index files.
Open both files.
Determine array size and read index file into array.
Begin loop.
  Display the command menu.
  Select a command: Quit, Edit, List, or Search.
  Branch to appropriate subprogram.
End loop if command is Quit.

The edit command allows a user to change any field (except the part number) in a specified record. If you don't know the record number, you can use the search command to find the record number corresponding to a given part number. A part number cannot be edited because a part number change would require re-sorting the index file, a procedure we wish to avoid in our simple program.

Information is stored in each inventory file record in a packed format to conserve space. *Packing* means storing the individual field strings as closely together as possible in the record. *Unpacking* means extracting the field values from a packed record. We will discuss later the procedures for packing and unpacking records.

Here is an outline of the edit subroutine:

Get record number.
Get field number.
If requested, display field names and numbers.
Read record from inventory file.
Unpack record string.

Begin loop.
    Display old field value.
    Enter new field value.
End loop when finished editing.
Pack record string.
Write new record to inventory file.
Return to menu.

The list command displays the contents of the inventory file. Each record is read, unpacked, and displayed on the screen.

Begin loop.
    Read record from inventory file.
    Unpack record string.
    Display record number.
    Display record fields.
End loop at end of inventory file.
Return to menu.

The search command uses a binary search to look in the index array for the record number corresponding to a specified part number. If the record exists, it is read, unpacked and displayed.

Get part number.
Search index array for record number.
If record exists,
    Read record from inventory file,
    Unpack record string,
    Display record number,
    Display record fields,
Else,
    Display failure message.
Return to menu.

THE MAIN PROGRAM

We call two subroutines from the main program in addition to the command subroutines. The subroutine Name asks the user for the name of the inventory file. If the user omits a disk drive designation, the prefix ''B:'' is added. If the user omits a three-letter type designation, the suffix ''.REC'' is added. An index file name is generated by adding the letter X to the beginning of the inventory file name. Note that only seven characters are allowed in the inventory file name to have enough space to generate the index file name.

Both files are opened in the main program, using error trapping routines. This program assumes that both files have already been created and loaded with information. If the inventory file does not exist, the user is asked to try again because the problem may be that the file name was misspelled. If the index file does not exist, the program is aborted because it will not work without a valid index file.

The size of the index file is determined and the index file is read into an array named Index$. Note the use of the MAT READ # statement to read the file and to redimension the array to the file size.

The subroutine Menu is called next and the menu is displayed. The CASE statement is used to call the selected command subroutine. If an invalid command is entered, an error message is printed and the menu is displayed again.

```
! Example Program 14-1.
! Inventory record file with index.

CLEAR
! If error in naming inventory file, let user try again.
DO
   CALL Name (Fname$, Xname$)
   WHEN error in
        OPEN #1: name Fname$
        LET NoFile$ = "false"
   USE
        PRINT "Inventory file "; ucase$(Fname$);
        PRINT " does not exist.  Please try again."
        PRINT
        LET NoFile$ = "true"
   END WHEN
LOOP until NoFile$ = "false"

! If index file for valid inventory file is not found,
! advise the user and abort the program.
WHEN error in
     OPEN #2: name Xname$
USE
     PRINT "The index file for "; ucase$(Fname$);
     PRINT " does not exist.  Program aborting."
     PAUSE 3
     STOP
END WHEN

DIM Index$(1)
ASK #2: filesize SIZE
MAT READ #2: Index$(Size)
LET Indent = 20

DO
   CLEAR
```

```
      CALL Menu (Command$, Indent)
      SELECT CASE Command$
      CASE "0"
           ! Exit command
      CASE "1"
           CALL Edit (#1, Index$, Size)
      CASE "2"
           CALL List (#1, Index$, Size, Indent)
      CASE "3"
           CALL Search (#1, Index$, Size, Indent)
      CASE ELSE
           PRINT
           PRINT tab(Indent); "Enter a number between 0 and 3."
           PRINT tab(Indent); "Press any key to continue."
           PRINT
      END SELECT
   LOOP until Command$ = "0"
   CLOSE #1
   CLOSE #2
   END


   SUB Name (Fname$, Xname$)
       DO
          INPUT prompt "Name of inventory file? ": Fname$
          LET X = pos(Fname$, ":")
          INPUT prompt "On disk in which drive? ": Drive$
          LET X = pos(Drive$, ":")
          IF X = 0 then LET Drive$ = Drive$ & ":"
          LET X = pos(Fname$, ".")
          IF X = 0 then LET Fname$ = Drive$ & Fname$ & ".REC"
          IF len(Fname$) > 13 then
             PRINT "File name cannot exceed 7 characters."
             PRINT "Please enter name again."
             PRINT
          END IF
       LOOP while len(Fname$) > 13
       LET N = len(Fname$)
       LET Xname$ = "X" & Fname$[3:N - 4]
       LET Xname$ = Fname$[1:2] & Xname$ & Fname$[N - 3:N]
   END SUB


   SUB Menu (Choice$, Indent)
       PRINT tab(Indent); "     Command Menu"
       PRINT
       PRINT tab(Indent); "0.....stop the program"
       PRINT tab(Indent); "1.....edit a record"
       PRINT tab(Indent); "2.....list all records"
       PRINT tab(Indent); "3.....search for a part number"
       PRINT
       PRINT tab(Indent); "Your selection.....";
       LINE INPUT prompt "": Choice$
   END SUB
```

THE EDIT COMMAND

The user is asked to enter a record number that is checked to make sure it is within the allowed range. The inventory file record is read and unpacked. The user is then asked to specify the field number to be edited in this record. Only field numbers between 2 and 8 can be edited. Entering a field number of zero produces a display of the field names and associated field numbers. The old field value is displayed and a new field value is requested. If the user presses the Enter key, the old field value is retained.

The process repeats and the user can change other field values. If a field number of -1 is entered, the process stops. The record is packed again and written back on the inventory file.

Figure 14-1 is a diagram showing a typical file record, with each field designated by its field number. Note that the field substrings have varying lengths.

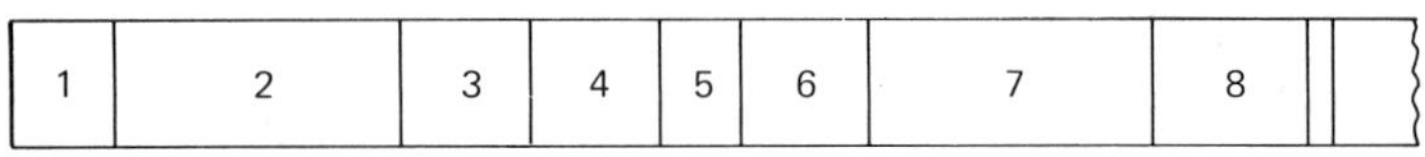

Figure 14-1 Schematic diagram of a file record.

We need to examine the packing and unpacking process in more detail. Each field is stored on the inventory file as a fixed-length substring. The 8 substrings are concatenated into a record string of 84 characters. Each field is displayed, in regular string format, as an element of a string array named Field$. The Pack subroutine converts the elements of the string array Field$ into a single record string Entry$. The Unpack subroutine converts Entry$ back into the elements of array Field$.

Several functions are used in the Pack and Unpack subroutines. The user-defined function Fixlen$(Str$, N) adds trailing blanks to the string Str$. It returns a substring, N characters long, of the resulting string. This function can handle a string of any length. If Str$ is longer than N characters, it is truncated to N characters.

Two new functions for converting between numbers and strings are introduced, in addition to the STR$ and VAL functions we discussed in Chapter 5. The NUM$(N) function converts a number N into an 8-byte string that stores the number in an internal string format. In contrast to the string produced by the STR$ function, **a string produced by the NUM$ function cannot be displayed.** The latter string is always exactly 8 bytes long, however, and thus allows any number to be stored in an 8-character substring. The complementary function, NUM(N$), converts a string of this type back into a regular numeric variable.

For example, if the value of NUM$(N) is assigned to the variable N$, then the value of NUM(N$) is equal to N.

Looking at the description of our inventory file record, we see that Part Number is always 6 characters long and is handled as a string. Quantity, Unit Price, and Reorder Amount are all numbers and are stored in the internal string format produced by the NUM$ function. They are converted to regular or variable-length strings for display. The two strings Description and Vendor Name have trailing blanks added to create fixed-length strings of 20 characters. We assume these two strings are originally 20 characters or less in length; if not, they are truncated to 20 characters. Vendor Phone is stored as a string of 10 characters, but displayed as a 12-character string in the format 123-123-1234.

Although we do not use the index file in the Edit subroutine, you should know how it is formatted. The record is 14 characters long and contains two strings. The first 6 characters are the Part Number. The last 8 characters are the record number, stored in the internal string format produced by the NUM$ function.

Here is the Edit subroutine, with the auxiliary subroutines Pack and Unpack:

```
SUB Edit (#9, Index$(), Size)
    CLEAR
    DIM Field$(8)
    DO
       INPUT prompt "What record number? ": Rec
       IF Rec < 1 or Rec > Size then
          PRINT
          PRINT "Record numbers are between 1 and"; Size; "."
          PRINT
       END IF
    LOOP while Rec < 1 or Rec > Size
    SET #9: record REC
    READ #9: Entry$
    CALL Unpack (Entry$, Field$)
    PRINT
    PRINT "Enter 0 for a list of record fields."
    PRINT "Enter -1 to stop editing this record."

   DO
      PRINT "What field number in record"; Rec;
      INPUT prompt "? ": FieldNum
      SELECT CASE FieldNum
      CASE 0
           PRINT
           PRINT "1.  Part Number"
           PRINT "2.  Description"
           PRINT "3.  Quantity"
           PRINT "4.  Unit Price"
           PRINT "5.  Bin Number"
           PRINT "6.  Reorder Amt."
           PRINT "7.  Vendor Name"
           PRINT "8.  Vendor Phone"
           PRINT
      CASE 1
           PRINT
           PRINT "The part number cannot be edited."
           PRINT
      CASE 2 to 8
           PRINT
           PRINT "Old Value:  "; Field$(FieldNum)
           PRINT "New Value:  ";
           LINE INPUT prompt "": Value$
           IF Value$ <> "" then LET Field$(FieldNum) = Value$
           PRINT
```

```
        CASE  ELSE
        END SELECT
     LOOP until FieldNum < 0
     CALL Pack (Entry$, Field$)
     RESET #9: same
     WRITE #9: Entry$
END SUB

SUB Unpack (Entry$, Field$())
    LET Field$(1) = Entry$[1:6]
    LET Field$(2) = trim$(Entry$[7:26])
    LET Field$(3) = str$(num(Entry$[27:34]))
    LET Field$(4) = str$(num(Entry$[35:42]))
    LET Field$(5) = Entry$[43:46]
    LET Field$(6) = str$(num(Entry$[47:54]))
    LET Field$(7) = trim$(Entry$[55:74])
    LET Phone$ = Entry$[75:77] & "-" & Entry$[78:80]
    LET Field$(8) = Phone$ & "-" & Entry$[81:84]
END SUB

SUB Pack (Entry$, Field$())
    DEF Fixlen$(Str$, N) = (Str$ & repeat$(" ", N))[1:N]
    LET Entry$[1:6] = Field$(1)
    LET Entry$[7:26] = Fixlen$(Field$(2), 20)
    LET Entry$[27:34] = num$(val(Field$(3)))
    LET Entry$[35:42] = num$(val(Field$(4)))
    LET Entry$[43:46] = Field$(5)
    LET Entry$[47:54] = num$(val(Field$(6)))
    LET Entry$[55:74] = Fixlen$(Field$(7), 20)
    LET Phone$ = Field$(8)[1:3] & Field$(8)[5:7]
    LET Entry$[75:84] = Phone$ & Field$(8)[9:12]
END SUB
```

THE LIST COMMAND

The list command simply reads each record from the inventory file and displays the record number and the record fields on the screen. It pauses after displaying each record and continues when any key is pressed. It calls a subroutine named PrintRec to display a record, and PrintRec in turn calls the subroutine Unpack to convert the record string to an array of display strings. PrintRec displays both the name of each field and the field value.

Here are the List and PrintRec subroutines:

```
SUB List (#9, Index$(), Size, Indent)
    CLEAR
    RESET #9: begin
    FOR I = 1 to Size
        LET Rec = num(Index$(I)[7:14])
        CALL PrintRec (#9, Rec, Indent)
        PRINT "Press any key to continue."
        GET KEY Dummy
    NEXT I
    PRINT "Press any key to return to menu."
    GET KEY Dummy
END SUB

SUB PrintRec (#9, Rec, Indent)
    DIM Field$(8)
    SET #9: record REC
    PRINT "Record"; Rec
    PRINT
    READ #9: Entry$
    CALL Unpack (Entry$, Field$)
    PRINT "Part Number"; tab(Indent); Field$(1)
    PRINT "Description"; tab(Indent); Field$(2)
    PRINT "Quantity"; tab(Indent); Field$(3)
    PRINT "Unit Price"; tab(Indent); Field$(4)
    PRINT "Bin Number"; tab(Indent); Field$(5)
    PRINT "Reorder Amt."; tab(Indent); Field$(6)
    PRINT "Vendor Name"; tab(Indent); Field$(7)
    PRINT "Vendor Phone"; tab(Indent); Field$(8)
    PRINT
END SUB
```

THE SEARCH COMMAND

A primary purpose of this program is to provide a fast way to search for a specified inventory record. The record is specified by part number, and the index array is used to determine the corresponding record number. A binary search technique is used to search the index array. This search procedure is somewhat specialized in the way it handles substrings and so is included as part of the search subroutine instead of as a separate subroutine.

The user enters a part number that must contain six digits. A failure message is displayed if the record for that part number cannot be found. If the record is found, it is displayed with the PrintRec subroutine.

Here is the Search subroutine:

```
SUB Search (#9, Index$(), Size, Indent)
    CLEAR
    DO
       INPUT prompt "Part number to find? ": Look$
       IF len(Look$) <> 6 then
          PRINT
          PRINT "Part number consists of 6 digits."
          PRINT
       END IF
    LOOP until len(Look$) = 6
    ! Binary search.
    LET Left = 1
    LET Right = Size
    LET Found$ = "false"
    DO
       LET Mid = round((Left + Right)/2)
       IF Look$ = Index$(Mid)[1:6] then
          LET Result = num(Index$(Mid)[7:14])
          LET Found$ = "true"
       ELSEIF Look$ > Index$(Mid)[1:6] then
          LET Left = Mid + 1
       ELSE
          LET Right = Mid -1
       END IF
    LOOP until Found$ = "true" or Right < Left
    PRINT
    IF Found$ = "true" then
       CALL PrintRec (#9, Result, Indent)
    ELSE
       PRINT "Part number is not in the file."
    END IF
    PRINT "Press any key to return to menu.";
    GET KEY Dummy
END SUB
```

The disk of example programs available from the publisher includes both an inventory file and an index file that are designed to be used with this program. The inventory file is named PARTS.REC and the index file is named XPARTS.REC. We recommend that you run the program with these files. In several of the practice programs, we suggest ways to expand this example program.

PRACTICE PROGRAMS

All the practice programs consist of enhancements or modifications to the example database program in this chapter.

1. Write a command subroutine to delete a record from the inventory file. Write a null string on the specified inventory record. This empty record in the inventory file will do no harm, although it wastes some space.

   Remove the corresponding entry from the index file (or index array) and adjust that file so there is no empty record. Will you need to sort the index file again?
2. Modify the DELETE command to allow a specified range of records to be deleted.
3. Write a command subroutine to add additional records to the inventory file. You should prompt the user with the field name for each field. As minimum error checking, make sure that numeric fields are valid numbers, that the part number contains exactly 6 digits, and that the telephone number contains exactly 10 digits.

   Ask the user to confirm the accuracy of a complete record before writing it on the file. Add an appropriate entry to the index file for each new inventory record. After you have finished adding records, be sure to sort the index file.
4. Write a command subroutine to create a new inventory file. After the inventory file and index file have been opened, call the ADD subroutine to start adding new inventory records.
5. Modify the PrintRec subroutine to allow optional printed reports on an attached printer. Add another parameter to specify whether the report should be displayed or printed. If you use networked printers, send your report to a text file for later printing.
6. Write a command subroutine to display or print the records of all parts supplied by a specified vendor.
7. Write a command subroutine to display or print all records of parts whose quantity is less than or equal to the reorder amount. The resulting report might be used as the basis for ordering new stock.
8. Write a command subroutine to purge all empty records from the inventory file. You will have to create and sort a new index file.

A Specifications for IBM PC Compatibles

IBM PC-COMPATIBLE LIMITS

Accuracy of numbers	14 digits
Accuracy of functions (sin, cos, tan, atn, log, exp)	10 digits
Smallest positive number (Eps(0))	1.11254e − 308
Largest positive number (Maxnum)	3.59539e + 308
Maximum string length	32,767 characters
Maximum number of files open at one time	5
Maximum number of dimensions in an array	255

TRUE BASIC LIMITS

Maximum length of variable names	31 characters
Maximum line number or label	999999
Maximum number of channels open at one time	10

TRUE BASIC DEFAULT VALUES

Default margin	80 columns
Default mode value	80

Default split value	17
Default zonewidth	16 columns

B Editing and Function Keys for IBM PC Compatibles

EDITING KEYS

left arrow	moves cursor one character to the left
right arrow	moves cursor one character to the right
tab	moves cursor one word to the right
shift tab	moves cursor one word to the left
up arrow	moves cursor up one line
down arrow	moves cursor down one line
Home	moves cursor to start of the program
End	moves cursor to end of the program
Ctrl left arrow	moves cursor to start of the current line
Ctrl right arrow	moves cursor to end of the current line
PgDn	displays next page in the program window
PgUp	displays previous page in the program window
Del	deletes the character under the cursor if on line tag, deletes the entire line
backspace	deletes character to left of cursor
Ctrl End	deletes characters from cursor to end of line
Ctrl Home	deletes word to left of cursor

Ctrl PgUp	deletes word to right of cursor
Ins	switches between insert and overwrite mode insert mode: small underline cursor overwrite mode: large box cursor
>	on line tag, indents line or marked block
<	on line tag, undents line or marked block
backspace	on line tag, joins line to end of previous line

FUNCTION KEYS

F1	Moves cursor into the program or editing window
F2	Moves cursor into the command or history window
F3	Finds a word between cursor and end of program
F4	Marks a program line or block of lines Press F4 again to unmark line or block
F5	Copies marked lines from one location to another
F6	Moves marked lines from one location to another
F7	Undeletes the last item deleted
F9	Runs the current program
F10	Provides help on use of commands

Type HELP or press the F10 key for further information on use of the FIND, MARK, COPY, MOVE, and UNDELETE commands.

C True BASIC Commands

MANIPULATE PROGRAM FILES

FILES	display a list of saved programs example: FILES B:*.* for all files on B
NEW	clear memory to create a new program
OLD	load a saved program from disk example: OLD B:HW01 (TRU suffix not needed)
REPLACE	replace saved program by current version example: REPLACE or REPLACE B:HW01
SAVE	save new program or new version to disk example: SAVE B:HW01A
UNSAVE	delete a saved program from disk example: UNSAVE B:HW01A

EDIT A PROGRAM FILE

CHANGE	change a word or phrase throughout the program example: CHANGE Num, Number

COPY	copy part of a program to another location (see use of F5 key, Chapter 2)
DELETE	delete part of a program (see use of Del key, Chapter 2)
DO FORMAT	reformat the current program, using the program FORMAT.
EDIT	restrict editing to part of a program (a seldom-used command)
INCLUDE	include a saved program within current program example: INCLUDE B:HEADING.TRU
KEEP	delete all but the specified subprogram example: KEEP Factorial
LOCATE	display all occurrences of a word or phrase example: LOCATE Name$
MARK	mark part of a program for later editing (see use of F4 key, Chapter 2)
MOVE	move part of a program to another location (see use of F6 key, Chapter 2)
TRY	like CHANGE command, but requires verification example: TRY Num, Number

CHANGE LINE NUMBERS

DO NUM	add line numbers to a program
DO RENUM	renumber all lines and line references
DO UNNUM	remove all line numbers from a program

DEBUG A PROGRAM FILE (SEE CHAPTER 6)

BREAK	insert a breakpoint, usually at a marked line
CONTINUE	continue execution after a breakpoint

MISCELLANEOUS

BYE	exit the True BASIC system
COMPILE	compile the current program to compiled code (CAUTION: destroys the current source code)
DO	run a preprocessor over the current program (see program FORMAT.TRU for an example)

HELP	get help on topics or a specific command example: HELP TOPICS
KEY	assign new meaning to specified key (see Chapter 10)
LIST	list the current program on an attached printer (may lock up the system if no printer is attached)
RUN	execute the current program file
SPLIT n	change number of lines in the program window example: SPLIT 0 displays only the command window
TO	move cursor to first line of a subprogram example: TO Factorial

D True BASIC Reserved Words

KEYWORDS

ELSE	NOT
ELSEIF	PRINT
IF	REM

FUNCTIONS

DATE	MAXNUM
DATE$	PI
DET	RND
EXLINE$	TIME
EXTEXT$	TIME$
EXTYPE	

SUBROUTINES

DIVIDE	PACKB
POKE	

E Format for Displaying Numbers

True BASIC has a set of built-in formatting rules for displaying numbers. In most cases, numbers are displayed in an appropriate format with no special effort on your part.

1. Positive numbers, and zero, are displayed with a leading space. Negative numbers are displayed with a leading minus sign. All numbers end with a trailing space, even if followed by a semicolon in the PRINT statement.
2. If a number can be represented as an integer with 12 or fewer digits, it is displayed as an integer:

   7
   1725
   −524185691

3. If a number can be represented by 6 digits or less and a decimal point, it is displayed in this format. Trailing zeroes after the decimal point are not displayed:

   1.4
   .377528
   −7041.37
   .000006

4. In all other cases, a number is displayed in exponential format, with only 6 digits or less in the mantissa or fractional part (the part before the letter ''e''). Trailing zeroes after the decimal point in the mantissa are not displayed. The leading digit will be between one and nine:

   1.27e+12
   -8.66667e-181

5. True BASIC rounds numbers to 6 significant figures, if necessary, before displaying them in exponential notation. For greater display precision, use the PRINT USING statement. Remember that True BASIC maintains an internal precision of about 14 significant figures for all numbers.

F The ASCII Set of Characters

ASCII value	Character	Control character	ASCII value	Character	
000	(null)	NUL	018	↕	DC2
001	☺	SOH	019	!!	DC3
002	☻	STX	020	¶	DC4
003	♥	ETX	021	§	NAK
004	♦	EOT	022	▬	SYN
005	♣	ENQ	023	↨	ETB
006	♠	ACK	024	↑	CAN
007	(beep)	BEL	025	↓	EM
008	◘	BS	026	→	SUB
009	(tab)	HT	027	←	ESC
010	(line feed)	LF	028	(cursor right)	FS
011	(home)	VT	029	(cursor left)	GS
012	(form feed)	FF	030	(cursor up)	RS
013	(carriage return)	CR	031	(cursor down)	US
014	♫	SO	032	(space)	
015	☼	SI	033	!	
016	►	DLE	034	"	
017	◄	DC1	035	#	

ASCII value	Character
036	$
037	%
038	&
039	'
040	(
041	)
042	*
043	+
044	,
045	-
046	.
047	/
048	0
049	1
050	2
051	3
052	4
053	5
054	6
055	7
056	8
057	9
058	:
059	;
060	<
061	=
062	>
063	?
064	@
065	A
066	B
067	C
068	D
069	E
070	F
071	G
072	H
073	I
074	J

ASCII value	Character
075	K
076	L
077	M
078	N
079	O
080	P
081	Q
082	R
083	S
084	T
085	U
086	V
087	W
088	X
089	Y
090	Z
091	[
092	\
093	]
094	^
095	_
096	`
097	a
098	b
099	c
100	d
101	e
102	f
103	g
104	h
105	i
106	j
107	k
108	l
109	m
110	n
111	o
112	p
113	q

ASCII value	Character
114	r
115	s
116	t
117	u
118	v
119	w
120	x
121	y
122	z
123	{
124	¦
125	}
126	~
127	⌂
128	Ç
129	ü
130	é
131	â
132	ä
133	à
134	å
135	ç
136	ê
137	ë
138	è
139	ï
140	î
141	ì
142	Ä
143	Å
144	É
145	æ
146	Æ
147	ô
148	ö
149	ò
150	û
151	ù
152	ÿ
153	Ö
154	Ü
155	¢
156	£
157	¥
158	Pt
159	ƒ
160	á
161	í
162	ó
163	ú
164	ñ
165	Ñ
166	ª
167	º
168	¿
169	⌐
170	¬
171	½
172	¼
173	¡
174	«
175	»
176	░
177	▒
178	▓
179	│
180	┤
181	╡
182	╢
183	╖
184	╕
185	╣
186	║
187	╗
188	╝
189	╜
190	╛
191	┐

ASCII value	Character	ASCII value	Character
192	└	224	α
193	┴	225	β
194	┬	226	Γ
195	├	227	π
196	─	228	Σ
197	┼	229	σ
198	╞	230	μ
199	╟	231	τ
200	╚	232	Φ
201	╔	233	θ
202	╩	234	Ω
203	╦	235	δ
204	╠	236	∞
205	═	237	Ø
206	╬	238	ε
207	╧	239	∩
208	╨	240	≡
209	╤	241	±
210	╥	242	≥
211	╙	243	≤
212	╘	244	⌠
213	╒	245	⌡
214	╓	246	÷
215	╫	247	≈
216	╪	248	°
217	┘	249	•
218	┌	250	·
219	█	251	√
220	▄	252	^{n}
221	▌	253	^{2}
222	▐	254	■
223	▀	255	(blank 'FF')

Microsoft, BASIC, IBM Manual. Appendix G. Reprinted with permission of IBM.

G True BASIC Standard Functions

MATHEMATICAL FUNCTIONS

ABS(X)	absolute value of X
DIVIDE(X,Y,Q,R)	divides X by Y, returns quotient Q and remainder R
EPS(X)	smallest number that can be added to X so that the result differs from X
EXP(X)	exponential function of X
INT(X)	greatest integer less than or equal to X
LOG(X)	natural logarithm of X
LOG2(X)	logarithm of X, base 2
LOG10(X)	logarithm of X, base 10
MAX(X,Y)	maximum value of X and Y
MAXNUM	largest positive number (see Appendix A)
MIN(X,Y)	minimum value of X and Y
MOD(X,Y)	X modulo Y (X − (Y * int(X/Y)))
REMAINDER(X,Y)	remainder left after dividing X by Y
RND	random number in the range 0 <= RND < 1
ROUND(X)	X rounded to an integer

ROUND(X,N)	X rounded to N decimal places
SGN(X)	1 if $X > 0$, 0 if $X = 0$, -1 if $X < 0$
SQR(X)	square root of X
TRUNCATE(X,N)	X truncated to N decimal places

TRIGONOMETRIC FUNCTIONS

ANGLE(X,Y)	counterclockwise angle between X axis and line from origin to point (X, Y)
ATN(X)	arctangent of X
COS(X)	cosine of angle X
DEG(X)	converts X radians to degrees
PI	the value of pi (3.14159. . .)
RAD(X)	converts X degrees to radians
SIN(X)	sine of angle X
TAN(X)	tangent of angle X

STRING FUNCTIONS

CHR$(N)	character corresponding to ASCII value N
LEN(A$)	length of string A$
LCASE$(A$)	changes string characters to lower case
LTRIM$(A$)	trims leading spaces from string A$
NUM(A$)	reverses action of NUM$(N), see below
NUM$(N)	converts number N to an internal string representation, not for display
ORD(A$)	ASCII value of first character in A$
POS(A$,B$)	position of first occurrence of B$ in A$
POS(A$,B$,N)	as above, but starts at character N in A$
REPEAT$(A$,N)	string A$ repeated N times
RTRIM$(A$)	trims trailing spaces from string A$
STR$(N)	converts number N to a string
TRIM$(A$)	trims leading and trailing spaces from A$
UCASE$(A$)	changes string characters to upper case
USING$(F$,V1,V2, . . .)	string containing variables V1, V2, . . . formatted by F$
VAL(A$)	converts string A$ to a number

DATE AND TIME FUNCTIONS

DATE	current date in YYDDD format, where DDD is day of the year
TIME	current time in seconds since midnight
DATE$	current date in YYYYMMDD format
TIME$	current time in HH:MM:SS format

H Run-Time Error Numbers and Messages

Extype	Extext$
1000	Overflow
1051	String too long
2001	Subscript out of bounds
3001	Division by zero
3002	Negative number to non-integral power
3003	Zero to negative power
3004	LOG of number <= 0
3005	SQR of negative number
3006	MOD and REMAINDER can't have 0 as 2nd argument
3008	Can't use ANGLE(0,0)
3009	Can't invert singular matrix
4001	VAL string isn't a proper number
4003	Improper ORD string
4004	SIZE index out of range
4005	TAB column not between 1 and margin
4006	Margin less than zonewidth
4007	ZONEWIDTH out of range
4008	LBOUND out of range
4009	UBOUND out of range
4010	REPEAT$ count < 0
4020	Improper NUM string
4501	Error in PLAY string
5000	Out of memory
6001	Mismatched array sizes
6002	DET needs a square matrix
6003	INV needs a square matrix

Extype	Extext$
6004	IDN must make a square matrix
7001	Channel number must be 1 to 1000
7002	Can't use #0 here
7003	Channel is already open
7004	Channel isn't open
7101	Unknown OPEN option
7102	Too many channels open
7103	File's record size doesn't match OPEN RECSIZE
7104	Wrong type of file
7202	Must be record or byte file for SET RECORD
7250	Can't SET RECSIZE on non-empty record file
7251	Must be byte file or empty for SET RECSIZE
7252	File pointer out of bounds
7301	Can't erase file not opened as OUTIN
7302	Can't output to INPUT file
7303	Can't input to OUTPUT file
7350	Can't PRINT to middle of text file
7351	Must be byte file for READ BYTES
8001	Reading past end of data
8002	Too few input items
8003	Too many input items
8011	Reading past end of file
8101	Data item isn't a number
8103	String given instead of number
8104	Data item isn't a number
8105	Badly formed input line
8201	Badly formed USING string
8202	No USING item for output
8301	Output item bigger than RECSIZE
8302	Input item bigger than RECSIZE
8304	Must SET RECSIZE before WRITE
8501	Must be text file
8502	Must be record or byte file
8601	Cursor out of bounds
8700	No GET MOUSE on this computer
9001	File is read or write protected
9002	Trouble using disk or printer
9003	No such file
9004	File already exists
9005	Diskette removed, or wrong diskette
9006	Disk full
9666	Program stopped
10001	ON index out of range, no ELSE given
10002	RETURN without GOSUB
10004	No CASE selected, but no CASE ELSE
10005	(CHAIN statement error, different error messages)
11000	Can't do graphics on this computer
11001	Window minimum = maximum
11002	Screen minimum = maximum
11003	Screen bounds must be 0 to 1
11004	Can't SET WINDOW in picture
11005	Channel isn't a window
11008	No such color

I GET KEY Numeric Codes

These keys return no numeric code when pressed alone:

Ctrl	Caps Lock
Shift	Num Lock
Alt	Scroll Lock

The character keys, alone or in combination with the Shift and Ctrl keys, return the ASCII set of numeric codes from 1 through 126. ASCII codes of 0, 127, and the extended character codes 128 through 255 are not returned.

Other keys return the following numeric codes:

Top row of character keys with the Alt key
Alt 1 through Alt = returns 376—387

First row of alphabetic keys with the Alt key
Alt Q through Alt P returns 272—281

Second row of alphabetic keys with the Alt key
Alt A through Alt L returns 286—294

Third row of alphabetic keys with the Alt key
Alt Z through Alt M returns 300—306

Function keys

F1 through F10 returns 315—324

Function keys with the Shift key
F1 through F10 returns 340—349

Function keys with the Crtl key
F1 through F10 returns 350—359

Function keys with the Alt key
F1 through F10 returns 360—369

Keypad keys with Num Lock off (cursor movement activated)

Home	327	End	335
up arrow	328	down arrow	336
PgUp	329	PgDn	337
left arrow	331	Insert	338
right arrow	333	Delete	339

Keypad keys with the Alt key

left arrow	371	PgDn	374
right arrow	372	Home	375
End	373	PgUp	388

J True BASIC Statements

Unless otherwise noted, in the following syntax descriptions, *var* signifies any variable, either string or numeric, and *expr* represents any expression, either string or numeric. The ellipsis (. . .) means that the statement may contain more or fewer items than are listed. For example:

```
PRINT expr1, expr2, . . .
```

means that a PRINT statement may contain any number of expressions to be printed, even zero.

H.1 Simple Statements

```
ASK MARGIN var
ASK ZONEWIDTH var

DATA item1, item2, ...

END
```

```
GET KEY var
```

var must be numeric.

```
INPUT var1 , var2 , . . .
INPUT PROMPT expr$ : var1 , var2 , . . .
LINE INPUT var1$ , var2$ , . . .
LINE INPUT PROMPT expr$ : var1$ , var2$ , . . .
```

```
LET var = expr
LET var1 , var2 , . . . = expr
LET var$[i : j] = expr$
```

```
PAUSE expr
```

expr must be numeric, and gives the length of the pause in seconds.

```
PLAY music$
```

music$ may be a string constant, variable, or expression, and must contain music commands and spaces.

```
PRINT expr1 , expr2 , . . .
PRINT expr1 ; expr2 ; . . .
PRINT USING format$ : expr1 , expr2 , . . .
```

format$ may be a string constant, variable, or expression, and must contain format fields and literal characters.

```
READ var1 , var2 , . . .
```

```
RESTORE
```

```
SET MARGIN expr
SET ZONEWIDTH expr
```

expr must be numeric.

```
STOP
```

```
SOUND freq , time
```

freq must be numeric, and gives the frequency in Hertz; *time* must be numeric, and gives the duration in seconds.

H.2 Loop Structures

In the following syntax descriptions, *var* must be a numeric variable; *first, last* and *size* may be any numeric expressions; *condition* may be any logical expression; and the blocks may contain any number of statements or structures.

```
DO
   ---
   ---  } block of statements
   ---
LOOP
```

```
DO WHILE condition
   ---
   ---  } block of statements
   ---
LOOP
```

```
DO
   ---
   ---  } block of statements
   ---
LOOP UNTIL condition
```

```
DO WHILE condition
   ---
   ---  } block of statements
   ---
LOOP UNTIL condition
```

A WHILE condition or UNTIL condition may appear in either the DO or the LOOP statement, or both, or neither.

```
EXIT DO
EXIT FOR
```

```
FOR var = first TO last STEP size
   ---
   ---  } block of statements
   ---
NEXT var
```

H.3 Decision Structures

In the following syntax descriptions, *condition* may be any logical expression; *statement* may be any one-line True BASIC statement except if; and *blocks* may contain any number of statements or structures, even zero.

```
IF condition THEN statement

IF condition THEN
   ---
   ---   block of statements
   ---
END IF

IF condition THEN statement1 ELSE statement2

IF condition THEN
   ---
   ---   block1
   ---
ELSE
   ---
   ---   block2
   ---
END IF

IF condition1 THEN
   ---
   ---   block1
   ---
ELSEIF condition2 THEN
   ---
   ---   block2
   ---
ELSEIF condition3 THEN
   ---
   ---   block3
   ---
ELSE
   ---
   ---   blockE
   ---
```

You may use any number of ELSEIF blocks, and zero or one ELSE block.

```
SELECT CASE expr
CASE test1, test2, ...
  ---
  ---  } block1
  ---
CASE test3, test4, ...
  ---
  ---  } block2
  ---
CASE ELSE
  ---
  ---  } block4
  ---
END SELECT
```

You may use any number of CASE blocks, and each CASE statement may have any number of tests. The tests may have the following forms:

```
constant
low TO high
IS operator constant
```

constant, low, and *high* must be constants of the same type (numeric or string) as the *expr* in the SELECT CASE statement. *operator* must be a relational operator.

H.4 Matrix Statements

```
MAT array1 = array2
MAT array1, array2, ... = array
MAT array1, array2, = expr
MAT array1 = array2 + array3
MAT array1 = array2 - array3
MAT array1 = array2 * array3
MAT array1 = constant * array2

MAT INPUT array1, array2, ...
MAT INPUT array(?)
```

MAT INPUT PROMPT *expr$* : *array1* , *array2* , . . .
MAT LINE INPUT *array1$* , *array2$* , . . .
MAT LINE INPUT PROMPT *expr$*: *array1$*, *array2$*, . . .

MAT PRINT *array1* , *array2* , . . .
MAT PRINT *array1* ; *array2* ; . . .
MAT PRINT USING *format$* : *array1* , *array2* , . . .

MAT READ *array1* , *array2* , . . .

H.5 Program Units

CALL Subr (*expr1* , *expr2* , . . .)

CHAIN *expr$*
CHAIN *expr$* WITH (*arg$*)
CHAIN *expr$* , RETURN
CHAIN *expr$* WITH (*arg$*) , RETURN

DECLARE DEF *func1* , *func2* , . . .

DEF Func(*var1* , *var2* , . . .) = *expr*

```
DEF Func( var1 , var2 , . . . )
   ---
   ---
   LET Func = expr
   ---
   ---
END DEF
```

EXIT DEF
EXIT SUB

LIBRARY "filename1" , "filename2" , . . .

PROGRAM name
PROGRAM name (*var$*)

```
SUB Subr ( var1 , var2 , . . . )
   ---
   ---
   ---
END SUB
```

H.6 Graphics

Unless otherwise noted, all coordinates (*x*,*y*, etc.) are window coordinates.

```
ASK BACK var
ASK BACK var$
ASK BACKGROUND COLOR var
ASK BACKGROUND COLOR var$
ASK COLOR var
ASK COLOR var$
ASK CURSOR var$
ASK CURSOR x, y
```

x and *y* are in character coordinates.

```
ASK MAX COLOR var
ASK MAX CURSOR x, y
```

x and *y* in character coordinates.

```
ASK SCREEN left, right, bottom, top
```

left, right, bottom and *top* are expressions in screen coordinates.

```
ASK WINDOW left, right, bottom, top
```

```
BOX AREA left, right, bottom, top
BOX CIRCLE left, right, bottom, top
BOX CLEAR left, right, bottom, top
BOX ELLIPSE left, right, bottom, top
BOX KEEP left, right, bottom, top IN var$
BOX LINES left, right, bottom, top
BOX SHOW var$ AT left, bottom
BOX SHOW var$ AT left, bottom USING constant$
BOX SHOW var$ AT left, bottom USING expr
```

constant$ may be "and," "or," or "xor", and *expr* must be numeric.

```
CLEAR
```

```
CLOSE #expr
```

expr must be numeric.

```
DRAW Pic
DRAW Pic WITH trans
```

```
DRAW Pic WITH trans * trans * . . .

FLOOD x,y

GET MOUSE: x, y, state
GET POINT: x, y

MAT PLOT AREA: array
MAT PLOT LINES: array
MAT PLOT POINTS: array
```

array must be numeric, and must have exactly two dimensions.

```
OPEN #expr : SCREEN left, right, bottom, top
```

left, right, bottom and *top* are expressions in screen coordinates.

```
PICTURE Pic (var1, var2, . . .)
   ---
   ---   block of statements
   ---
END PICTURE
```

block may not contain any SET WINDOW or OPEN SCREEN statements.

```
PLOT x, y
PLOT x,y;
PLOT x1,y1; x2,y2; . . .
PLOT AREA: x1,y1; x2,y2; . . .
PLOT LINES: x1,y1; x2,y2; . . .
PLOT POINTS: x1,y1; x2,y2; . . .
PLOT TEXT, AT x, y: expr$

SET BACK expr
SET BACK expr$
SET BACKGROUND COLOR expr
SET BACKGROUND COLOR expr$
SET COLOR expr
SET COLOR expr$
SET CURSOR expr$
```

expr$ may be "off" or "on."

```
SET CURSOR x,y
```

```
SET WINDOW left, right, bottom, top
```

the four expressions must be numeric, and give the left, right, bottom and top window coordinates.

```
WINDOW #expr
```

H.7 File Handling

Unless otherwise noted, the following statements can be used with any type of file: text, record, or byte. *#expr* signifies a required pound sign and any numeric expression representing a channel number between 1 and 999.

```
ASK #expr: ACCESS var$
ASK #expr: FILESIZE var
ASK #expr: MARGIN var
ASK #expr: NAME var$
ASK #expr: ORGANIZATION var$
ASK #expr: POINTER var$
ASK #expr: RECORD var
ASK #expr: RECSIZE var
ASK #expr: ZONEWIDTH var
```

MARGIN and ZONEWIDTH apply to text files only; RECORD and RECSIZE apply to record files only.

```
CLOSE #expr
```

```
ERASE #expr
```

```
INPUT #expr: var1, var2, ...
LINE INPUT #expr: var1$, var2$, ...
MAT LINE INPUT #expr: var1$, var2$, ...
```

#expr must be a channel to a text file.

```
OPEN #expr: NAME expr$, ACCESS accmode$,
                        CREATE crtmode$,
                        ORGANIZATION orgmode$,
                        RECSIZE recsize
```

ACCESS, CREATE, ORGANIZATION, and RECSIZE are optional; NAME is required. The possible strings are:

Option	String	Meaning
ACCESS	input	Read-only
	output	Write-only
	outin	Read and/or write (default)
CREATE	new	Create new file
	old	Use existing file (default)
	newold	Use existing file or create new one
ORGANIZATION	text	Text file
	record	Record file
	byte	Byte file

recsize must be numeric.

```
OPEN #expr: PRINTER
```

```
PRINT #expr: expr1, expr2, ...
PRINT #expr; expr1: expr2; ...
PRINT #expr, USING expr$: expr1, expr2, ...
```

#expr must be a channel to a text file.

```
READ #expr: var1, var2, ...
MAT READ #expr: array1, array2, ...
```

#expr must be a channel to a record or byte file.

```
READ #expr, BYTES expr: var1$, var2$, ...
```

#expr must be a channel to a byte file.

```
RESET #expr: BEGIN
RESET #expr: END
RESET #expr: NEXT
RESET #expr: RECORD expr
RESET #expr: SAME
```

NEXT, RECORD *expr*, and SAME apply to record files only.

```
SET #expr: MARGIN expr
SET #expr: POINTER BEGIN
```

```
SET #expr: POINTER END
SET #expr: POINTER NEXT
SET #expr: POINTER SAME
SET #expr: RECORD expr
SET #expr: RECSIZE expr
SET #expr: ZONEWIDTH expr
```

MARGIN and ZONEWIDTH can be used with text files only; NEXT, POINTER, RECORD and RECSIZE can be used with record files only.

```
UNSAVE expr$
```

```
WRITE #expr: expr1, expr2, ...
MAT WRITE #expr: expr1, expr2, ...
```

#expr must be a channel to a record or a byte file.

H.8 Error Handling

```
CAUSE ERROR expr
CAUSE ERROR expr, expr$
```

```
CAUSE EXCEPTION expr
CAUSE EXCEPTION expr, expr$
```

```
EXIT HANDLER
```

```
WHEN ERROR IN
    ---
    ---   protected block
    ---
USE
    ---
    ---   error handler
    ---
END WHEN
```

```
WHEN EXCEPTION IN
    ---
    ---   protected block
    ---
```

```
USE
   ---]
   ---}  error handler
   ---]
END WHEN
```

J.G. Kemeny & T.E. Kurtz, TRUE BASIC, Reference Manual, © 1985, Addison-Wesley, Reading, Massachusetts. Appendix H. Reprinted with permission.

K How to Use the Example Program Disk

INSTRUCTIONS FOR READING PROGRAM FILES

Example programs are stored in separate directories on the example program disk. For example, programs for Chapter 3 are stored in a directory named CH03.

To examine these programs, put the example program disk in drive B and change to that drive with the B: command. At the B> prompt, change directories by entering CD \CH03. The command CD means change directory. If you now enter DIR, the names of all files in directory CH03 will be displayed. For example, the file containing Example Program 3-2 is named EX03-02.TRU. If you want to examine another directory, say containing the example programs in Chapter 4, enter CD \CH04 and then DIR.

When using True BASIC, you can access any example program on the disk by specifying its pathname, a combination of the drive name, directory name and file name. For example, to access Example Program 3-2 in Chapter 3, use the True BASIC command:

```
OLD B:\CH03\EX03-02.TRU
```

As always in True BASIC, the .TRU suffix is optional.

INSTRUCTIONS FOR READING TEST FILES

The practice programs in Chapter 9 and beyond often use test files. These files are stored in the same separate directories as example programs on the program disk. For example, the test files for practice programs in Chapter 9 are stored in a directory named CH09.

When using True BASIC, you can access any test file on the program disk by specifying its pathname, a combination of the drive name, directory name and file name. For example, the OPEN statement for a text file named TEST.DAT, located in directory CH09 on the disk in drive B, is:

```
OPEN #1: name "B:\CH09\TEST.DAT"
```

You may need to modify the file names in your practice programs to conform to your particular situation.

INDEX